DOOLEY'S DAWGS

DOOLEY'S

25 Years of Winning Football

To Guy & Ben's Dad — Big Guy! Merry Christmas '89

Vince Dooley

LONGSTREET PRESS

Atlanta, Georgia

DAWGS

at the University of Georgia

VINCE DOOLEY

with Loran Smith

For my family,
Barbara, Deanna, Daniel, Denise, and Derek,
and for the entire Georgia family,
especially the players
who made it all possible.

Published by
LONGSTREET PRESS, INC.
2150 Newmarket Parkway
Suite 102
Marietta, Georgia 30067

Text copyright © 1989 by Vince Dooley
Foreword copyright © 1989 by Lewis Grizzard

Printed in the United States of America

1st printing, 1989

Library of Congress Catalog Number 89-084530
ISBN 0-929264-60-6

This book was printed by Arcata Graphics, Kingsport, Tennessee. The text type was set in Palatino by Typo-Repro Service, Atlanta, Georgia. Cover photograph by Wingate Downs. Cover design by Paulette Livers Lambert. Text design by Bob Fruitt.

FOREWORD

I am grateful for this book and for the fact that Vince Dooley and "Whatayagot" Loran Smith decided to write it.

I know some of it, but I want to know all of it—Vince's firsthand account of how he took a tired and tattered University of Georgia football program in 1964 and proceeded over the next twenty-five years to win 201 games, six Southeastern Conference championships and one glorious national championship, which remains a highlight of my life.

Vince Dooley is a private man. I think he realized just how much of his privacy would be invaded if he went into politics, as he threatened to do at least twice, and that is one reason he eventually chose not to run.

But in this book, Vince has allowed his window shades to be lifted. He turns out to be, as you will read, a man of strong emotions, a man who loved to win and hated to lose, and a man whose loyalty to Georgia has been fierce.

Vince Dooley and I arrived at the University of Georgia the same year. I was a skinny seventeen-year-old kid who wanted to study journalism. He was a thirty-one-year-old unknown who had played at rival Auburn and had no previous experience as a head football coach.

As I have mentioned often, when Vince got to Georgia he got a car and a house. I got a small room on the fourth floor of Reed Hall that overlooked Sanford Stadium. But Vince had the tougher row to hoe: I had to pass freshman English, while he had to turn the Georgia football program completely around.

I was often hurt over the years when I heard Georgia fans criticize Dooley. What they obviously had forgotten was just how bad the program was suffering when he inherited it.

There had been the Wally Butts-Bear Bryant scandal, and Georgia football was a house divided. Butts, who had been head coach at Georgia for twenty-two years, was forced out after the 1960 season.

He was succeeded by Johnny Griffith, who didn't have a chance and who would coach Georgia for three years and win a total of ten games. Things were so bad that the Bulldogs played a conference game at night against Mississippi State in Atlanta on Georgia Tech's Grant Field to attempt to improve attendance.

Georgia was in a desperate situation. First, the house was cleaned, and then Joel Eaves was summoned from Auburn as athletic director. One of his first moves was to find a new head football coach. Georgia fans wanted a name. What they got was "Vince who?"

Eaves had been impressed with Dooley at Auburn, both as a player and, later, as an assistant coach. And, knowing Coach Eaves' tightness with the athletic department dollar, one must also think that he knew he could get young Dooley for a song.

At a press conference announcing Dooley's appointment, the late Dr. O.C. Aderhold, Georgia's president, couldn't remember Dooley's name. When the press asked him a question, he would refer to Dooley as "our fine new coach."

It's a long story about how I happened to be in Tuscaloosa, Alabama, watching Vince Dooley's first team open the 1964 season.

It's a long story about how I happened to be in Tuscaloosa, Alabama, watching Vince Dooley's first team open the 1964 season.

I worked for the First National Bank in Atlanta during the summer of '64, prior to entering Georgia in the fall. I had a fierce, long-standing desire to succeed in sports journalism, whether it be as a writer or a broadcaster. On a whim, I phoned WAGA-TV one afternoon and spoke to sports director Ed Thilenius, who was also the radio voice of the Bulldogs.

I told him I simply would like to have some of his advice, and he was nice enough to agree to see me. Not only that, he needed somebody to spot Georgia's opposing teams for his broadcast, and he offered me the job. He would pay me ten dollars a game and expenses. I was thrilled beyond words. Working for Thilenius would help me make contact with other sports journalists, and that was how I got my start in the business. Ed Thilenius, who died a few years back, gave a kid a chance.

A warm night—Denny Stadium on the campus of the University of Alabama in Tuscaloosa. The date was September 19, 1964.

Georgia kicked off to start the game. I sat on Thilenius' right. John Withers, who spotted the Bulldogs, was on his left. On my right was Bill Munday, the pioneer sportscaster who did color for the Bulldogs.

I trust my memory here: On the first play from scrimmage, defensive tackle George Patton swept past the Alabama offensive line and threw the running back for a loss. Munday screamed into his microphone, as only he could, "Gawja's ready! Gawja's ready!"

Then Joe Namath, the Alabama quarterback, cranked it up, and the result was a 31-3 loss for Georgia and a less-than-

impressive debut for Dooley. But, as the conventional wisdom went the next week, "What did you expect?"

What they *didn't* expect was for Georgia to win six games that first season, including a glorious 7-0 victory over Georgia Tech in Athens. Tech's Bobby Dodd would coach two more years. He never did beat Vince Dooley.

Georgia, 6-3-1, went on to a Sun Bowl victory over Texas Tech. Dooley had worked a miracle. In one season, he had righted the program.

I could recite chapter and verse of great Georgia victories for hours, but I'll just do my top five favorites:

1. GEORGIA 17, NOTRE DAME 10. New Year's Day, 1981, in the Sugar Bowl. Georgia's first national championship.

2. GEORGIA 26, FLORIDA 21. 1980. Belue-to-Scott, ninety-three yards in the closing seconds in the Gator Bowl. Without that win, Georgia would never have made it to the championship game.

3. GEORGIA 18, ALABAMA 17. 1965. The flea-flicker. Moore-to-Hodgson-to-Taylor. That game said '64 was no fluke.

4. GEORGIA 15, MICHIGAN 7. 1965. Upset in Ann Arbor. Athens went wild.

5. GEORGIA 20, AUBURN 16. 1986. Between the hoses. The ride back to Atlanta that night was on a magic carpet.

I like to count Vince Dooley as a friend of mine. We are close by no means—I still can't greet him without a little awe on my part getting in the way—but I think he knows I was one of those who was there when it all began, and it has often been my pleasure to set doubters straight on the magnitude of what Dooley accomplished at Georgia.

Before I left school in 1968, I would see two SEC Championships, not a single loss to Georgia Tech, and trips to the Cotton, Sugar and Liberty bowls.

I would see the first of two expansions of Sanford Stadium, and, even more importantly, I would see the coming together of the Georgia people again and the subsequent Red Sea that rocked the stadium on many a Saturday.

There would be a few, but very few, losses that wrenched the guts of Georgia fans during the reign of Vince Dooley. The 'Dogs lost to Nebraska, 45-6, in the 1969 Sun Bowl. Vince called it an "embarrassing loss." The last-gasp Dan Marino pass that gave Pittsburgh a 24-20 victory over Georgia in the 1982 Sugar Bowl was devastating.

And who can't yet picture John Dewberry's uplifted arm when he crossed the goal line in Sanford Stadium for Georgia Tech and led the Yellow Jackets to a 35-18 rout? Dewberry had once been a Bulldog but later transferred to Georgia Tech. I went to Colorado and skiied for two weeks after that. Some might have called it going into hiding.

Although I was there when the Dooley party started, I didn't dance until later. As a young sports editor of *The Daily News* in Athens during my college days, I was never able to sit in the stands and cheer. I had to maintain proper press box decorum at all times. As my friends partied into the night and celebrated another victory, I was back at the paper, heading toward deadline.

I would become executive sports editor of *The Atlanta Journal* three years out of college. Unfortunately, being in charge of producing a Sunday sports section during football season kept me in the office and away from most Georgia games.

Then I was off to Chicago to become sports editor of the *Chicago Sun-Times*. It was hard to get worked up over Ohio State vs. Michigan when I knew the 'Dogs were playing Auburn.

All that changed in 1978, however, when I began writing a life-as-I-see-it column for *The Atlanta Journal* and *The Atlanta Constitution*. I was no longer sentenced to the press box. I bought season tickets, put on my red, and hunkered down with the same resolve as the next guy. And I have made up several-fold for the missed partying.

I have missed fewer than ten Georgia games in person in the last eleven years. Three of those were because I was busy having open-heart surgery.

Remember Georgia-Alabama on national television in 1985? Vince and Barbara Dooley called me a few hours before the game in the hospital where I lay in what was described by my doctors as "very poor condition." They told me they loved me and wanted me back as soon as possible.

I came close to death twice—once when Alabama hit a last-second pass to beat Georgia that night, and again a few days later when doctors determined they had to go into my heart to stop an infection that raged there.

I was at Emory Hospital in Atlanta for four weeks, recovering. When I was discharged my doctor said, "Try not to get overly excited, and stay in the vicinity of your home for awhile."

What? When Georgia is playing South Carolina in Athens Saturday? They took me to my seat in a golf cart, and I got to see Georgia win, 35-21. The excitement did me good.

So now, after a quarter of a century of the good life, we get the story from the source. This book absolutely needed writing, and the Bulldog faithful absolutely need to read it. Not to do so would be an even bigger sin than not showing up in Jacksonville.

And Loran Smith, who has been at Dooley's side for the entire ride, and who still roams the sidelines on Georgia broadcasts and reports dutifully when Larry Munson asks, "Loran, whadayagot?"

was the right person to team with Dooley on the project. He knows the territory. And he knows Vince Dooley and what makes him tick. Dooley-to-Smith. It may be uttered in the same breath as Belue-to-Scott.

Thanks, Vince. You have given us precious memories, and how they do linger.

You took us to the mountaintop, and the view from there took our breath. You restored our pride and rekindled our faith.

We will love you for it for a thousand autumns to come.

—*Lewis Grizzard*

CHAPTER 1
The Right Place, The Right Time To Say Farewell

Memories of the 1989 Gator Bowl game keep flashing back through my mind as if it were yesterday. Warm, even tender moments to savor and enjoy. Memories that remind me of the good times of a tough and demanding job. Memories of my last game as a head coach after twenty-five rewarding years.

Our captains — Todd Wheeler, Wayne Johnson, Mike Guthrie and Wycliffe Lovelace — stand in the middle of the field for the toss of the coin. My adrenalin is flowing. My heart is thumping. My anticipation has seldom been keener. In that respect, my last game is no different from the other 287 of my career.

Our entire team moves out onto the field with the captains. They are eager, intensely motivated. I sense that this is one time the team has peaked just right. They are ready. So am I.

We win the toss, elect to receive in the second half, and immediately John Kasay's booming kick settles into the Michigan State end zone. At last it is time to play ball. Our players are yelling and screaming. Every player on the sideline is on his feet, totally involved from the start. The crispness of the night air seems just right for a football game. Normally it is not cold in Jacksonville the first of the year, but this night of January 1, 1989, has a crispness, and so does my football team. I am grateful for that, because . . . despite my mental efforts, the thought sneaks in again— *this is my last game.*

For the most part, that thought had been put aside during the last month of my career, and for good reason. It was too much of a distraction, and it would have taken away from the team concept which we worked so hard to promote and preserve — not just for this game, but from the beginning of my career.

But I'll confess. A little earlier in the night, my guard slipped down. I did look back. Reminisced. But nobody knew.

Stalking the sidelines one last time

It happened when we first arrived at the Gator Bowl and I took my customary pre-game walk on the field, a ritual that dates back to my first game as Georgia's coach against Alabama in Tuscaloosa, September 19,

1964. That was a hot night, and the competitive crispness belonged to Bear Bryant, Joe Namath and the Crimson Tide, who started my coaching career with a 31-3 pasting.

While the players got taped and dressed, the coaches and I walked the Gator Bowl field, getting a feel for things, surveying the stadium. We always check the turf and the conditions. We determine which way the wind is blowing and, if it is late afternoon, we study the sun's position and reckon how it might affect receivers and punt returners. On that final walk, the first thing that hit me as I looked up into the big arced lights was that we were playing at night — very unusual for a Georgia team in the Gator Bowl. We did finish up one year after dark because of a four o'clock kickoff for television. Suddenly the dominating performance of Herschel Walker in the 1981 and 1982 Florida games burst into focus. I sometimes think about such things, even though they don't mean much to the task at hand, but it is best to keep them private — at least until the game is over. I am reminded of omens all the time, but omens never block, never tackle. And on this New Year's night, Herschel was in Dallas, Texas, where he wears the blue of the Dallas Cowboys.

I enjoyed my pre-game stroll on the field. I was relaxed and excited because of my confidence in my last team playing that final game. I knew they would render a championship performance, expertly utilizing those football fundamentals of blocking and tackling, playing the game the way it ought to be played. But as the late Governor Gene Talmadge used to reply to a leading question from an incognito supporter in the crowds on his campaigns, "I'm a-comin' to that."

I bumped into a few friends, photographers, writers and officials here and there on the field, but there was also time for a little bit of privacy and recollection.

For the previous month, my aim had been to play down as much as possible the fact that this would be my last game. But when I was alone, I couldn't help reminiscing. I fought the urge because of a long-standing emphasis on self-discipline and self-control. I always expected my players to keep their minds on the task at hand, and I should have been able to do the same. But under the circumstances, who could not think about the past twenty-five years and all the fun and excitement?

Suddenly the question of retirement intruded into my thoughts. Would it be a problem? "Certainly I can handle it, if I discipline myself," I mused. "Everything in life is an adjustment, and I'll just have to adjust." It wouldn't be easy, I was well aware of that, but I also knew the time had come to quit. I was positive of that, which is why I knew then and know now that there will never be any looking back. There will be much reflection on the past, as during my pre-game walk, but I'll never second-guess the decision. My coaching career would be over in about four hours.

I was almost thinking out loud. "Can it be that I've been coaching at the same place for twenty-five years? The time has gone by so quickly. Wonderful times, prosperous and fulfilling years, but so fleeting. One day I am an assistant, the next a head coach with babies at home in diapers. Two were not yet born. That seemed like yesterday and now they are all grown, getting married, starting families and I am retiring. I am a grandfather." I was on a reminiscing roll, almost oblivious to the preparation around me.

All the things I had ever wanted to accomplish in coaching had come about. Indeed, I was a very fortunate man. But now it was good-bye time, farewell to a profession and a

Sanford Stadium, one of the most beautiful arenas in America

generous university which had rewarded me and my family handsomely. I was leaving the beautiful hedges of Sanford Stadium. Those Saturday afternoons overflowing with emotions — excitement, exhilaration and anticipation. What a glorious experience it had been to establish a program that could compete with the best, one that was recognized for its quality and success. It was good-bye to a tradition of great players: the Chandlers, the Pattons, the Stanfills, the Scotts, the Johnsons, the Robinsons, the Hoages, the McClendons, the Walkers. There would be no more Dooley's Dawgs. Never again would I jog onto the field with a Bulldog team or stand on the sideline and hear the faithful fans on one side yell, "Georgia!" and cock an ear to the other side which answers back, "Bulldogs!" I wouldn't hear the Redcoat Band play

the national anthem again as I stood underneath the east stands and waited for the officials to come and tell me we had five minutes, at which time I'd call for our captains.

I wouldn't ever go inside and look at those young faces of young men from Waycross and Valdosta and Toccoa and Wrightsville and Macon and Savannah and inner-city Atlanta. Big-town kids, small-town kids, black kids, white kids, kids with heart, kids with talent, kids who have little more than a fighting spirit — all motivated by a common goal, which was to win football games for the University of Georgia.

"That's enough," I reminded myself. I had had my little walk down memory lane. There would be plenty of time for that later. For now I had to think of the team concept that we preached throughout my years at Georgia. I

3

could not permit self-indulgence. Football is not an "I" game; it is a "we" game. The team. The team is what counts, just as General Douglas MacArthur in his farewell speech at West Point kept emphasizing "the Corps." We have to keep the team emphasis our highest priority. It must be paramount. Even when alone, you must not put your personal goals ahead of the team. And if a head coach can't discipline himself, even on a pre-game walk, how can he effectively underscore the team-comes-first theme to his players? I had to concentrate on the challenge of the evening, playing Michigan State, a most worthy opponent from the Big Ten, a team that had won the Rose Bowl a year earlier. Putting distractions aside had been my primary mission the week of the Gator Bowl. I, too, would have to stick to the game plan.

For years I have been asked on game day or the days leading up to Saturday, "How does the team feel?" "Are they ready?" "Are they up?" In the hotel lobby all week in Jacksonville, people asked that question, but this time there was a more pressing query: They wanted to know what I knew about who would succeed Vince Dooley. Just as I never knew for sure whether the team was up or not, I didn't know for sure who would be my successor. I had offered some thoughts and opinions but hadn't made a specific recommendation to the search committee.

Everybody was aware that things had changed rapidly in the few days leading up to the Gator Bowl. The search committee had been told by Erk Russell of Georgia Southern and Dick Sheridan of North Carolina State that, for various reasons, they had no interest in the position. It was fairly obvious that the new coach was to come from inside, which was what I had recommended in the first place — either one of our own or someone very familiar with the program, potential

candidates like Erk and Mike Cavan, who had played and coached for me and had moved on to Valdosta State in 1986. Initially, of all the possibilities, I felt Erk was the best candidate, but he took himself out of the picture. Then it came down to choosing one of our assistants, which is not a good situation for a team preparing for a Bowl game.

On the whole, the team had handled all the distractions extremely well, but naturally I was concerned that it had been a problem for some of our players. They hear and they react. If players were allowed to nominate an assistant, they naturally would vote for their own position coach. And why not? The players and their coaches develop a close rapport. They spend considerable time together on and off the field. The rules permit coaches to entertain players in their homes under certain circumstances and at specific times, and periodically each position coach has his players over to his house for dinner. Strong personal and athletic bonds develop between assistants and players these days.

But even with all the distractions, I felt confident. I was not about to change my pattern and predict victory, but even though you never really know, you sometimes get that certain feeling about a team. Your instincts give you good vibes. You believe that the team will be up and ready, that it is peaking just right. But what your instincts never tell you is whether the other team is reaching an emotional peak at the same time. Neither do your instincts give you the feel for the pattern of the game or who will make which mistakes, and when and how these little developments will ultimately determine the outcome.

One thing I am certain of is that in my twenty-five years of coaching, I never felt better about a team being ready to play. Seldom had a team of mine been as up as the 1988

Bulldogs were when we took the field against Michigan State in the Gator Bowl New Year's night.

What did I do to get them ready?

Nothing. Absolutely nothing.

Why were they so ready? What were the factors that brought this about? I must confess that I don't know.

On the subject of preparation for a game, there is an interesting story about Bill Yeoman, the long-time coach at Houston. Bill was a hands-on, offensive-oriented football coach. On the Cougar sideline, he kept the headset on and called the plays. He was in on every decision and, in fact, pretty much made the decisions, getting input from his coaches upstairs who had a better view of what was taking place on the field.

Bill Yeoman meant no disrespect when he once said he wouldn't walk two doors down the hall to hear Bear Bryant lecture on football. Bill didn't consider Coach Bryant that much of an X's and O's coach. But when talking about the psychological part of the game, at which Bryant was the master, Yeoman said, "I would crawl on my hands and knees from here to Tuscaloosa, Alabama, if I could learn what he [Bryant] gets in those kids' minds the day they are playing a game." Incidentally, Bill was in Los Angeles when he made that statement.

I agree with Bill about Coach Bryant's great way with the mental side of the game, but I suspect that even Coach Bryant, if he were with us today, would say that you can never be sure. You sense things, but you never are absolutely certain.

That was the way it was most of my career, but this time, my last time out, I felt good. I kept the feeling close inside, although not to let on was a challenge, even for someone as private as I am. My team had sent me a silent message I could not misunderstand.

Perhaps the team was so ready to play because it was my last game. That made it special for many of the players, especially the seniors who called themselves the "Silver Seniors." It might have had something to do with the fact that we were playing at the Gator Bowl, where we had had so many glorious performances on so many November Saturdays over the years. Georgia teams have always enjoyed playing in Jacksonville. I didn't know we would win this game, but I knew beyond a doubt that this team on this night in the Gator Bowl was primed for a peak performance. And that is a great feeling for a football coach.

All of the practice sessions leading up to the game were sharp. There was that edge, that crispness. I can't remember better practice sessions nor do I recall having more fun at practice, except perhaps in the early days of my career at Georgia. In fact, I thought that if it were this much fun all the time, one would never tire of coaching. You would want to do it forever.

This was a special time when our team truly enjoyed being on the practice field. They had fun knocking each other dizzy and smiling about it. There were some tremendous licks passed. The final scrimmage in Sanford Stadium was as enjoyable as any in my career. Both sides of the ball were sharply competitive. Naturally, we needed a good game plan, but there wasn't any worry about playing well. This team would give a good account of itself.

The Silver Seniors had provided excellent leadership. It was a point of pride for them, being the leaders of my last football team. They set the tempo. They showed us the way. They took nothing for granted.

Nobody ever said, "Let's win this thing for Coach Dooley." If they had, that would have been discouraged. I certainly never would have brought it up because I believe it would have been counter-productive. I knew they were going to play hard and that any sentiment used as motivation would have hurt more than it would have helped. They had enough incentive. Just let 'em play.

My final day leading up to the Gator Bowl game was like so many others. My biological clock had me up a little after 5:30 A.M., which is about normal. Oftentimes a swim is part of my early-morning agenda, but not this time.

After a fruit breakfast and a quick perusing of the *Jacksonville Times Union* sports page, I headed downstairs for the team devotional conducted by our chaplain, Claude McBride.

We consider our devotionals a team function. At one point in my career we made them optional, but whether it is a few moments for meditation or time to review opponents' film, you have poor participation if you make it optional. Especially if the meeting is the first thing of the day, which devotionals usually are. Give nineteen- and twenty-year-old college athletes the option of attending a meeting of any kind or sleeping in and you know what many of them will do every time.

The devotional is an opportunity for us to meet for the first time, get our game day underway and allow for private reflection for each player. This is a routine which has become traditional at Georgia and is one that all our senior leaders have approved of enthusiastically. We've never had any complaints because the entire weekend for a game is conducted under the team banner. We do everything as a team. We eat as a team. We meet as a team. We take in a movie as a team, and we hear a short devotional as a team.

Four years ago when Bill Goldberg, who is Jewish, became a Bulldog, I asked him how he felt about what we were doing. I didn't

want our devotionals, normally presented by a Christian minister or layman, to be a problem for Bill. I asked him if he had any objection to our devotionals, and he said no. "I appreciate your asking me how I feel," Bill said. "I appreciate your thinking about me, but I am happy and have no problem in doing whatever the team is doing." Our services, whether special for a bowl game Sunday or a fall Saturday, are always ecumenical in nature anyway, since we have a variety of faiths on our team.

Several years ago, we began inviting ministers from around Georgia to join us on game day and speak to our team. It gave us an opportunity to hear some very inspirational messages from representatives of various denominations, and the practice has included several of our former players who became ministers.

Claude McBride, an ordained Baptist minister who is a member of the university's alumni staff, has been our chaplain for twenty years. Claude is a former Bulldog cheerleader and spends considerable time creating and developing weekly inspirational and motivational points for our team during the season.

His subject on Gator Bowl Sunday was "possessing of the land." It had to do with Moses making his farewell speech to the Children of Israel, and while Claude didn't appeal to the players in his devotional to win the last game for Coach Dooley, he did emphasize that it was a great opportunity for the team and compared it to Moses' last journey. For our seniors, there would be no second chance. This was an opportunity to make the last game for so many of us a memorable one. An historical opportunity, Claude suggested. Obviously, I didn't think winning that last game was as important as the Children of Israel possessing the promised land, but it was nonetheless important to me for us to win.

I have never felt that there is any divine intervention involved in the outcome of college football games, but on January 1, 1989, I participated in two religious services prior to the game. Being the cautious type, I appreciated any advantage.

In Jacksonville with sister Rosezella, brother Billy

After leaving the team devotional, I went back upstairs for a private Mass conducted by Father Russ Biven, who had come over for the game from Mobile with my sister, Rosezella, and her children. Barbara and her mother and her sister, Karen, and her brothers, Johnny and Mike, her Aunt Barbara, and all of our kids were there, and so were my brother, Billy, the head coach at Wake Forest, and his family. It was a nice family get-together which left me with warm and grateful feelings.

After Mass, Barbara says I turned into Mr. Hyde immediately, that I became irritable and edgy. I began focusing entirely on the game and was restless during the long afternoon, not being able to enjoy the professional games televised that day.

I was anxious to get on with the show, ready to play the game, and I wanted to go out a winner. I was fortunate to have won my last game in Sanford Stadium — my two-hundreth victory — but it was a big personal goal to finish my career with a victory.

Maybe it would be a little like Ted Williams hitting a homer in his last time at bat. I've always thought that was one of the great performances in sports. You announce your retirement, and then your last time at the plate, you connect with the ball and it soars over the right field fence and you jog around the bases. You tip your hat, the curtain falls, lights flicker out. They play taps on your career. Cheers and no tears. That is exactly the way I wanted it.

A few years earlier, I had agonized for my old coach Ralph "Shug" Jordan at Auburn. He announced in late summer of 1975 that he would quit at the end of the season, but his last hurrah fell far short of what he had anticipated. Auburn had a miserable year, losing in its final game 28-0 to Alabama, and finished with a 4-6-1 record. This was a great football coach, the one whose influence formed the base for my own coaching philosophy, and he deserved better. You can't dictate the circumstances, but I passionately wanted a different ending from my old coach's in my final outing.

For Coach Bear Bryant, his career concluded in the Liberty Bowl after he had become the winningest coach in the history of college football, but the Liberty Bowl was below his long-time standards. Even so, his last team finished 7-4, and he enjoyed a victory ride that last time out in Memphis, 21-15 over Illinois. Not a bad way to finish.

The worst case that comes to mind is that of Darrell Royal of Texas and Frank Broyles of Arkansas, good friends who often played golf together. Their respective retirements were either announced or widely rumored as the 1976 season neared a close. The Texas-Arkansas game, played in Austin, had been moved to early December for national television, which led to a lot of pre-game hype. Texas and Arkansas entered the game with 4-5-1 and 5-4-1 records respectively, below Royal's and Broyles' standards. But it was not the classic Texas-Arkansas confrontation that these two great schools had put on for so many years as they fought for dominance in the proud Southwest Conference.

Texas won the game, 29-12, in something less than the usual Longhorn-Razorback thriller. One of them had to lose, of course, but both of these great coaches deserved to go out a winner. That game was no way for distinguished coaches to exit.

My last team not only gave me my two-hundredth win in the game against Georgia Tech, which was very important, but at the Gator Bowl, it sent me to the permanent sidelines with No. 201. What a way to go! I'm proud of all my teams, but when I've finally lost all my hair and am idling time away with a rod and reel on the intercoastal waterways of Southeast Georgia, I'll reflect often on that last game. I appreciate all the championships, I am grateful for all the big wins, but I don't think I'll ever be more grateful to a football team than that last one in Jacksonville — the one that hit a homer for me in my last at bat.

As usual, our fans were ready for the game, too. We were playing a different opponent than our usual Gator Bowl foe, Florida, but the atmosphere for the Georgia people was the same — festive and anticipatory. Georgia fans like the Gator Bowl and they love Jacksonville.

Our players have always been comfortable there, too, and I was pleased with their mood as they moved into the east side locker room,

which normally is the visitor side for the Georgia-Florida game. The last time we were here we had been the visiting team dressed in white. On New Year's night, we were the home team in our familiar red, even though we used what we know as the visitor's dressing room at the Gator Bowl.

All during pre-game, I thought about the fact that we had to put the ball up. We had to throw. Who would ever believe that? Who would think that I — a coach noted for preferring the run — would take that position? From some of the post-game comments, there seemed to be a feeling that since it was my last game I just sat back and let the coaches and players have fun and was not involved with the game plan. Not true. That would not be my style. Granted, the atmosphere of the situation made things different, but there is no way I would change the routine for my last game, even though that two-hundred-victory plateau had been achieved and my retirement had been announced.

As I have already admitted, winning that last game was something special. It was an important objective to go out a winner, and our offensive staff concluded that there was no way we could beat Michigan State without throwing the ball. I heartily agreed. Throughout the game when I talked with offensive coordinator George Haffner — him in the press box calling the plays and me on the sideline — I kept reminding him to throw the ball.

George agreed in the Gator Bowl game, but my mind flashed back to one fortunate time when he had disagreed. It was the Cotton Bowl of 1984, when we upset Texas 10-9 to knock them out of the national championship. We had not moved the ball on the Longhorns all day. Then they fumbled a punt late in the fourth quarter and handed us that one last opportunity at their twenty-three yard line. It was third and eight, our last chance, when I told George on the phone that we had to throw. It was our only hope.

George argued; he wanted to run the option. I relented. Third and eight, and we run the option into that tough Texas defense. Nobody now cares about who wanted to do what. All they remember is that John Lastinger scored the winning touchdown with 3:22 left in one of Georgia's greatest victories.

George Haffner has good judgment as a play caller. Many fans suspect that George and I didn't see eye to eye on pass versus run philosophy, that George supported a more open attack while I leaned to a ball control game. But one thing about George Haffner that makes him such an outstanding football coach is that he subscribes to the same rule that I do: "Don't beat yourself."

George Haffner, a man of class

After interviewing George for our offensive coordinator's position in 1980, I called Bobby Bowden, for whom George had worked at Florida State. The first thing Bobby said was, "George is a sound, fundamental football coach who understands you must be balanced on offense to win."

George is a man of class, too. Not getting the Georgia job was tough on him, but one of Ray Goff's smartest decisions was selling George on staying in Athens to run his offense. It took a big man to make that decision without bitterness, and that is George Haffner. He deserves a head coaching opportunity, and I hope he gets one soon.

Much of the offensive problems we experienced during the 1988 season stemmed from the fact that we were never really settled at quarterback until late in the year. Once it became apparent that we had to go all the way with Wayne Johnson, we became a more consistent offensive football team. Unfortunately, it was not until after the Kentucky game that we made the decision to stay with Wayne. As the season progressed, our coaches did a fine job of directing Wayne in not only which passes to throw, but which ones not to throw. We also gained a better feel for what he could and could not do. We felt that minimizing the on-the-field decision-making was important. By the end of the year, we were realizing our objective.

Auburn was too much for us physically, but we would never have beaten Georgia Tech without putting the ball up. We could not have consistently lined up and run the ball right at them. We had to throw and did. We knew it was the same with Michigan State.

We had Wayne Johnson as a regular for only one year. He was always the back-up. We were always taking somebody else's offense — James Jackson's most of the time — and fitting Wayne into it, because you can't develop two different offenses. If Wayne had not been hurt in his final spring practice season and if we had become more aware of how best to use him earlier in the season the out-

9

come might have been different for us at Columbia and Lexington, especially the latter.

Losing to Kentucky was as frustrating a game as I have ever experienced. Taking nothing away from them and their coach, Jerry Claiborne, one of the closest friends I have, we should have done better jobs as coaches. Winning that game would have thrown a much different light on our season. As it turned out, had we won over the Wildcats, we would have at least tied for the conference championship. But then a glance back over all the twenty-five years we played in Lexington reveals that we lost only twice, so we were very fortunate against them over the long haul. You keep lining up against a team often enough, and sooner or later they will get it going their way and whip you.

But that was all behind us. The season was over except this last time out in the Gator Bowl. I had walked the field, had flipped through the game program and now was preparing to make my final remarks to the team.

From the beginning of my career, I have never been a proponent of last-minute emotional and inspirational pep talks. That is not the way to win football games, in my opinion. Emotion can enhance the performance of a team strong in fundamentals, but it cannot make up for fundamental weaknesses. I looked across the young faces in that lockerroom, faces with anticipation, faces of big, robust young men who will know victory and disappointment in their lives just like the rest of America's college-age youth, and I suddenly realized that this was the last time I would talk to a team. But I was true to form. I didn't say a lot; I simply reminded them to play hard and to have some fun.

The shouts went up as they always do when that moment comes to hit the field, and suddenly we were moving through the door

to prepare for the kickoff. I stood by the door and slapped each one of them on the back as they filed out.

At home in Athens there is a sign over the Sanford Stadium dressing room door that reads, "Be worthy as you run upon this hallowed sod, For you have dared to tread where champions have trod." Players reach up and tap that sign as they file out for home games. That sign was not over the door as my last team moved out for the 1989 Gator Bowl, but they were more than worthy. They played like champions and brought me my last championship, the Gator Bowl championship of 1989.

You know the story. You know how exciting the victory was. Some felt it was the best game of the bowl season. It was the largest audience ever to see a college football game on ESPN — 6.3 million homes viewed the game for a 6.6 Nielsen rating.

Early on, I realized that not only was our team up and ready, but that Michigan State was, too. That crispness of the night had carried over to the blocking and tackling of both squads. Stand around on the field in Jacksonville on last New Year's night and you would get yourself flattened in a hurry. This was no game for the faint of heart. Both sides had their chin straps buckled and their belts cinched. They were girded for battle.

We got field position on our third possession at the Michigan State forty-five and scored on a touchdown pass from Johnson to Rodney Hampton. Hampton would be busy all night. Of all the backs I've ever coached, none could stop and start as quickly as Hampton. From dead stop to top speed was only a couple of steps for him. Glynn Harrison could change directions without slowing his speed better than any back we had at Georgia, but Rodney was the best at stopping and starting. Healthy, he gives the offense an added dimension. Just get him the ball and get him open.

But the big play in that drive was a pass to Keith Henderson to the one-yard line. It was one of the exceptional catches that Henderson seemed to make so often. Great extension to get to the ball and the ability and awareness to keep his feet in bounds. He is versatile and probably has the best instinctive awareness of any back I coached. He really had a feel for where he was on the football field. That is something you don't coach and is why the pros were high on him. He weaves and flows, whereas Tim Worley was a pounder, a blaster. Worley could blast off a tackle and go seventy-five yards with the best of them.

We soon got the ball again and moved for a field goal — 10-0. On our next possession, Johnson scrambled and hit Hampton who danced by a few defenders and scored on a thirty-yard play. That made it 17-0. I was right: This team was ready to play.

But just when you begin to feel good in a football game, things often tighten up, especially if the other side is prepared to play, which Michigan State was. If there were any doubts about the Spartans as a team, there certainly were none about Andre Rison. I don't think we've ever played against a better receiver. He caught nine passes for 252 yards and three TDs. We reached a couple of points where we might well have put the game away early, but Rison wouldn't let us.

In the second quarter, quarterback Bobby McAllister hit Rison for his first TD pass, and our lead was cut to 17-7 at the half.

In the locker room, I usually speak to the team while the offensive and defensive coaches are in conference. All I said during the Gator Bowl half-time was, "You are playing well. Don't let up. Thirty more minutes." Not exactly Patrick Henry style oratory, but it

never is for most football coaches. You often say the obvious, but you want the players to know you feel good about their performance and to underscore the importance of their realizing it is always a sixty-minute game. Leading at the half doesn't always mean that much.

After a brief moment of encouragement for the team, I listened to what the respective coaching staffs were saying — first to Dale Strahm, who was named defensive coordinator when Bill Lewis became head coach at East Carolina in early December, and then to George Haffner and the offensive coaches.

Halftimes go by quickly unless you are not in the game and you sense that your team lacks sharpness. In those situations, time drags, your worries intensify. Fortunately, that seldom took place for us in the Gator Bowl. During my years at Georgia, we played in the Gator Bowl stadium twenty-seven times, winning nineteen and tying one. There were only three times that we were not in the game in the fourth quarter: In 1977 Florida beat us 22-7; in 1984 they shut us out 27-0; in 1986 the Gators were on top 31-19. The rest of the time we either won the game or lost by seven points or less.

If I had as good a record everywhere as I had in the Gator Bowl, I might have stayed on and challenged Coach Bryant's career victory total of 323.

In the second half against Michigan State, we picked up where we left off, scoring on our second possession to make it 24-7. We were making big plays on offense, which was exactly what we had to do. We had to keep the ball in the air. Yes, this is Vince Dooley talking, and I'm reminding you that in my last game I wanted to see the ball in the air. Like our offensive coaches, I knew that was what it would take to win the game.

George Perles, the Spartan coach, must

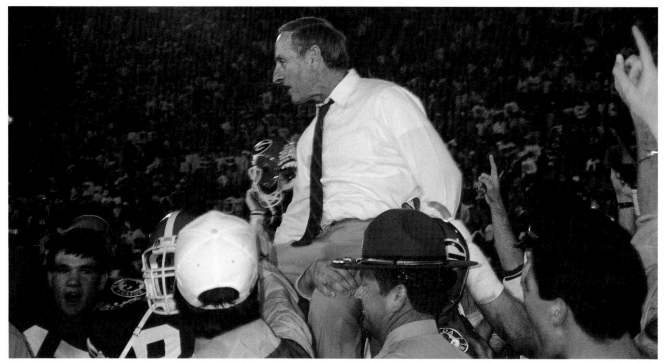

A satisfying victory ride after whipping Michigan State in the Gator Bowl

have felt the same way, and his man Rison kept his team close on our heels.

McAllister to Rison on the fly for fifty-five yards and a touchdown, and it's Georgia 24, MSU 13 after their kick was wide. Then we got a field goal from Steve Crumley to make it 27-13, which is the way the third quarter ended with the Spartans on the attack. They scored on the second play of the final quarter to make it 27-20.

But Hampton was hot. In our next drive, he took the option to his right and cut back across the grain to his left for thirty-two yards and a touchdown. Kasay's kick gave us a 34-20 lead.

However, Rison was not finished and neither were the Spartans. In their next possession they moved it down to our twenty-five, first and ten. They got another first down, but finally our defense began to stiffen. After a fumble for a loss of ten, MSU was caught

holding and Richard Tardits sacked McAllister for a sixteen-yard loss. It was third and forty-six at midfield, and on the sideline I was thinking, "There is no way they can get forty-six yards." I was right. They got fifty when Rison went up with our defenders and came down with the ball for a touchdown.

Our lead was 34-27 with 3:42 left when the Spartans kicked to us.

Quickly I was on the phone and reminded George Haffner, "Their defense has to be tired. We need to keep the ball and run out the clock." George did a superb job of keeping the ball on the ground for nine plays and killing the clock. We had thrown enough passes. In fact, we got it just right. You always want to throw just enough to win.

What a great way to wrap up a charmed career — good old-fashioned ball control football. I couldn't have been happier or prouder.

CHAPTER 2
The Lessons Of Jackson Street, The Basis Of Success

On Monday, January 2, 1989, I awakened as head football coach at the University of Georgia for the last time. The decision on my replacement had been made, but it would not be announced for several hours. Later that morning at a press conference, University President Dr. Charles Knapp ended all the speculation and presented Ray Goff to the media as Georgia's fourth head coach since the beginning of World War II.

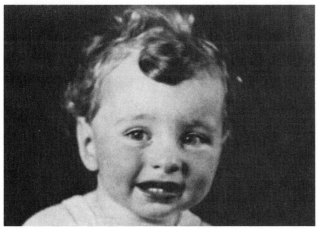

Baby Vincent in Mobile

When that war began, I was in grade school in Mobile, Alabama, my hometown, and had little or no knowledge about the Peach State and its flagship university in Athens. I knew a good deal more about the war. One of my earliest childhood memories is the reports on radio of what was taking place overseas on two fronts. Since that time, I have finished high school and college, spent two years in the Marines, and coached for thirty-three years without another major war, although those who suffered from the "conflicts" in Korea and Viet Nam probably scoff at anyone who says those wars were not major.

Through the years, I have always been sensitive about wars and their influence on our lives and history, and that sensitivity probably stems, in large measure, from my childhood memories of World War II.

Every night we would turn on the old radio and listen to the news commentators like Gabriel Heater tell us how our troops were doing. Early on, the news was all bad. I remember the headlines about the courage of our first hero, Colin P. Kelly, a brave pilot who ordered his crew to bail out and then went down with his plane. I remember how much that impressed me. He became a real hero to me, as well as to an entire nation.

We saw a lot of newsreels and war movies. One that really touched me was the story of the ship sinking with the five Sullivan brothers aboard. I might have fought with my younger brother, Billy, but I couldn't imagine how a family could cope with losing all its sons. When a family lost an immediate relative in action, a star was hung in the window of the home. I remember seeing photographs of the Sullivan home with five stars hanging about. The pathos of that scene really touched my conscience.

Perhaps those war memories had some influence on my appreciation for the military and stimulated my historical curiosity about wars. It is difficult for me to make a trip to Europe or the Far East and not relate where I go and what I see to the two World Wars which so drastically affected lives everywhere.

When I was growing up nothing was more important than doing your job, providing for your family and serving your country. You put the family and church first, and you kept the school right in there with them. Life was very simple and orderly. Not a lot of material things to enjoy, but a great background when it comes to values. I have often thought about my background and what it meant to me, and I have always concluded that the most important things I gleaned from growing up in the tough times on Jackson Street in Mobile were the values learned.

We weren't exactly destitute, but there is one haunting memory that still lives with me. My mother was afraid we were going to be evicted once because we couldn't pay the rent. We also couldn't pay our utility bills and were told our lights would be turned off. We looked at the landlord as a mean person. When you're eight or nine years old in a situation like that, you don't quite understand. I had visions of my clothes and personal belongings being out in the street, and I lay awake at night really bothered.

Out of such experiences is born a fierce drive to succeed.

Funny thing — we didn't consider ourselves poor. We weren't aware that we were struggling that much. Nobody was hungry. In fact, I wasn't aware of my poverty until twenty years later when I read about it in the newspaper. Nobody really suffered, although I learned later that both my parents had failing health. A more liberal income may have allowed for more medical rehabilitation and a better diet, but by and large ours was a good life even though it was a challenge for our parents.

Former Secretary of State Dean Rusk once said about a similar upbringing in Cherokee County, Georgia, "There was no question, the so-called work ethic was important to those growing up in the circumstances in which I grew up. We didn't sit around too much. We were always doing whatever was at the ends of our fingertips to do. We were poor, but if anyone else had called us poor, we would have killed them. We were comforted by the

BILL HARTMAN — *"I have had the feeling for many years that Vince experienced such a hard time from a money standpoint at a young age that he became used to overcoming adversity and realized that he had to do it with hard work and discipline. I believe that the Catholic priests and nuns in Mobile had a great deal to do with forming his good habits at an early age. And then, of course, his Marine training was a positive influence in this regard. One of his most remarkable assets is stability. He really thinks through anything he attempts, gets it well organized before tackling it. He has persistence, and that is outstanding in the fourth quarter of a football game. I've seen the time when, in the fourth quarter, I couldn't imagine how he was going to win, but with the combination of persistence and a little luck, he has won more than his share.*

"He rehearses everything that he is going to do, and this is particularly true in football maneuvers. He goes through every phase of the game methodically. He rehearses on Thursday for the actual game on Saturday and covers all phases of the game. He probably rehearses his speeches and his actions whenever he makes a public appearance or meets with an organized board of any sort. He has become a polished public speaker, where at first he was not too good. He's gotten where he has very good rapport with the public and is extremely cooperative with the public, particularly young people. In the last few years he has cultivated a good rapport with his football players, and he motivates them extremely well. At the end of nearly every paractice, he has something unusual to say to them.

"Most importantly, you can rely on his word. If he tells you something, you can count on it, which is a great attribute. He has great discipline, both personally and with his football team, and he does not hesitate to take any action even though it might be a negative factor in winning a football game on Saturday.

"Lastly, I think he has great curiosity about many subjects. He has an inquiring mind and is very, very curious about what makes the world go around in many fields."

statement in the Bible that it was easier for a camel to pass through the eye of a needle than for a rich man to get into heaven." When I think about my early life, I relate to what Mr. Rusk said.

Living in a town or small city as Mobile was back then was not like life on a farm or rural environment where there were constant chores and field work to do, but we learned responsibility early. A variety of assignments faced us every day.

We sought any opportunity to make money by applying for odd jobs. I recall being given a job selling Liberty Magazines door-to-door. The company offered a prize for the person who sold the most magazines — a baseball bat and glove which I wanted very much. As I sold the magazines, I was fortunate to get a few tips, which soon mounted up. I was so anxious to win the glove and bat that when the deadline came, I bought all of my leftover magazines with my tip money and just tore them up. I won the prize, but it didn't take me long to discover what a poor business man I was. If I had kept the tips, I could have simply bought a bat and ball and still had money left over. That was my first experience in learning to make good business decisions. But the important thing was not the money; it was the competitive desire to win first prize.

In high school, one of my most important jobs was delivering laundry for the Sam Joy Laundry with my friend and high school teammate Bobby Duke. This job had a very important fringe benefit. Since we had no car, my first dates were in a Sam Joy panel truck, doubling with Bobby.

For two summers and after school certain days of the week, I worked at a meat market and earned $56.00, which my mother put into a savings account. One day she took me for my first visit to the dentist, and I recall hav-

ing two teeth pulled and fourteen filled. Later on when I asked my mother where my money was, she said, "Open your mouth," and she pointed to my dental work.

Nowadays after lunch, you'll find me headed to the washroom with my toothbrush in hand. I learned to take care of my teeth.

Today, one of the things that I appreciate about the success of our athletic program at Georgia is that I see a lot of kids coming to school with bad teeth, just like it was with me, and we're able to offer them some relief without taking their life's savings.

In my childhood, we always had to sweep floors and make up the beds. We also learned to iron our own pants and to assume a number of other household duties as well as work in the yard. But the thing I remember most about those early days was washing dishes.

It was my job to wash the dishes and Billy's to dry them. He got to dry because he was the baby. I never did understand that. He grew up to become a successful college head football coach, but he never grew up to wash dishes. I bet to this day my younger brother, who is the best friend I have, has never washed any dishes. Probably hasn't dried very many lately, either.

When Billy and I were not washing dishes or working at our home chores, we took to the streets. In a city, especially a port city like Mobile, you are faced with a lot of temptations and grow up fast. There were a lot of bars and a lot of sailors, which meant that we were aware of alcohol's influence and that what we often heard down at the waterfront was not to be repeated at the dinner table or in front of the nuns and the brothers at school. I can't begin to imagine what it is like for young boys today. There were plenty of things to tempt us when we were growing up, but there were no violent gangs, no drugs, no guns. The streets were where the action was but the action was sports, not crack or criminal activity so pervasive now. There was a game of some kind going on all the time, and I loved to play games. I loved to compete and enjoyed being involved in any kind of sport, even those we invented. The only time I would ever stop playing was when a lady who lived next door — Grandma Leon — would finish baking hot Syrian bread. She was Lebanese, and her hot bread with butter was the greatest delicacy I had known. I loved it so much that she took great delight in baking it for me. There was no game circumstance crucial enough for me to continue when Grandma Leon's bread came out of the oven and she yelled, "Come and get it, Vincent!"

Incidentally, nobody in my family or any of my close friends has ever called me Vince. They all call me Vincent, including my wife, Barbara. Everybody refers to my brother as Bill, except me and the family. He has always been Billy, just as I am Vincent to him. He has never called me Vince.

Brother Billy, "my best friend"

Billy and I have a very close relationship, which has grown over the years. I have a high regard for him and his coaching ability. He is an excellent football coach, and it has been a great thrill for me to see him turn the program around at Wake Forest. That was a tough assignment, but Billy has benefited from the Jackson Street experience and principles, too. He has put them to good use. Billy is a hard worker, good communicator and a coach who knows his X's and O's. And more.

We fought a lot as kids, as all brothers do, but that began to change in high school when he got big enough to hold his own. By the time we got to college, the bonds really strengthened. Today, as I say, he is my best friend, and we enjoy getting together as often as our schedules permit.

Billy is very much a competitor too, dating back to those Jackson Street games. We always enjoyed competing against one another, except for the time our teams met in the Gator Bowl following the 1971 season. He was at North Carolina at the time. Georgia won the game 7-3, and our friend Rex Edmondson, then sports editor of the *Jacksonville Journal*, accused me of winning the toss and then running out the clock.

What is interesting about that game is that all my family — sisters, nieces, nephews, cousins — was pulling for baby brother, Billy. That didn't sit too well with Barbara.

It wasn't a lot of fun for either Billy or me. You don't enjoy being in those situations. I was naturally very happy to win the game, but I felt bad for Billy. I'm sure he would have felt the same if he had won. Whenever you win a football game and walk across the field to shake hands with the coach, you naturally feel good about winning. But you always have empathy for the other coach because you have been there yourself.

When I walked across the field in Jacksonville on December 31, 1971, and saw the expression on Billy's face, I realized it was not just an opposing coach. It was my brother. The competitor in you stimulates a "better he than me" emotion, but in a situation like that you are overcome with compassion. It is something I would never want to go through again.

Billy and I share a lot of pleasant memories. After college when he was an assistant at Mississippi State and I was coaching the Auburn quarterbacks, we both scouted athletes in our hometown of Mobile. We would wind up staying at home on Jackson Street. Even as grown men, we slept in the same bed we slept in as boys.

We would lie awake at night and reminisce about the Jackson Street games and our childhood experiences. But when we got around to talking about recruiting, who we were interested in and what we thought about the abilities of several players we both were pursuing, that coaching competitiveness returned. We lied to each other about prospects. Even when a coach shares a bed with his brother, his best friend, he can't give away recruiting secrets.

On a trip to Mobile in the spring of 1989, I rode through the old neighborhood, feeling the urge to reminisce about the past. Our home was where the parking lot of the Mobile City Auditorium is today. There isn't much left to remind me of what it was once like, but I do have those memories, and I enjoyed riding around for several minutes and thinking about all the games we played. Like stoppers, which was somewhat akin to baseball. We played stoppers with a broomstick and a bottle cap. I still have a chipped tooth that resulted from my diving for a stopper and landing mouth-first on the street curb.

For a family that watched its pennies closely, it was a disturbing thought that such games could result in unaffordable medical bills, but that chipped tooth was a badge of honor. I caught the stopper and won the Jackson Street championship for my team.

I remember something else from that period that was not significant at the time but later was to make me realize what was happening in my life as an athlete. During one of those street games, a neighbor who said he had played pro football — I could never remember his name — stopped me one afternoon and said, "Son, I've been watching, and you can play. You've got a quick change of pace."

"What does change of pace mean?" I asked. I had no idea, but later on I realized that there is nothing like athletic quickness to carry an athlete in any sport. Great speed I didn't have, but when it came to quickness, I was blessed. And if you line up at quarterback, which was my position, quickness was perhaps the most important asset.

Master of quickness, Fran Tarkenton

Look at Fran Tarkenton, who played at Georgia and then set numerous career records in the National Football League: most attempts — 6,467; most completions — 3,686; most yards — 47,003; most touchdowns — 342. Fran got by on desire, determination, brains, cunning, guile, quarterback arrogance and quickness. I can identify with those attributes. Fran was durable, playing for nineteen years, but he would have never gotten off a number of those passes if he had not had the quickness to escape the rush and gain a second opportunity to find a receiver.

But playing in the games on Jackson Street, I was not concerned about quickness or developing any athletic skills. I was just playing and having fun. Competition was keen in the streets and I thrived on it. I played to win, and when it got rough, I didn't mind being in the middle of it. If somebody took a whack at me, I whacked back.

In high school I developed a responsible attitude about my grades and homework, but in the lower grades it was recess that was most important to me, as it is with all kids growing up.

Once when Georgia baseball coach Steve Webber checked into the possiblity of recruiting Pete Rose's son, Petey, he was informed that Petey would probably sign a professional contract out of high school. "There are not but three things that Petey likes about school," Webber was told, "lunch, recess and baseball." In the early forties in Mobile, Petey's philosophy fit me to a T.

I remember one day when we all raced out of the classroom at recess and headed to the vacant lot across the street. Suddenly we realized that there was a new locked gate blocking our path. "Okay," I said, "no gate is going to stop us." And like a platoon leader faced with an unexpected obstacle, I barked out a command to my buddies. "Over the top,

men." About twenty grade-school kids tried to scamper over the gate at one time. It collapsed.

When the nuns learned of the incident, they conducted an investigation and discovered that I was the one who had given the "over the gate" order.

In those situations, corporal punishment was very much the order of the day. I had had my backside tanned a number of times at home. The nuns would wrap your knuckles or pull your ear or pinch the fatty part of the sides of your waistline. I was never abused, but I got my share of physical punishment and deserved every bit of it. After the gate incident, however, the nun chose to "interview" me.

"Why did you do that?" she asked.

"Well," I responded, "I read in a book about a leader taking charge, and I thought that was great. I want to be a leader."

She thought for a minute and said something which I have never forgotten: "It is great to be a leader, but the important thing is to lead in the right way. What you did was the wrong way. If you want to lead people, you must lead them in the right direction."

Not only did my truthful answer save me from humiliation and physical punishment, it left a lasting impression.

Even with that sister's indelible analysis, which I look back on as a significant lesson in life, I was far from learning to control my emotions and my quick temper.

I had problems my first couple of years in high school. I was uncooperative in school and ignored homework. I was arrogant and resented authority. The Brothers of the Sacred Heart did not care for me at all, but they knew how to handle the situation. They understood that I was testing them, so they did not exactly use kid gloves.

They were tough, but what made the difference was that they were patient and never lost faith in me. Brother Phillips once said to me, "Dooley, you're No. 1 on my hit parade." He was a boxer, and I knew that he meant business. On another occasion I recall yawning in class without putting my hand over my mouth, an arrogant response which he didn't appreciate. He spoke words that still ring in my ears: "The next time you open your mouth like that," he said, "I'm going to put my fist down it."

That scene was repeated in a meeting a couple of years ago when a big tackle kept popping gum as I addressed the team. I gave him the same warning Brother Phillips had given me, promising to ram my fist down his throat if he ever popped gum in a squad meeting again. Sometimes the arrogance of youth and the impatience of adults clash rather emphatically and without warning.

Just like Brother Phillips got his point across to me, I got my message across to the big tackle. Sometimes that kind of shock discipline is needed. I just hope that tackle will someday appreciate what I did as much as I appreciate Brother Phillips for threatening to literally knock the arrogance out of me. Then, too, I don't want to think about what would have happened if the big tackle had popped his gum again. I had made a commitment.

Something else I learned from Brother Phillips was that responsibility can work wonders with young people. I eventually gained his confidence as he offered me responsibility, and he actually became a dear friend. Then I did not want to disappoint him.

Brother Phillips, Sister Patricia — the nun who taught me the hesitating jump shot by making me jump over a chair — and my coach Ray Dicharry saw something worthwhile in me and gave me a chance.

My pressing problem was learning to control my temper. I was always getting into fights, even during games. It was mostly over competition, but it reflected a defiant and arrogant attitude, and they knew that they had to demonstrate faith in me as I learned how to cope and grow out of it.

Ray Dicharry's patience is something that made a monumental difference in my life. I remember that in the state basketball tournament one year a team from Selma had been defeated and was watching our game from the stands. One of their players kept heckling us. I had him spotted in his seat, and at the half as we headed into the locker room, it suddenly got to me. I simply could not take it any longer. When we got to his end of the court, I took off after him with Coach Dicharry right behind me. Before I could get a couple of swings in, my coach had jerked me back and gave me a dressing down that I still remember. He really gave me hell. But he was patient, too. He understood that I just could not stand to lose.

Many times, when I have felt that a second or third chance was in order for an undisciplined player, I remember what my coach and others did for me, and I have always tried to go the last mile with players to help them learn to overcome their problems and weaknesses. I've been criticized for doing that many times, but criticism never bothers a coach if he thinks through carefully and believes in what he is doing. If people like Ray Dicharry had given up on a hot-tempered, big-nosed kid back then, I shudder to think what would have happened in my life. I needed patience and understanding.

That incident in the basketball game stuck with me. I was embarrassed and began to gain self-control, which is why I've always expected my teams to handle themselves with class on the football field.

The angriest I suppose I have ever been with a team was following the Florida game in 1967. Florida beat us 17-16 in one of those games you feel you should have won, and a fight broke out at the end of the game. When we got our team in the locker room, I gave them as tough a tongue lashing as I have ever given any Georgia team. I was embarrassed. I was livid and wanted them to understand I didn't appreciate what they did and that such conduct would not be tolerated if they played for me.

One of my basic rules has always been that there would be no profanity on our practice fields — from coaches or players — but sometimes your anger overwhelms you. You lose control and violate your own rules, as I did in the Gator Bowl locker room in 1967. "Fight your ass off on the field, but when the damn game is over, act like gentlemen and represent the University of Georgia like you are supposed to." Of course, I ad-libbed a little here and there with a few phrases I learned back in Mobile at the waterfront.

The problems I had with my temper were pretty much gone by my junior year of high school. The explosive temper was being brought under control.

In my junior and senior years, I was exhibiting leadership on the football field and the basketball court and my grades were consistently good. The priests and nuns had forgotten about my bad years when along came brother Billy, who was rowdy as hell.

McGill High School stars (L-R) Dooley, Bobby Duke, Bubzy Partridge

Billy couldn't believe his ears when the teachers began saying, "You ought to be more like your brother, Vincent."

Even though I was streetwise, there were many important influences in my life. There was a father who impressed upon me at an early age that a "commitment is a commitment." Be a man of your word, he always taught me. Do what you say you are going to do. And it was my mother who always said, "Manners will take you where money won't."

The nuns at grade school, Sisters of Charity, the Brothers of the Sacred Heart, and my high school coach Ray Dicharry — they all stressed the right values. And they in return had the fullest cooperation from my parents. A paddling at school would have been okay with them. I date back to the time when the teachers were in charge of the classroom, that era when parents often said, "If you get a spanking in school, count on getting another one when you get home."

In fact, at our house, if Billy and I did something really bad, our rears were often in double jeopardy. If Mama gave us a spanking, Daddy administered one when he got home. I never understood that.

Over the past twenty-five years, I have seen many kids come through our program with problems, and I've seen them wrestle with a lot of emotions, but the ones who had the right training at home and those whose parents stressed discipline and respect are the ones who usually learn to properly control their lives and achieve balance and direction. There are some exceptions, of course. Some kids with proper training at home get off track in college and have difficulty recovering. There are no guarantees, but "train up a child in the way he should go" most often produces positive results.

When people suggest to me as I travel about the country that they believe the wild rumors about illegal recruiting, I remind them that it is not as bad as they hear. But I also like to point out that I have never heard of anything illegal taking place in recruiting when the parents were truly against such practices.

If athletics were a motivating influence for me personally — self-development and improvement — they also provided opportunity. Growing up, I never thought much about what I would do in life. I was too busy having fun in the streets and playing sports at McGill Institute. It never crossed my mind that college would be an option. Neither of my parents had even gotten beyond grade school. It was a matter of great pride that my sisters Margaret and Rosezella finished high school. That was a big accomplishment for our family.

Most likely I probably would have sought employment in the shipyards if I had not gone to college. That was the preferred line of work in my neighborhood. It paid better than the rest.

One thing is for sure, I would have never attended college one single day without an athletic scholarship. But again that never crossed my mind. We lived one day at a time and never looked beyond Jackson Street.

Then I played football and basketball well enough to be named athlete of the year in Mobile, and suddenly I received invitations to visit a couple of college campuses. Only then did I realize that a scholarship was possible, and only then was there the awareness that a college education was within my reach.

So you can see why I might express such great appreciation for college athletics. I know we have problems. I know we've got to be better custodians. I know we have to police ourselves more effectively and keep trying to strengthen the rules and keep the game healthy. But just as I graduated from Jackson

Street to McGill to Auburn, there are countless young men out there today who could not get into and through college without athletic aid. Many of them turn out to be model and productive citizens in our society, but unfortunately they don't often make the headlines.

It disturbs me that there are so many problems facing our schools and our teachers today. If I had run for governor of Georgia, as I contemplated, and had been fortunate enough to be elected, education would have been my No. 1 priority. We must never neglect education if we are going to succeed with our children, and athletics can be a valuable part of an education. There are abuses, sure. But athletics offer youngsters opportunities. Conducted with the proper emphasis, they can make a positive difference in a young person's life.

Even though times and mores have changed and discipline is a problem, I believe that there are high school coaches out there today who are doing a great service for our communities and are not always properly appreciated and rewarded. At a recent educational symposium that included all of our living former presidents, it was recommended that education return to teaching values. After reading that, my first thought was, that is why high school coaches like Ray Dicharry are so important — they teach values.

One thing I believe has been overlooked in recent Southern history is the influence of athletics in the integration of our school systems in the late sixties and early seventies. There were some problems, and some tension probably remains, but I don't believe the successful integration of our school systems in the South would have ever come about as orderly as it did without athletics. A lot of people objected to the idea and resisted, but

by and large, the transition and adjustment were made with a minimum of problems. Athletics gave students and their communities something to relate to and rally around. Athletics became a common bond that kept peace and reduced major problems. And when there is a discipline challenge in our high schools today, the first person consulted is often the coach.

We must find ways to reward and promote teachers and coaches. They mean so much to our society. It thrills me to see a player for whom I have great respect come and tell me he is planning to coach. I think that is a noble calling, and we need to encourage more of our qualified young men and women to consider a career in education.

Certain athletes also make good role models. One of my early heroes was Stan Musial of the St. Louis Cardinals. I really admired the way he played, but I also admired him as a person and decided to write him a letter, working the sentence construction over and over, making sure that I got it just right.

I have no idea what I said in the letter other than expressing my feelings for him, but I naturally assumed that he would write me back. He didn't.

That disappointment was tough for me as a young boy to accept, but I never lost faith in him. I don't know that he even got the letter. He might have felt that a response was not necessary. He might have gotten so much fan mail that he could not find the time to answer his mail. I don't know.

While I have never resented the fact that he didn't write back, I used that experience to shape one of my professional attitudes. To my knowledge, I have never failed to answer any letter that has crossed my desk. I have always made it a point to answer all my mail, including what I call "hate mail" or "nut mail," provided the author signs his or her name and includes an address.

After I had become successful at Georgia, I was in St. Louis for a coaching convention, and several of us went out to dinner at Stan Musial's restaurant. He was in the restaurant that night and came over to our table. He seemed to know something about Georgia and showed an interest in me as the head coach, which made me feel good, since he had been my boyhood idol.

I was pleased to meet him and told him again how much I had admired him as a baseball player. I had long forgotten about not receiving a reply to my letter. There are two reasons for my getting over it. One, even as a youngster, I learned never to carry grudges and harbor ill-will; it's not productive. And

A dog lover, even in college

two, I remember Jesse Outlar, long-time sports editor of *The Atlanta Constitution*, telling me about an experience he had with Musial in spring training. Jesse remembered that when a Cardinal workout ended in St. Petersburg, it was the rookies and younger players who didn't have time for the kids gathered around for autographs. But Musial, the old pro playing in his last couple of seasons, waited and patiently signed for every kid.

Even though he didn't answer my letter, Stan Musial was a good role model, like the heroes and role models of Jackson Street who taught teamwork, humility and understanding.

I am thankful for all the lessons learned back then. They were the bases of the skills I needed to become a successful football coach.

At Auburn, I enjoyed college life. It was an opportunity to remain in athletics on a higher level and naturally I was anxious to see if I could compete.

I also had matured enough that there was no problem with my attitude about classwork. I intended from the beginning to obtain a degree and did so in four years — on time — without ever attending summer school.

The only problem I had was one that many college freshmen encounter: loneliness. It traps the best of them.

I can't tell you how many times Mike "Moonpie" Wilson quit at Georgia before he settled in with us and became an All-America tackle in 1976. He'd leave and we'd go get him. He'd strike out again and assistant coaches Doc Ayers and Mike Castronis would talk him into coming back one more time. Finally he stayed, and after thirteen years in the NFL, including playing on a Super Bowl team, I'm sure he is glad that somebody kept coaxing him back to the campus.

There was somebody at Auburn who kept me from making a similar mistake — Joel Eaves. He was freshman end coach and always willing to counsel me. When I was discouraged, he understood and offered me confidence and support. We had ten quarterbacks and I was at the bottom of the list. I felt that I was not doing anything right on the field and that when I did, nobody seemed to notice or care.

But Coach Eaves continued to listen patiently and kept encouraging me.

Finally I made up my mind to leave Auburn and go back home to play basketball in Mobile at Springhill College.

Basketball was always my favorite sport. In high school, my junior year, I never would have played football if my friend Bobby Duke had not come by the first day of fall drills and badgered me into going out for the team. I went to practice that day just to get him to leave me alone. That is when I took a serious interest in football and began to really enjoy the sport. It was fun to play quarterback, to be in the center of the action, to be in control.

But basketball not only was my favorite, it was the sport that I felt I was best at, those being the days before the game changed to the fast-paced style of today and when there

was a role, physically, for a short, stocky guard.

I set two records in Alabama state tournaments. In 1949, I was the leading scorer in the state tournament with an eighteen points per game average, and a year later in 1950, I broke it with an average of nineteen points per game. That record stood for many years.

Being at the bottom of the quarterback list, plus nobody's noticing anything I did, was bad for my confidence in football at Auburn, and I was certain that it would be a different story if I went back to basketball and enrolled at Springhill College.

But in the spring football game of my freshman year, I intercepted a couple of passes and returned a couple of punts for good yardage and gained some attention. That motivated me to come back the next

Quarterback Dooley led Auburn to its best record in seventeen years

year, but I don't think that I would have reached that point of staying around if it had not been for Coach Eaves' encouragement.

A year later, an interesting development took place in my life that further helped me to mature and see things more clearly. I had become a starter in football and basketball, which took up a lot of time if you paid any attention to class responsibilities.

A Mobile banker, Ken Lott, had recruited me to Auburn, and at the end of my sophomore year, I went to see him about some campus rumors.

I told him I heard that some of the players, several of whom were not even starting, were getting a few considerations under the table. I was starting in two sports and working harder than anybody else, but I wasn't getting anything. In fact, in my flawed thinking, I felt I was worthy of two scholarships.

Mr. Lott said, "Well, if the rumors are true, you have a point. But you'll be better off in the long run if you take only what you deserve and do what is right." That was some of the best advice I ever had, and I'm proud to say I never again thought about any under-the-table inducements. I was playing and starting and making decent grades, and that was all I was ever promised when I signed. As a matter of fact, after talking with Mr. Lott, I concluded that what I was getting was all that I deserved.

My senior year I was voted captain after missing all of spring practice with a bad knee. This put pressure on me to get the knee well. I did not want to be a captain sitting on the bench.

We finished with Auburn's best record in seventeen years (7-2-1) and were invited to the Gator Bowl, where we were defeated by Texas Tech, 35-13.

My college football experience was one I enjoyed and now recall with great affection.

We turned the program around under Coach Shug Jordan. We fielded Auburn's first bowl team in sixteen years, and when it was over, I had the good fortune and honor to be invited to play in the college all-star game in Chicago. About this time, I began thinking more about my future. My mother, who so ardently looked forward to my graduation from college, died when I was a freshman. With the friends I had made in college, I began to move away from my Mobile roots and began putting down roots at Auburn, although I knew where I would be the next two years — the United States Marine Corps.

Not only did I look forward to military service, I enjoyed it and considered making it a career. At the end of two years, my options included an offer to re-enlist for a tour of duty in Europe as a colonel's aide, joining Ken Lott in the banking business in Mobile, or returning to Auburn as an assistant coach. All along I had prepared myself for business because everybody said there was no security in coaching, but I was not married and had the itch to give it a try. I joined Coach Jordan's staff thinking it would be temporary.

Initially I worked with the quarterbacks and later asked to become freshman coach, which many considered a demotion. My thinking was that it would be good for me to have the responsibility of running a team. But during all this time, an important assignment for me was scouting our opponents with Coach Eaves.

A football coach at the time worked hard during the season — seven days a week — and in the spring, but in the off-season there wasn't anything to do. You literally just sat around, which I could not stand. I had to be doing something, so I decided to return to school.

My plans were to obtain a Master's degree with a major in economics and a minor in history. After taking the history courses first, which really excited me, I enrolled in economics and discovered that I had to make myself study. Those courses were not as enjoyable as history. I voiced my concerns to my counselor, who advised me that since I was seeking a Master's on the side, so to speak, I would be far better off to do what I enjoyed even though it would take me twice as long. It was great advice, even though it took me five years of attending class in the winter, spring and summer quarters to earn the degree.

After awhile, Coach Jordan began to ques-tion me on just how long it was going to take to complete that Master's. He was very patient, but the man most patient with me was the Auburn basketball coach and chief football scout, Joel Eaves. Other than with Barbara, whom I met when she was a fresh-man at Auburn, I spent most of my time with Coach Eaves. I was to learn a lot about him on those football weekend scouting trips for five years.

Fortunately for me, he was watching, studying and observing me. Later events sug-gest he thought reasonably well of what he saw.

CHAPTER 3
A New Kid In Town, And New Fight In The Dog

November 22, 1963, is a pivotal date in American history — the day President John F. Kennedy was assassinated in Dallas, Texas. It also is a pivotal date in the athletic history of the University of Georgia — the day University President Dr. O. C. Aderhold hired Joel Harry Eaves as athletic director.

For some time the word had been spreading in Auburn that Joel Eaves was going to give up coaching basketball, which he loved, and become an administrator, taking over a distressed program at another unnamed school. Coach Eaves had become irritated at some of the things that were happening to him at Auburn. He didn't enjoy having to work as the head basketball coach and football assistant and scout, any of which could have been a full-time job, and I think he saw no improvement on the horizon for him at Auburn. He considered himself a basketball coach first and a football coach second, but he found out from Coach Jordan and Jeff Beard, athletic director, that they considered him first a football coach and secondly a basketball coach. Too, he had experienced a heart attack and obviously felt that he should consider an alternative to the pressures of day-to-day coaching. The temporary tension between him and Coach Jordan, as well as the other factors, forced him to change his thinking and make what seemed, at the time, a drastic move. Although the position of athletic director today is a very powerful one, in 1963 it was just becoming prominent in college athletics.

Coach Eaves and Dr. Aderhold had met at the Heart of Auburn Motel to hammer out the details of the contract, and soon word of Coach Eaves' decision and plan spread quickly about the little town. Auburn's president was Ralph B. Draughon. When the news about events in Dallas broke, a neighbor of Coach Eaves was raking leaves when a friend drove by and said, "Did you hear the news? They just shot the president."

Coach Eaves' neighbor, unaware of the national headlines but familiar with the Eaves situation, leaned forward on the rake and said, "Which one? Draughon or Aderhold?"

When I heard that Coach Eaves was headed to Athens, it never dawned on me that he might call me about the head coaching job at Georgia. The first time we talked, late one afternoon at Auburn, I began to realize that he wanted to offer me the job, but I also saw that he was afraid to recommend me, considering the predictable reaction in Athens to the idea of hiring an unknown freshman coach.

"How would you like to come as maybe an assistant head coach?" was his first comment. I think he had in mind hiring a highly regarded assistant like Gene Stallings, who then was Coach Bryant's top assistant at Texas A&M. "That sounds pretty good," I said in reference to the assistant head coach idea. "I'd like to talk further with you about it."

I didn't hear anything from him for a couple of days until he called while I was on a recruiting assignment in Memphis. Right off the bat, he said, "I want to offer you the job as football coach here at Georgia and give you a three-year contract." Coach Eaves never beat around the bush. He always got right to the point. Before the shock of his offer set in and I could react, he added, "By the way, Frank Broyles is looking for you. He wants you to

come to Arkansas as backfield coach. Tennessee is hiring Doug Dickey as head coach. What do you want to be, an assistant at Arkansas or head coach at Georgia?"

What is interesting about the Broyles call is that I had come to the conclusion a year or so earlier that my best interests would be served by applying for an assistant's job at another school. Coach Jordan and I talked about it, and I told him that I planned to write letters to both Broyles and Darrell Royal of Texas, inquiring about the opportunity to work for them.

My thinking was that this additional experience would broaden me as a coach and would be a step in the right direction. If that had worked out, I would have been taking a step toward a head coaching position. The way I had it figured was that after I had moved up the coaching ladder, my timing for succeeding Coach Jordan at Auburn might be favorable. As it turned out, the day that important break — to be an assistant coach at the "right" school — came was the very day Joel Eaves decided he wanted me as the head coach at Georgia.

There was no question what I wanted, but I tried to think things through carefully as we talked. I was immediately concerned about the three-year contract. "Can you get me four years?" I asked Coach Eaves. "I think I need four years. I don't care about the salary."

He said, "I'll see." And then he added, "Do you want to come?"

I said, "Give me five minutes to talk to Barbara, and I will call you right back." When I called Coach Eaves back, I said, "If you are crazy enough to stick your neck out, I'm crazy enough to come."

The next day I was in Athens. Dan Magill picked me up at the airport and took me to

Facing page: Eaves and Dooley, architect and builder

the Holiday Inn with instructions not to leave the room — not even answer the door. Since I could have walked down Broad Street without being recognized, I was amused at the secrecy, but Dan wanted to make sure that nobody broke the news before the press conference. At the time the Atlanta papers, even though they were under one ownership, were very competitive. There had been widespread speculation on both the athletic director and the head coaching jobs, as a matter of fact.

The hiring of Coach Eaves had surprised a lot of people. There was some sentiment for an athletic director with Georgia ties or an established football coach who would take both jobs. On top of that, Coach Eaves was generally considered a basketball coach, and you can imagine how that rankled people in Athens. There was just nothing in the hiring process that suggested Georgia would be gaining any football credibility in the deal.

While Coach Eaves did not appreciate the stepchild relationship that often characterized basketball in the Southeastern Conference at the time, he not only enjoyed football, he knew that it was the sport which had to sustain the athletic program. Even though he was annoyed with his personal relationship in regard to his football assignment at Auburn, it did not diminish his feelings for football nor his understanding of its importance, especially at Georgia.

Now, all of a sudden, my experience as a basketball player for Coach Eaves and five years of football scouting with him on weekends were about to change my life dramatically. Coach Eaves felt that he knew me and had an understanding and appreciation for my ability. In fact, nobody knew me better than he did.

On all those scouting trips, it was nonstop work. We would arrive at the site where the team we were scouting was playing and pick up their game film in the afternoon. Then we went to a motel room, turned out the lights and began watching film, using the old Kodak analyst projectors and hanging a bed-sheet on the wall for a screen. We would chart our opponent's games, play by play, noting what they did in certain situations and what had or had not worked for them. He scouted the opponent's offense, and I took the defense. Sometimes we would work until 10:30 P.M. and then get up early and spend another couple of hours with those projectors grinding away before we headed to the

The Auburn Staff: (front, L-R) Shot Senn, Vince Dooley, Shug Jordan, Buck Bradberry, Joe Connally, (back row) Gene Lorendo, Joel Eaves, Dick McGowen, Hal Herring

game. I was single at the time, but there was no question about where I would spend Friday nights in the fall. Spending them with Joel Eaves turned out to be the biggest break in my career.

Joel Eaves was the best of coaches when it came to teaching. He was highly organized and very technical. He had high standards and was very much a gentleman. Above all, he was a man of unsurpassed integrity.

It was from Coach Eaves that I learned the importance of respecting your opponent. Once we were scouting Wake Forest at a time when ACC football was obviously not on the same level as the SEC. Additionally, ACC films were shot at a slower speed, all of which gave me a false impression of the Deacons. I mean, they really looked slow. "Boy, they look terrible to me," I said to Coach Eaves. He didn't like it at all and replied irritably, "I'm pretty much impressed myself," and he began building them up, much to my surprise. When they came down to Auburn and played us a close, tough game, I realized how I had fooled myself. Thanks to Coach Eaves, I learned a valuable lesson: respect your opponents. I have since that time.

And I'll always be grateful to him for indeed sticking his neck out for me. That took courage in the face of the turmoil at Georgia, but he believed in me because of our long-time association. He not only learned what I knew about the game, he taught me what he had accumulated over the years. Joel Eaves had a fine understanding of football fundamentals. He knew the game.

In every sense, you could say that my timing was remarkably good when I arrived in Athens in December of 1963, and not just from the standpoint of coaching the football team. The community and the Georgia supporters were ready for something positive, and we had everything going our way, one of those nothing-to-lose-and-everything-to-gain situations.

But there was more. The university was poised to emerge into an era of significant expansion and academic growth that would bring it national recognition for excellence. The sleepy little town of Athens was soon to experience noticeable growth, too. The town and county didn't suddenly explode, but progress was about to take place, and you could see that there was enormous potential everywhere.

To tell the truth, I was a little disappointed in the campus initially. And I say this with no disrespect, because I came to understand why there was not a lot of emphasis on certain things like landscaping and maintenance.

Dr. Aderhold had a rural background and had administered through the changing times of the fifties. The state of Georgia was not affluent by any means, and there wasn't an abundance of money for education for its colleges. In those austere times, landscaping that seemed important to an ex-marine was not a budget priority. But Dr. Aderhold was a splendid salesman for the university and sold Governor Marvin Griffin, with the help of former Agriculture Commissioner Phil Campbell and a few others, on the importance of developing the science center on the south campus, a building program that was continued under the administrations of Governor S. Ernest Vandiver and Governor Carl Sanders, who had played quarterback for Coach Butts in the early forties. Governor Sanders was an ardent supporter of our program in the early days. Before the state began to put any significant money up for education, the university really operated on a shoestring budget. There wasn't enough money to recruit and pay outstanding teachers, let alone fret about the upkeep and maintenance of buildings. New construction was usually out of the question. But as someone newly arrived, I didn't understand the presence of bare paths across the campus. I felt that things could have been neater and that it wouldn't take much to improve the landscaping. I always complained privately about a lack of emphasis in that area.

What Georgia had in those days was an abundance of potential, and I am proud to say that amazing progress has taken place since then. Not only has there been efficient landscaping, maintenance and construction, Georgia leaped forward in recruiting outstanding faculty. We became a quality educational institution, and today everybody likes the way we look. You won't find a prettier campus than Georgia's, with its blend of the traditional and the modern.

While all this was going on, downtown Athens really took on a new look. A tree-planting campaign developed under a downtown beautification program, which began under Mayor Julius Bishop in the early seventies (and continued during the administrations of Upshaw Bentley and Lauren Coile), gave the city an attractiveness that makes it a delightful place to browse around. A number of shops and new stores have sprung up, making Broad Street, which borders the north side of the campus, an active neighborhood with a lively vitality and a pleasing ambience.

Today we have a lot to sell when we talk to a prospective athlete, and not just the athletic facilities and tradition. The campus, faculty and the community add to our portfolio, and that is very important.

So I arrived in Athens when the community and the university were about to experience their greatest growth and progress. It's good to be where things are looking up. Growth meant more youthful energy and optimism, resulting from rapid increase in enrollment. That was obvious as the student body grew from 7,538 in 1960 to 21,873 by 1970.

Like a lot of people who know Athens only because they followed their favorite team to Sanford Stadium to play a football game with the Bulldogs, I knew very little about the school and campus. My knowledge was pretty much confined to the Georgia athletic program and Sanford Stadium.

I based my decision to come to Georgia in terms of the opportunity to win as a football coach. You don't have to be a genius to understand that a state university has a tremendous advantage in recruiting.

My brother, Billy, who joined me in 1964 and left to become the head coach at North Carolina after the 1966 season, always marveled at the unique educational options in Athens. Georgia is the only school in the South, one of the few in the country, where every academic program of study, except engineering, is offered. Billy thought that provided great recruiting opportunity and flexibility, and he was right.

At the time, the rules permitted the signing of forty-five players to football scholarships annually, so we didn't worry too much about tryouts, as we called them then. As time went by and the scholarship limitations became more restrictive, we began to depend on walk-on players, and there is no question that our academic programs helped in that regard. You get a lot of kids coming to a state university for academic reasons. Many of them consider taking a crack at football. Even though we encourage athletes not quite good enough for a scholarship to walk on — which now is a very important part of our program — a state university like Georgia's just naturally has a lot of walk-on players to show up on their own, without being recruited for that purpose.

The most interesting thing about those early days at Georgia is that we were able to work in relative obscurity. There were a few locals who made an effort to get to know the new coach and to offer good, neighborly assistance, but by and large nobody knew us, so we were left alone to prepare to coach a football team we knew little about.

Coach Eaves was quite concerned about outside relationships. By nature, he was very private and was not inclined to heavy socializing, but he knew that the Georgia people had really been split over the changing of coaches — Johnny Griffith succeeding Wallace Butts, and the subsequent court case involving Coach Butts and the _Saturday Evening Post_. The _Post_, in a sensational article by Frank Graham Jr. — "sophisticated muck raking," the magazine called its editorial theme of the time — accused Coach Butts and Coach Bear Bryant of Alabama of trying to fix the 1961 Georgia-Alabama game.

Bryant later settled out of court after Coach Butts won a $3 million libel judgment, but the trial and related events left a lot of people dismayed and bitter. The Georgia people were as down as they could possibly be, and Coach Eaves knew that there had been much choosing of sides, either for or against this person or this plan, and he didn't want us to be affected by those rancorous divisions.

We chose our friends very carefully, knowing that there were many true Bulldogs out there who put the school first; we would try to learn who they were. Mainly we felt that we should stick to ourselves and get the job done. If we did that, everything else would be okay.

Of course, opportunity for a football coach usually comes when something has gone wrong in the past. Changes open doors, but when opportunity knocks, you go to work. Stick to yourself and stick with the basics.

In any case, you gain the confidence and support of the friends and supporters of the school by building a strong and competitive program. Winning on Saturday afternoon works wonders for a coach's credibility, and I knew that it really didn't matter whether people liked me or not. They would respond based on the performance of the football team.

Since nobody really knew me in those early years, I was left alone to coach the football team. There weren't a lot of distractions.

Watching Ray Goff the first eight months of 1989, I sometimes wondered if the Georgia people would ever give him enough time to coach. He took over an established program after having played, coached and recruited for his alma mater and was immediately and affectionately embraced by the Georgia people. They were pulling and tugging at him from the very beginning. He has not had — nor will he have — the luxury of being left alone to get his program started. By his second day as Georgia's head coach, he had an unlisted phone number. I coached ten years and won a couple of Southeastern Conference championships before having to take that step.

One of the reasons that I was left alone in the beginning was that not only did nobody know me, they didn't want to know me. Most Georgia fans considered the state of affairs so bleak that they felt the only way out was for the university to have hired a name coach, one who had already produced, one who brought established credibility. They were in shock when they learned the news that a freshman coach from Auburn had been hired.

Johnny Griffith, my predecessor, had been a freshman coach when he was hired, and when it didn't work out with Johnny, there was a lot of public opinion that if one former freshman coach couldn't get the job done, how could you expect anything better from a second freshman coach? Especially one who knew nothing about Georgia.

But in Johnny's defense, and I think everybody who really knows would agree, he had no opportunity. There was too much of a rift with the Georgia people, and there was not a person on the face of the earth who could have healed the split that existed from 1961-63.

Johnny Griffith with Ray Clark (L), Don Blackburn

Johnny was one of the first people I met when I got to Athens. Even though he resigned as coach with a year left on his contract, Johnny offered to spend some time with me to help familiarize me with various aspects of the program as much as he could. There is the perception over the years that Coach Eaves fired Johnny, but that is not right. Coach Eaves would not extend his contract, so Johnny resigned.

I've always been grateful to Johnny for his help. He didn't have to assist, and if he had gotten mad and skipped town, I surely wouldn't have blamed him. His behavior was, however, just the opposite.

He told me where we stood in recruiting, offering details on every player his staff had scouted. He also reviewed the current players on the Georgia roster, advising me of certain problems, attitudes and concerns. Then we went recruiting. Johnny Griffith drove me to Atlanta to see a high school playoff game involving Cedartown. Georgia had been working hard to sign Edgar Chandler, a lanky lineman with amazing speed and quickness. We watched Cedartown, coached by Doc Ayers who would eventually join us in Athens as freshman coach, and Edgar Chandler. Johnny sat in the stands with me only a few days after he had resigned. Then we drove home. How many people would do that? Johnny Griffith showed a lot of class in that situation.

Over the years, Johnny and I have enjoyed a cordial relationship. I know it was tough for him, a Georgia man, to go through what he did. It must have been hard on him seeing things break so well for us. However, I have always felt that he contributed to our getting off on the right foot by giving us his time and honest opinions and making himself available to us in those early weeks of the job.

The first month or two, though my phone was generally quiet, I did get some interesting calls. One in particular, I won't forget, came from an eccentric graduate who lived up in the mountains. He was well connected and was never loathe to allude to his associations and ability to get something accomplished. "Listen, Vince," he said, "whatever you want, we'll get it for you. If you need money, let us know. If you want a million, we'll get it. Just let us know what you need." Though flabergasted, I was listening patiently when all of a sudden he says, "The first thing we gotta do is get rid of O. C."

I said, "Who?"

"O. C.," he repeated.

"O. C. who?" I said again.

"O. C. Aderhold," he snapped.

"What have I gotten myself into?" I asked aloud. My first month on the job and a Georgia alumnus wants to fire the president and buy us a football team.

It didn't take me long to get off the phone and to avoid that alumnus after that. A rookie coach siding with anybody wanting to bounce the president, not to mention buying players, would have to be out of his mind. Even if the coach agreed, it would not be very smart to become involved in those conversations.

Besides, I had in a short period of time come to appreciate Dr. Aderhold. He took a lot of criticism about the handling of athletics, and like some of my coaching decisions, he could be second-guessed. All I know is that nobody could have been fairer with Coach Eaves and me in getting our program underway than Dr. Aderhold. He wanted us to have every opportunity to win. He was an honorable man, but he truly enjoyed football and enjoyed seeing the team do well on Saturday afternoons. But I think there was a more compelling reason. He knew that if we could win a few games, it would unite the Georgia peo-

Dr. O. C. Aderhold (C), a supporter of Dooley and Eaves

ple again. It wasn't that he wanted that so much to ease his own headaches, I truly believe that he loved his school and knew it would be healthy and positive for Georgia's future for people to unite. His widow, Bess, and her daughter, Bebe, remain warm friends of mine and Barbara's.

One of the first things that I did when I got to Athens was call on Coach Wallace Butts. I didn't really know him, but I knew a lot about him, that he had been very successful and meant a lot to many Georgia people. He was truly one of college football's colorful characters.

Most Georgia alumni probably would not have accepted this viewpoint over the years, but indirectly I am a product of the Bulldog football system. A lot of the style and philosophy I employed as Georgia's coach actually began in Athens, a place I never really expected to be. When Ralph Jordan arrived from Athens as the Auburn head coach in 1950, who did he bring with him? Buck Bradberry, Homer Hobbs, Gene Lorendo and Joe Connally — all Bulldogs. They brought along the Georgia system. Coach Butts greatly influenced the coaching career and philosophy of Coach Jordan, who influenced mine. Jordan didn't share Butts' predeliction for the passing game, but there was no question but that Coach Butts left an impact on Coach Jordan.

I had heard about all those long, tough practices that took place in Athens, and I can tell you about a few at Auburn. As a matter of fact, I'll never forget Coach Jordan's first spring. Earle Brown, who was the head coach my freshman season at Auburn, was fired and Coach Jordan was hired to straighten out the football program in 1951. He was an old War Eagle coming home. Everybody loved Shug, except, of course, the players that first spring. Those were the toughest drills you

could imagine. The lengthy headknocking practices seemed to last all spring, so when I hear the old Georgia players talk about difficult spring practices, I always say, "I know. I went through one or two myself." I am sure that there are many Georgia football graduates out there today who can tell you about some tough practices sessions during the Dooley era.

That first spring under Coach Jordan was one I really didn't like, but who could have? I remember Frank Sinkwich saying that when he returned from the Orange Bowl in 1942 after setting the total offensive record of 365 yards as a single-wing tailback — a record which still stands — there was a note on the dormitory bulletin board saying, "Report for Spring Practice Next Week."

"Not me," Frank said, and he quit the team. Spring drills in those days were almost year-round. After Tennessee upset Oklahoma in the 1939 Orange Bowl, the game that experts said made the Orange Bowl, General Bob Neyland said to his team that he was "damn well pleased with the result. Be ready to report for spring practice January 15th."

That is the way it was with spring practice in the old days, and it carried over to a large degree in the fifties.

If Coach Jordan was an extension of Coach Butts' philosphy, which he was, then I am an extension of both men. When I got to Athens there was something of Georgia in me, but nobody knew it or would have accepted such a premise.

But back to my visit with Coach Butts. I called on him at his office on Milledge Avenue. My opinion was that he represented a long and great tradition at Georgia, and I wanted him to know that I appreciated his contribution and respected the job that he had done with his great teams.

Wally Butts, "the nicest man in the world"

There in his modest office I saw another side of him that so many were familiar with. He was surrounded by several friends including the great Charley Trippi. We sat and listened while Coach Butts entertained us with stories and anecdotes. He was a master storyteller, and I remember that it was a delightful experience for me.

Right after I went by to see him, he called on us. Actually he called on Barbara. One day I when I got home, Barbara was all smiles and there was a bouquet of flowers on the kitchen counter. As I walked in the door, she said, "I met the sweetest little man today, the nicest man in the world."

When I asked who, she replied "Coach Butts." Having heard all those stories about how tough he was on the practice field, I asked her if she had met the wrong person.

Through the years I have had fun telling that story to some of his old players and even

his family. And I think it says something about the man. You ask his daughters — Faye, Jean and Nancy — and they will tell you that Barbara saw the important side of Coach Butts.

When we dedicated the Butts-Mehre Building, which houses the athletic offices, in the spring of 1987, we asked Harry Mehre Jr. to speak on behalf of his family, and Nancy Butts Murray was chosen to represent the Butts family.

I'll never forget her touching remarks about her father:

> We all have memorable, unforgettable days. There's that first day of school, and mine was right across the street; the time of first love; marriage; children; important milestones in life. Those of us who are the ordinary members of the Butts family have enjoyed an extraordinary coattail ride to fame through our association with Wallace Butts. He truly lighted up our lives. Because of the "little round man" our memories are overflowing. There were Orange, Sugar, and Gator Bowls, even that Rose Bowl, and if you've never ridden through a city with police sirens blaring ahead announcing that the Georgia Bulldogs have arrived, then you haven't really lived. Then, too, all of the family are certified Bulldog fans. In 1980 many of us had the sheer unmitigated joy of returning from New Orleans across the entire states of Alabama and Mississippi waving our pennants and our shredded crepe paper and screaming, "We're No. 1!" Dressed in our wrinkled red and black outfits, too proud to make a change, we shared that unique event along with thousands of our fellow Bulldog fans. What a memory! We owe that one to you, Vince. Please allow a vintage cheerleader, Class of '59, to echo the words of the present-day cheerleading squad, "It's great to be a Georgia Bulldog!" ... [Wallace Butts] never bore grudges nor nursed resentment. He was generous to a fault, especially with the University of Georgia. Having observed his courage, his tenacity, and his fighting spirit firsthand, I feel that all the attributes, awards and honors he received during his lifetime, all the respect he commanded from his players and coaches, yes, even the naming of this great Heritage Hall in his honor, he so richly deserved. He was only five-feet-six-inches tall, but in my estimation never was there a

man so short in stature to stand so tall. He had players well over six-feet tall who honestly thought they were looking up when they talked with the coach. Faye, Jean, and I have always been proud to be the daughters of Wallace and Winnie Butts. Proud on the days when he rode off the field on the shoulders of his players with those Georgia yells and chapel bell ringing out the victory. Proud even on the days when his battling Bulldogs suffered those few defeats. Proud when he made witty after-dinner speeches. Proud when he fought back in life and restored his good name, and never prouder than at this moment.

I hope my own children will remember their parents with the same affection that Nancy and her sisters have for Wallace and Winnie Butts.

After the swapping of those first visits, Coach Butts and I had a lot of contact. He was very supportive. He dictated a letter every week which was always on my desk early Monday morning. If we had won the game, it was congratulations, and if we lost, he offered encouragement. As a coach, he was a tough disciplinarian, and those who stuck it out truly loved him. I always believed those players who stuck it out and became his staunchest allies saw that he gave unabashedly of himself, that he put his heart and soul in coaching. There are no more loyal players anywhere than those who are loyal to Wallace Butts. If he were a disciplinarian, I'd have to say so was Coach Jordan. Come to think of it, I sorta land in that category to some degree myself. Coach Butts taught his teams to pay the price, and during my twenty-five years as the Georgia coach, I benefited from the tradition that he established.

One of Coach Butts' enduring traits was his remarkable sense of humor, and I will never forget a scene at the annual jamboree of the Athens Touchdown Club one evening

in January of 1968. John Stembler of the Georgia Theater Company annually donates a beautiful silver service to Georgia's outstanding back and lineman. In 1968, the lineman to receive the award was All-America Edgar Chandler, who had just finished his senior year and was headed for a distinguished career as a middle linebacker with the Buffalo Bills.

Edgar, who stood 6'4", brought some levity to his remarks by saying to me, "Now that I am finished and will soon be an alumnus, Coach Dooley, I'll expect you to make sure that Georgia fields winning teams." When it came my turn to speak, I chided Edgar for his remarks, saying, "Edgar, I didn't expect you to join the ranks of critical alumni so soon."

Coach Butts followed me and said, "Vince, don't worry about Edgar. You can see him. What you have to worry about in this business are those you can't see." That was a special quality that Coach Butts had. He could not only tell a story and embellish one, he could make a point with humor that went right to the heart of the matter.

As we settled in with our new regime in Athens, we felt that Coach Butts sincerely wanted us to succeed. He may have been embittered with events prior to our coming as many suggest, but when we got our program underway, we felt that he wished the best for us. I have always appreciated that.

That first year went by so quickly, but it was one of the most enjoyable that I have ever experienced. Our staff worked long hours and devoted overtime toward putting together a new system while buying houses and bringing their families to town. It was a new adventure, a new experience, and even though there were a lot of doubters out there, I don't think it ever crossed our minds that we would not succeed.

CHAPTER 4
With A Little Help (And A Lot of Work) From My Friends

When I arrived in Athens incognito in December of 1963, I was preoccupied with hiring a coaching staff and signing football players.

If you recall, colleges were allowed to sign forty-five freshmen in those years, but the SEC signing date was in early December. We were in trouble already. Everybody was way ahead of us with evaluation, contacts and commitments. You can't recruit without a coaching staff, and hiring coaches is not anything you rush into. You need to learn as much about a candidate as possible, seeking every available evaluation. Any successful head coach will tell you quickly that the key to winning over a long period begins with hiring and maintaining a capable staff of assistants.

In that regard, I have always been fortunate, and I am certain that the reason we got off to such a good start in 1964 was that we recruited an outstanding coaching staff.

Coach Eaves and I met frequently in the days following my hiring to discuss staff positions. We both agreed that our first objective was to bring Sterling DuPree back to Georgia. When Wallace Butts resigned in 1960, DuPree left, anticipating that there would be a lot of dissension and turmoil with the Bulldog supporters. He preferred to remain in Athens, but he felt that it would be best for him and his family to accept an attractive recruiting offer from Ray Graves at Florida. His comment to a close friend expresses that rare loyalty that so few possess: "I couldn't hang around here with them cuttin' Wally up."

We had a hunch that Coach DuPree might be ready and anxious to return home. He had

Sterling DuPree agreed to come home

never sold his house when he left, and when I called, it was obvious right away from his disarming and infectious laugh that he was keen on the idea of moving back.

Selling Sterling on the recruiting position was very important, but we wound up with a package deal in the process. He recommended that we hire John Donaldson, who was to become my long-time fishing buddy. I knew a lot about Donaldson. He was a sound, fundamental football coach with good experience coaching both sides of the football. John was familiar with high school coaches in the state and would work well with the man I had in mind for offensive coordinator — Bill Dooley.

There was no question — I knew I had to bring my brother in from Mississippi State, where he had played for Darrell Royal and was then coaching for Paul Davis, who had coached the Georgia defensive line in 1960. At the time there was no nepotism rule with the

BILL DOOLEY — *"The first thing I remember about Vincent at Georgia was that, not having coached with him before, I was impressed with his organizational ability. He organized down to the most minute details. He assembled a very good staff, a staff that was young and enthusiastic and really didn't have that much experience. But a very congenial, compatible staff that I thought did a tremendous job.*

"One thing that impressed me about Georgia was that there was some talent there. We had just gone to a bowl with Mississippi State and there was, I'd say, as good a talent at Georgia as there was where I had just come from. I can remember players like Ray Rissmiller and Jim Wilson, two excellent offensive tackles. Preston Ridlehuber and Lynn Hughes at quarterback. Fred Barber at fullback and Bob Taylor at tailback. It was good talent, and it was the same on the other side of the ball defensively. I think they were determined to be successful. With fairly good talent and good attitude, which was a tribute to Vincent, assembling and directing and guiding the team and assembling the staff, I thought that we would be successful.

"In 1964, we worked hard, pulled together. Like I say, it was a young staff without a whole lot of experience, but we had a great deal of fun. It was a staff that was close-knit. We played and enjoyed sports together and socialized together. And that made it that much more enjoyable."

How much did Vince influence Bill as a head coach?

"From an organizational standpoint, I think a great deal. I'm not too proud to admit that. I don't mind saying that I borrowed some from Darrell Royal, Bear Bryant, Bowden Wyatt and my brother — all of the coaches who have been successful. You kind of pick and choose the things that work for you. You've got to coach to suit your own personality, but Vince had an influence from an organizational standpoint, no doubt about it."

Athletic Association. Nonetheless, there was some criticism of my hiring my brother, but I knew he was exactly what we needed. He already was one of the finest offensive line coaches in the country. But even Billy wasn't sure he should come. He was worried about the brother thing more than anybody. But I told him I needed him, and he later remarked that his blood called and he had to go.

If that was a wise decision, then I was probably even wiser to have brought Erk Russell in as the defensive coordinator. However, his situation was different from Bill's. Erk was as eager to come as Bill was reluctant.

In fact, we didn't offer Erk the job at first, but he called more than once to express his interest. He really wanted to come to Georgia. "If you were coaching at Vandy, wouldn't Georgia appeal to you?" Erk often said later.

Bill Dooley: Blood called, he came

The Bulldog Staff: (L-R) Erk Russell, Howell Hollis, John Donaldson, Bill Dooley, Ken Cooper, Joel Eaves, Jim Pyburn, Vince Dooley, Sterling DuPree, Doc Ayers, Hootie Ingram, Frank Inman, Mike Castronis

Frank Inman was retained from Johnny Griffith's staff to work with the offense, and Hootie Ingram, who was then at Virginia Tech, and Jim Pyburn, whom I had played with in college and was then head coach at Columbus High School, completed our defensive staff. We hired Doc Ayers to coach the freshmen, and Ken Cooper, a graduate assistant with Johnny, was retained to work with Doc. Dick Copas, still with us as an academic counselor, was our first trainer. Mike Castronis, who was joining the Dean of Men's staff, also worked as a part-time coach assisting Billy with the offensive line.

When we started out only Donaldson, Cooper and Ayers had Georgia backgrounds, not the ratio that I prefer. But my knowledge of coaches with Georgia backgrounds was limited, and we needed time to grow our own. I believe it is best if one-half to two-thirds of your staff comes up through the program. They are part of your tradition, they understand your base system and were trained through that system. One-third then comes from the outside, which always keeps a fresh flow of new ideas to supplement the base.

My last staff, for example, included Georgia graduates Steve Greer, Charlie Whittemore, John Kasay, Ray Goff, Joe Tereshinski, Dicky Clark, Robert Miles and Robert Goodwin. Those with non-Georgia backgrounds included George Haffner, Joe Hollis, Bob Harrison, Bill Lewis, Dale Strahm and Hornsby Howell.

In the eighties, we enjoyed an enviable reputation in college football. If there was an opening at Georgia, applications flooded in. We had our pick of coaches. Our tradition, success, facilities and record were partly responsible. Being in the Southeastern Conference was a positive factor, and so was the fact that Georgia is recognized as an outstanding state for recruiting.

Word gets about, too. Athens is a great place to live. And I'd like to think that the word was out that at Georgia you would be allowed to coach.

That first staff was allowed to coach. It was keen on fundamentals. It was a sound thinking group. We worked hard and paid the price. I have never enjoyed a coaching staff more than that one. When the Athens Touchdown Club surprised me by getting that staff together for a reunion in the fall of 1988, it was one of the most enjoyable nights I can ever remember. Seeing all those first assistants together again brought back warm and grateful memories. It was truly one of the highlights of all the celebrations of my Silver Anniversary year.

A lot of the fun with that first staff had to do with our new situation. That always creates excitement and stimulates enthusiasm. We were young and energetic. I was only thirty-one, which meant that I wasn't that much older than some of our five-year seniors. And linebacker LeRoy Dukes, who had spent four years in the military, was practically a contemporary.

We worked hard but enjoyed ourselves. Football was our life, and if there were distractions, we would have had to hunt them up. One of my most vivid memories of that first year in Athens was that we sat for long hours on metal folding chairs in our meeting room putting together a complete new system. Even when you are a young man, sitting on a metal slab for hours leads to a rump ache that makes working a challenge. "Fatigue makes cowards of us all," Vince Lombardi once said, and I agree. I will always have a special feeling for those assistants on that first staff who fought off fatigue and discomfort even though they succeeded while "sitting down" on the job.

What we soon learned about our football players was that they were pretty good hitters and had no interest in sitting. They were eager and ready to play. I have never seen a team respond any more positively than the team we inherited at Georgia. They lacked mobility, but they were a hardnosed lot who never gave up the fight, a decided asset in establishing a winning program.

There are no guarantees in this business, but I realized immediately that we were blessed with a capable coaching staff and that it would get the job done. It was also a staff that recruited well, and when I look back over my twenty-five years at Georgia, I realize how great it was for my future as a coach to get off to a good start and how much those first coaches had to do with it. Four members of that staff became head coaches: Billy at North Carolina, Virginia Tech and Wake Forest; Hootie Ingram at Clemson; Ken Cooper at Ole Miss; and Erk at Georgia Southern.

Through the years there were many capable assistants to join the Georgia program. You can't win 201 games without coaches who can teach and provide leadership. They must learn to work together. There were problems at times, and there have been tensions, frustrations and strained relationships, but we always seemed to remain focused on our objectives and kept moving forward. We got along with a minimum of problems.

A head coach is not always aware of what people are saying. He doesn't hear every detail nor is he privy to the raw criticism, but he senses the mood and picks up on the chief complaints. One of the criticisms that I have endured over the years is that I never fired anybody. If you check the record, you will find that is true.

The way I look at it, loyalty is a two-way street. If you hire somebody, unless they embarrass your program and really do something that is absolutely wrong and indefensible, then you have an obligation to stick by them in the difficult times. That is an old coaching philosophy, and maybe I'm the last of a breed. I must earn loyalty and earn it by defending my assistants in the hard times. My way of firing has been to move coaches to other positions when a change was in order. I have strong feelings about a man's dignity. To fire anyone is a tremendous blow to him and his family. I hired the man in the first place. I made a commitment to him, and unless he does something legally or morally wrong, then there my obligation is to help him, motivate him and stimulate him to do the best job he can do.

However, I can see that attitude changing with the high salaries that assistant coaches are making today. The bottom line expectations are intensifying, and the attitude that "If you don't produce, you are gone" is coming on strong in college athletics. This is something I regret very much.

I have always believed that it was best to hire good people, that is, people with good character. Sometimes their knowledge of football is secondary if they're basically good people. Once you hire good people, the next thing is to let them coach. I always appreciated that in my old coach Shug Jordan. He allowed me as an assistant at Auburn to coach, and I have never forgotten it.

You let them coach and you want them involved. I tried to keep my coaches informed as to what was going on, and in return, I expected to be kept informed. Communication is very important in developing a winning program.

It was a tradition for the last twenty years at Georgia that immediately following spring practice each coach would organize on paper his opinions as to how we could coach and teach more effectively. I wanted each coach's candid evaluation. If there was something bothering him about what we were doing, or if he had suggestions on how I could do my job better, that was his opportunity to speak up. I wanted his advice, his constructive criticisms. I wanted him to share with me what he thought would be important in improving our program and our relationship. We also evaluated recruiting.

Communication must flow down as well as up to be successful. I always encouraged our assistants to become involved with the players beyond coaching, to develop an interest in them after football is over. It was standard that in position meetings, the coach would devote the first five minutes to academic matters. What courses are you taking? How are you doing? Any problems?

Our coaches were required to meet with the players after spring practice for an evaluation and critique. Each player filled out a form which included his goals, what he planned after college, what his ambitions were as a football player, what he could do to become a better student or better person. After that form was completed, each position coach met with each player for a discussion and review. The coach would then make this form available to me along with any written thoughts or comments. I used this form as a basis of discussion with our players when I met with them for any reason, whether it involved discipline or simply our getting together to talk. During pre-season practice before the first game in the fall, I always met privately with every player on our team, and that form and the coach's evaluation of his players offered an insight into the athletes who made up our team. This practice, begun in 1975 and continued until my retirement, allowed our coaches to participate in the overall decision-making responsibility.

One of the unfortunate things about being a head coach these days is that you cannot really coach. For the first five years at Georgia, I coached the quarterbacks. It was fun to work with the players on the field. That is one of the reasons I enjoyed those early years so much. We were winning, everybody was pleased to see us making progress, and our coaches and players were having fun. The head coach was part of all that. Right after the second championship, however, I realized that I couldn't devote the time to a position responsibility. There were too many demands on me and the game had changed too much. It was unfair to the players and it was unfair to the program, so I had to go out and hire a quarterback coach. That was a personal disappointment to no longer remain directly involved in the individual teaching on the field. Coaches, I have always said, are teachers first, and I missed that teaching involvement.

Coaching today is much different from what it was when we started out at Georgia twenty-five years ago. The resources are so much greater, both in college and professional football. Coaches of today have access to printed matter — great numbers of magazine articles, books and films, both technical and motivational — on all phases of the game. There are dozens of clinics, and college coaches visit other colleges and professional camps. The opportunity for self-improvement in college coaching is remarkable. But there is a down side to all this information.

Since assistant coaches are so much more knowledgeable today than they used to be, there is a natural tendency to attempt to teach too much, setting up rules of thumb for every situation and then providing exceptions both for the rules and the exceptions. They ignore that solid base. Winning execution comes only through repetition and becoming consistently good at what you do.

I often remember what Fran Tarkenton told me about Vince Lombardi's Green Bay Packer offense in the 1960s. They basically had five running and five passing plays, and that was enough to win the National Football League title. Green Bay could execute its plays better than any team in the NFL. Everybody knew what the Packers were going to do but could seldom stop them. If Lombardi were coaching today, I am sure he would use far more plays than in 1960, but you can be sure that he would still be keeping things simple. Chances are he'd still be winning, too. Lombardi never strayed from fundamental football.

Just as resources are so much greater today, so is the pressure to win. One of the reasons for this is the media. There are more media columnists with liberal opinions than ever before, and this brings pressure to coaching. These opinionated media experts offer solutions based on observation, not experience, all speculating how they would solve a problem. And there is a sports radio talk show every hour of the day somewhere or other featuring those who are convinced of their genius and enjoy hearing themselves talk. There is more second-guessing by the public than ever before. Coaches just have to learn to deal with such things.

Investigative reporting also has come into the coaching life. While I admit that some probes lack balance and fairness, I believe a coach should be held accountable for his program. This is good for college athletics, even though some coaches consider investigative journalism a harassment. I'm for it.

Even with all the pressures and problems, what better life is there than coaching football? I can't think of anything. You may recall what Erk Russell often says about coaching: "Beats workin'."

Erk Russell. What a coach! What an unforgettable character! What a man! During my twenty-five years at Georgia, I hired a total of forty-three assistants, and each of them made an important contribution to the Dooley era's 201 victories. Each can take pride in what has been accomplished, and I am grateful to every one of them. What I enjoy today are the fruits of the labors of many.

But I would be unfair if I didn't pay special tribute to Erk for the exceptional contributions he made to the Dooley era. Each of the

Erk Russell, a hard-charging disciplinarian with experience

assistants who worked with Erk would agree that he transcended all the rest. He was the cornerstone of our staff for seventeen years.

In the beginning, his influence was important from several standpoints. I was a hard-charging disciplinarian, and Erk benefited from age and experience which I lacked. He had coached in high school, headed a freshman team in college and had been a position coach with a varsity program. He, through his varied experiences, had seen kids grow up. He had older kids of his own, which influenced his thinking. Mine were still pretty much in diapers. He brought to the staff a maturity that was very important, and I think we complemented each other. I pretty well knew what I wanted to do. I was confident and believed strongly in what I was doing, but I also respected Erk and was able to counsel with him about things that would

be helpful in dealing with our players. I was straight down the line and he was more relaxed and had that special touch, that captivating sense of humor. Yet, he was a serious competitor. A lot of people overlooked that at first, but Erk had a strong desire to win, as strong as I've ever seen. He was just quiet and undemonstrative about it.

As time went by, Erk became our dominant assistant and was promoted to assistant head coach. He and I worked well together, mainly because he was easy to work with, but I'd like to think my flexibility in a number of areas was also important. For example, he had his own radio show. Every head coach I talked with kept telling me that was a mistake. That would have probably been true in most cases, but Erk was different.

The problem with his hosting a show was that we could have wound up with two

45

coaches speaking for the program instead of one. If you get to the position where an assistant becomes as influential as the head coach, that undermines the leadership. But I made my own decision and never regretted it. I had confidence in Erk, knew that he was loyal and would never undermine the program. I had no serious ego problems with his having his own show. I didn't feel threatened by Erk, a very popular individual and a unique person. Because of our mutual trust and respect, we never had any friction or conflicts.

Erk could relate to the players and leave me in a position to remain aloof to some degree. A head coach has to look out for the entire family, which prevents him from becoming too close to the players. Erk could develop rapport with them as well as any assistant coach I've ever known. He was good for them, he was good for me, he was good for our program. Erk could motivate and inspire, but most of all he was a competitor who enjoyed a grass-roots affection for coaching, one who could teach and produce on game day.

Early on he would butt heads with our players in pre-game warmups, his bald head against their chests. He would enter the locker room with blood streaming down his face and you could see the fire in his defensive players' eyes. He was going to war with them. They truly believed that. They had confidence in him and they loved him because they knew he loved them. Erk motivated through leadership and teaching, not enforcement. Yet he had the macho image.

Erk quit butting with the players for awhile, but once when our defense dropped off, I suggested that he bring his butting act back. He informed me that his wife, Jean, had asked him to quit. I told him not to tell Jean I had asked him to butt again, but that the players were motivated by his butting and that he was not relating to them like he once did. He went back to butting again immediately. The blood began flowing and our defense perked up once more.

What did all that really mean? It was nothing more than symbolism, but it was important to the team. We never wanted anyone to play mean or dirty, but football is a physical game. It is a spartan game which requires total commitment and dedication. The players were inspired by a coach, older than their own fathers in some cases, who would get out there and crack heads with them in pre-game warm-ups. Erk was one of a kind.

That is why his slogans were so influential. It was Erk who came up with the Junkyard Dog theme in 1975-76. The players really took to that one. He could work up something in spring and summer when the schedule was more relaxed, or he could create something

---

FIGHTING BACK — *During Erk's time: From 1964 through the 1980 season when Erk Russell was the defensive coordinator, it became something of a habit for the Bulldogs to come from behind when down at halftime. Twenty-eight times during this period, Georgia was down at the half (two games when the Dogs were behind at half ended in a tie) and came back to win. On eight other occasions, the Dogs were tied at the half and went on to victory (two games when the Dogs tied at half ended in ties). That is an average of two games a year that Georgia came from behind (or from a tie) to win in the second half. This does not count coming from behind in the last two quarters.*

on the spur of the moment. We were not playing well against Georgia Tech in 1965 in Atlanta, and during the halftime Erk saw something stenciled on some equipment in the visitors' locker room which read "G.T.A.A." This stood for Georgia Tech Athletic Association. Erk went over and pointed to it and said, "Men, let's move one of those A's over here between the G and the T and make it GATA, which means "get after their ass." We dominated the second half and won the ballgame. GATA became a symbol for our team for several years. We would see it on motel marquees when we pulled in from the airport, and it was certainly true that if you get after an opponent's rear on the football field, you were likely to win more than your share of games.

The year of the national championship, Erk produced shirts during the pre-season with the word TEAM spelled in big bold letters and the word me in small letters underneath. That was one of the most popular tee-shirts on our team. Big team, little me.

Of course, his calendars were priceless. He sent reminder calendars to the players over the summer with humorous notations designed to motivate them to work hard and return to Athens in peak condition for the season. Those calendars kept a lot of players from procrastinating and succumbing to laziness in the summer. Erk always looked for that motivational angle.

While the defensive players would die for him on the field, he also related to the offensive players. The entire team loved him. On Fridays before games, I always asked the offensive and defensive coordinators to speak to the team, the offensive coordinator always going on first. This meant that when Erk finished reviewing the defensive game plan, he would tell one of his many jokes. The players always looked forward to that. It was

an important time of the week for our team. It kept them loose and relaxed.

When he ran the defense, I always met with him and the defensive staff each week just as I did with the offense. If things were going well, I seldom asked questions. If we were having problems, I would probe more. But if Erk ever got mad at me, he never told me. Coaches disagree, and I have disagreed with some of the things he did with the defense during a game, but I never got mad at him. How could you get mad at Erk? No coach ever had a bigger heart for the game than he did.

There was a time when there was a feeling that we tried to stack the offense with the better players and left Erk with lesser talent. I don't think you could say that Bill Stanfill or Jake Scott or Jimmy Payne or Scott Woerner or Eddie "Meat Cleaver" Weaver or Freddy Gilbert were short on talent. There may have been times when we might have shaded things a bit for the offense, but you don't find too many players who could play on either side of the ball equally well. It is sometimes easier for certain players to play defense than offense. A defensive player has got to run and redirect. Not every athlete can do that.

If we did give Erk the "neck of the chicken," as he would say, or the "rumble seat," he was using it for an advantage more than to complain. He fought for the underdog role, and no coach has ever used that role any better. It never bothered me if the defensive players felt they were second-class citizens. It gave them a rallying point, and teams with rallying points often play winning football.

When we were shown little respect by pre-season polls, Erk would always remind the team that, "You know what dogs do to polls."

The Junkyard Dog idea came about over a

ERK RUSSELL — *"If you had been coaching at Vanderbilt in '63 and had an opportunity to go to Georgia, what would you think of the offer? Hey, I was delighted. Very delighted to have the opportunity to go to Georgia. As a player at Auburn, as a high school coach in Atlanta and then back again as an assistant coach at Auburn, I knew that Georgia was something special. I felt like it was a wonderful opportunity to come to a school with great, great tradition, like there was an opportunity to really do something.*

"Everybody [the staff] was eager to go to work, and I don't think anybody ever thought about any problems that Georgia might have had in the past. We were a new bunch ready to go to work. And let me say this about the people that we were introduced to on the field, the Georgia players: they were ready to go to work, too. You know, a lot of people had said that, boy, we really got those guys hitting in a hurry. They were ready to do that. Whoever had coached them in the past had done a wonderful job of teaching them what those helmets were for. And I'd like to take some credit for that, but those guys were already ready to do that.

"I think the best thing about Vince is that he lets his assistant coaches coach. This is not to say he turns everything over and backs away. He knows a little bit about what's going on with every group of people and with every individual. But I think he was very, very smart in letting his assistant coaches coach. He did that throughout the time I was there, and I assume that he is still doing it. And I think that's the way to do it.

"We really didn't have to spend a great deal of time together because I think our basic philosophy of defense, and I think offense, too, was the same. Both of us felt like we had to play good defense in order to win. I think by nature both of us are conservative in knowing that mistakes will get you beat quicker than mismatches. And that if you don't turn the ball over, and don't make mistakes, you've always got a chance to win — if you've got a good defense. Let me tell you about an experience in 1964 after our first game. I was coaching the ends and linebackers, Jim Pyburn was coaching the down linemen, and Hootie Ingram was coaching the secondary, and Alabama really just beat the slop out of us. They beat us 31-3. The score wasn't indicative of how bad the defeat was. And I guess it was the next day or the day after that Vince made a reassignment of coaching responsibilities. And that was an indication that he was going to take things in hand, that he was mentally tough and able to make decisions like that. It wasn't an easy decision, but it was one that proved to be a great decision, because we went on to steadily improve every week."

beer with Jimmy Matthews, an alumnus from Albany, at Erk's favorite hangout, the Rockwood Inn. There was one particular story about the Rockwood Inn that Erk enjoyed telling. When the Cotton Bowl game of 1967 was over, our tight end, Frank Richter, came up to Erk and said, "Coach, it has been so much fun playing for the Bulldogs, and the only reason I am glad my career is over is that I won't ever again have to hide in the men's room at the Rockwood Inn until you leave."

Erk was such an unusual individual that he probably was the one coach I've known who could have had a few beers with his players without its becoming a problem. If anyone could have pulled that off, it would have been Erk.

Whenever Erk's defense was off, the critics in the profession kept suggesting that our even front, our base 60 defense, was the problem. Many considered it old-fashioned. Erk and I often talked about that, and we went to an odd alignment one year, but it was the worst mistake we ever made. We had a great big strong tackle Dan Spivey in the line and Danny Jones at noseguard, so we gave the odd front a try. But we lost those two players, and things soured quickly for us. We made some variations from time to time, like when Sam Mitchell came in to coach our secondary in 1975 and we used the four/four defense, which was an eight man front with a variation.

After Erk left, Bill Lewis developed very effective defenses in '81, '82 and '83. You don't win championships as we did in '81 and '82 and the Cotton Bowl of '84 if you aren't playing great defense. It was great for Georgia and for me that Bill and his staff produced as they did after Erk, our most popular assistant, left.

Then we experienced a drop-off in talented personnel, and all of a sudden everybody began to say we were outdated again. It is amazing how outdated you get when you line up without great players.

An area of particular excellence for Erk was his ability to make halftime adjustments. This was possible because he and his staff knew their defense inside out. They had all grown up with the eight-man front, and as a result they had a history to draw from and could make effective halftime adjustments. Our football team's ability to come back in the second half accounted for many of our biggest victories.

When I was interviewed by Auburn before we went to the Sugar Bowl in 1980, Erk was pushed by everybody in the state to seek the head coaching job. The consensus was that I was leaving, and I am sure Erk believed that, too. Erk did tell the appropriate officials that if I left, he badly wanted the job. Some say that he was never as comfortable after that. I don't know. All I know is that when he confirmed in the spring of '81 that he was taking the Georgia Southern job, I was disappointed. I really hated to see him go, but I didn't try to talk him out of leaving. I just told him to make sure he got the right kind of contract with nothing left to chance.

Georgia Southern President Dale Lick and Athletic Director Bucky Wagner were tremendous recruiters. They were great salesmen.

"I knew it was going to be tough at Georgia Southern," Erk joked after he had made his decision. "When we went out for dinner to finalize everything, I got the check. Then the athletic director spent the night at my house."

When Erk got his program established at Georgia Southern, he won back-to-back national championships. I enjoyed his success. I loved watching his teams play on TV and was fortunate to arrange my schedule to see them play a couple of times in recent years. I've been happy for him and proud for him with the good job he has done in Statesboro, but like everybody else in Athens, I miss him. Erk is one of those unforgettable characters, and he certainly had a lot to do with the 201 victories posted by the name of Vincent Joseph Dooley.

In 1964, Vince Dooley was barely older than some of his players

CHAPTER 5
Too Much Success Too Quickly; The Hunger Wanes

Many factors led to our initial success at Georgia, including the good fortune to win close ball games, but I think it's important that I begin with the players.

We had some quality players, although I preached that winning would be quite a challenge. But haven't I always done that? As time went by, people expected that out of me, but back in 1964 nobody had any indication of what my pre-game analysis of football teams would typically become. They were accustomed to "Weepin' Wally," but some said I took the dismal pre-game outlook to a new level. Remember, however, what Chuck Daly of the Detroit Pistons said after winning the NBA title in the spring of 1989: "A pessimist is an optimist with experience."

GEORGE PATTON — All-America tackle and captain in 1966, George Patton of Tuscumbia, Alabama, came to Georgia as a quarterback.

It didn't take him long to get the message that he was out of position. If he were going to play, he knew he had better move on.

When Vince Dooley took over, Patton was given the opportunity to try other positions and quickly found a home at tackle. "They tried me at end, but my hands were like bricks. They told me I could try defense and I just lined up at tackle. All I wanted was an opportunity to play, to be a part of the team.

"It was not that much of an adjustment, and I had an advantage having played quarterback. Sometimes I felt that I knew what they were thinking. The biggest thing was that I had quickness. I was able to get by a lot of people and get into the backfield. The main thing was that I wanted to play. That was the way it was with our entire team. We had desire, and it started with Coach Dooley and his staff. They were young like we were, they were eager and taught us to believe in ourselves.

"What they did was bring organization to our practices and our program. They knew what they were doing, they were very businesslike and they got our attention. They believed in what they were doing which made us believe in them.

"They made me proud to go home to Alabama. I had a brother who played on one of Alabama's national championship teams and one that played on a great Ole Miss team. After we began to win at Georgia, it was nice to go back and talk about my championship team. Respect. That is so important and that is what Vince Dooley brought to us in 1964."

"General" George Patton

I don't think you should ever be caught off guard in this business by being foolishly optimistic. You need to proceed in every case with caution, and that was my style for which I make no apology. One thing was certain: I was not going to be a coach who let his mouth cost him or his team any football games. They could laugh at me all they wanted. I didn't care and still don't. I believe you must prepare for the prospect that your opponent might be at its very best. That philosophy may not have won many games for us, but one thing I am sure of — it did not cost us any.

Privately, after we were established in 1964 and got a grip on things, we realized that we did have some talent to work with. The Georgia football team lacked organization, direction and morale, but that was understandable with all the dissension and confusion that had taken place around it.

We had in our camp some solid players who knew how to hit. Remember, that has always been a Georgia tradition, and it certainly was a big plus for us. Having been where the athletes were physically superior, I was surprised — actually shocked — at the overall lack of mobility, particularly on defense. Our mission the first spring was to find the best twenty-two players, regardless of position, and work on developing quickness and speed. This resulted in one of the greatest decisions we ever made, moving George Patton from quarterback to tackle.

While the decision appeared to be a stroke of genius, it really was out of necessity. Our first team was eager — very eager, in fact. They were very coachable, too, reliable and ready to roll up their sleeves along with the young coaching staff.

After the Alabama opener, where we lost 31-3, things changed dramatically for us. I felt that some changes were in order for our

coaching staff. I gave Erk Russell the down lineman responsibility and put Jim Pyburn with the ends, reversing their roles. That was a move which benefited our defense and, as it turned out, a decision which was to produce positive results for many seasons. Jim had been a great defensive end at Auburn, and Erk just fit with the down guys. Erk knew how to communicate and relate to them; his trench warfare mentality was just right for the job. After that, we began to get maximum efficiency out of our personnel.

Another thing which we emphasized early turned out to make a big difference with our team. College football was still under limited substitution rules. You were allowed unlimited substitution when the clock stopped, but when it was running you could send in only two substitutes each play.

We decided to practice our offensive unit on offense eighty-five percent of the time and fifteen percent on defense. With the defense, we practiced them eighty-five percent of the time on defense and fifteen percent on offense. We really had a specialization system

Sun Bowl officials extend invitation in '64

Accepting the Sun Bowl trophy from an official with Rissmiller (L) and Ridlehuber (R)

going and got the jump on a lot of teams which still practiced all their units fifty percent offense and fifty percent defense.

After the opener, we allowed seventeen points to Florida State in a heart-breaking loss in Athens and fourteen points at Auburn, but nobody else scored more than eight points on our defense. We won every close game we played except Auburn (7-14) and the tie with South Carolina (7-7). We beat Vandy 7-0, Florida 14-7, Georgia Tech 7-0 and Texas Tech 7-0 (Sun Bowl). Those close games were games that Georgia had often lost in previous years.

A good start was a big factor in getting our

new program established. We earned everybody's respect. Most important of all we were able to go out and recruit one of the best freshmen teams in 1965 that we recruited during my time in Athens. This group was capable enough as sophomores to help us claim a share of the SEC championship in 1966 and then to win it again when they were seniors in 1968.

Those first five seasons were wonderful. We beat Georgia Tech every year, won two championships and played in four bowl games. Had it not been for injuries to so many front line players in 1965, we would have contended for the title and for sure

53

BILLY CLOER — *"Not a lot of people remember that I recovered the onside kick that enabled us to beat North Carolina in a high scoring game in Chapel Hill in 1965. But my teammates remember. That is what's important after all these years. Sometimes when I bump into somebody I haven't seen in years, they still say, 'Nice job on the kick, Bill.' Memories of that play will swell my head for a long time. I was 150 pounds, but Coach Dooley convinced me I could play and that I could make a contribution."*

would have received a bowl invitation. That team upset Alabama and Michigan. We had quality athletes on our team but no depth — one of the best 6-4 teams I have ever been associated with. If freshmen had been eligible, we'd have been an outstanding team in 1965 with freshmen like Jake Scott and Bill Stanfill.

Now that I have had an opportunity to reflect on those early years, I think that perhaps we suffered from too much success too quickly. We reached a point where the thrill of victory wasn't as exciting as it once was. We experienced some heady moments in a short period of time, winning big games against great coaches like Bear Bryant of Alabama, Johnny Vaught of Ole Miss, Bobby Dodd of Georgia Tech and my old coach Shug Jordan. Those conference titles and big bowl invitations can blur your vision when you are still maturing as a coach. Our team had appeared on national television, and I had received a flattering offer from the University of Oklahoma. But believe me, that thrill comes back after the agony of defeat. When things didn't go well for us in 1969 and we lost to Tech for the first time and then were swamped 45-6 by Nebraska in the wind at El Paso, I began craving the thrill of victory again. Badly, too. This game humbles you in a hurry.

Maybe things came too easy after that first year. But one thing I know for sure: after 1969, even though I experienced some tough seasons, I never again lost that thrill of victory. Every win became special and I never took any good fortune for granted. You have to work and prepare and play the percentages if you want to win over the long haul, and while I may not have handled success as I should have in the sixties, on the field we were doing the right things. We were coaching fundamental football and working hard as a staff to get the job done each Saturday.

After 1964, I realized more than ever the potential that Georgia had. There were many outstanding football players in the state and when the Bulldog program is in fine fettle, you notice the whole state taking notice. The Georgia graduates are not the only ones who

DEAN TATE — *It is customary, when Georgia wins a football game, for the freshmen students to ring the chapel bell. When Coach Dooley turned down an offer to coach at Oklahoma following the 1965 season, the happy students began ringing the chapel bell. Soon Dean William Tate, one of the university's best known and best loved characters, joined them, taking his turn at ringing the bell to signal one of Georgia's greatest victories.*

BILL STANFILL — *"Spring practice in my freshman year, the coaches could not decide who would play offense and who would play defense between me and David Rholetter, who was a hell of a player. During those long scrimmages, it was No. 1 offense against No. 2 defense and vice versa, but when they changed teams everybody got a break except me and David. If he was on offense, he switched over to defense, and I would go from defense to offense. I took matters into my own hands during the next big Saturday scrimmage. When they put me on offense, I knew who to block, but I always blocked the wrong guy. The next Monday I went permanently to defense. They had thrown Br'er Rabbit into the briar patch."*

take pride in the state university's team; there are the many friends of the institution who are pleased to see the Bulldogs succeed.

When he became interim president of the university in 1986, Dr. Henry King Stanford often opened his speeches wherever he went in the state by saying, "Welcome to the Campus of the University of Georgia." He was right, the state is the university's campus, and the pride in the school and Georgia football is far-reaching — from Hiawassee to Hahira and from Rabun Gap to Tybee Light. If you live in one of Georgia's 159 counties and didn't attend the university, chances are that your lawyer or your accountant or your doctor or your county agent did. In many cases your brother or your cousin or your best friend became a Bulldog, and close ties to the university are myriad.

No doubt that always helped us in recruiting, and getting off to a good start with our team in 1964 enabled us to bring in players like Bill Stanfill, Brad Johnson, Kent Lawrence, Bruce Kemp, Happy Dicks, David Rholetter, Billy Payne and Jake Scott, who was from Virginia but had Georgia ties, having once lived in Athens. Even during troubled times before I came, somebody at Georgia influenced good, solid players to enroll in Athens, and those players helped us turn things around in 1964.

But after a taste of success, many fans don't exactly understand when you fail to maintain the standards of your most recent success. That's the downside.

In many respects, 1965 was one of our most disappointing years at Georgia. Before the season began, I had promised that it would be a more difficult year. After all, we had won those close games the year before and had lost some very outstanding seniors, especially tackles Ray Rissmiller and Jim Wilson. But the 1965 team was an opportunistic outfit. We could make the big play on defense as well as offense. In our opening game against Alabama, we scored first on an interception return of fifty-five yards by George Patton, the quarterback who moved to tackle and eventually made All-America. On the other side we had Jiggy Smaha, who was a tremendous lineman. He was the one who hit quarterback Steve Sloan while he was attempting to throw and made him cough up the ball. George gathered it in and sprinted fifty-five yards into the end zone to put us ahead. Then after we lost our poise and made mistakes which enabled Alabama to gain the lead 17-10, we came up with the never-to-be-forgotten flea-flicker play. Quarterback Kirby Moore passed to Pat Hodgson who flipped the ball to Bob Taylor who went seventy-three yards for the touchdown. We won it with a two-point conversion on the next play, Moore to Hodgson, and by the defense keeping the Tide from getting within makeable field goal range in the closing seconds of the game.

When Alabama missed a desperation field goal attempt, I, in my excitement, turned and kicked Howard Beavers, our equipment manager, right square in the rear. Howard had a habit of squatting down on the sideline when he was watching the game, and he unwittingly became a convenient target for my enthusiasm.

My sideline conduct became rather topical after that, but only among our coaches and players. Nobody except those on the sideline knew about my gyrations because I was shielded from the stands by our players, who always stood up close to the sideline during the games.

The first time my exaggerated body English went public was after we beat South Carolina in 1977, which was our one-hundredth career victory. Prior to the South Carolina game, a member of my TV staff sent a cameraman, Clate Sanders, to the opponent's side of the field for the Clemson game a week earlier, and all Clate did was point his camera in my direction. Then on Sunday after the Carolina game, when I went to the television

Congratulations from Bear Bryant following the 1965 upset

BOB TAYLOR — *"People still talk about the flea-flicker that beat Alabama. I'm in sales, and when I travel the state and tell people my name, they say, 'Did you score the touchdown against Alabama?' You can't imagine how thrilling it is to me to say, 'Yes.' Funny thing, the play never worked in practice, and we even tried it earlier in the game against Alabama in 1965. But when the play came in, and they called my number, I knew I had to produce. We all did. Somehow or other we knew that it would work. It was going to work because Coach Dooley had told us we could play with anybody, and we believed him."*

KIRBY MOORE — *"When the flea-flicker came in, I couldn't believe it. 'Coach Dooley said run the flea flicker,' said the guy who brought the play in. I said, 'C'mon. What is the play? This is no time to be joking around.' He said again, 'Coach Dooley said run the flea-flicker.' I said, 'Okay, guys, we are going to run the flea-flicker.' And we ran it. I wanted to make it interesting, so I threw it low, but Pat [Hodgson] picked it off the grass and flipped it to Bob, and the stadium went crazy. When we scored, we knew we would go for two points. We had a two-point play. We had practiced it again and again. We knew, from all that training under Coach Dooley and his staff, that when we got into a critical situation, we would know what to do."*

PAT HODGSON — *"When I caught the ball, I never thought about my knees being on the ground or anything. All I did was follow through. Since the pass was low, it turned out to be an advantage. Alabama played a lot of pursuit on defense and really came after me. When I got the ball off, I was immediately hit by several defenders, at least four or five, which helped take them out of the play. I didn't know what was happening for a few minutes until I heard the roar of the crowd. It was then that I knew Ert [Elton Robert Taylor] was going all the way."*

station for my weekly show, that sideline footage was edited into the "Dooley shuffle" with music. I didn't know anything about it until the show began and my co-host, Ernie Johnson, told me to sit back and watch. There was a message from Barbara and the kids congratulating me on my one-hundredth win and a couple of highlight features of my years at Georgia, but the thing that grabbed my attention was my sideline dancing act.

After that it became my trademark. At first I was a little chagrined about seeing it on TV and was not particularly excited about the public exposure, feeling that the sideline is

The Dooley Shuffle

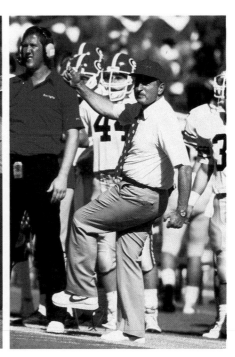

You put your left foot in, you put your left foot out . . .

the coach's domain and therefore should be somewhat private. Then Bill Simpson, later president of the Athens Touchdown Club, pointed out that it showed a side of my personality that people were generally unaware of and demonstrated that I cared. Most people were more familiar with my reserved manner and never expected me to display such emotion on the field.

Actually, body English comes natural with me. I was kidded about it by my teammates in college because it was part of my running style.

On the sideline, I had always been relatively calm before the snap of the ball and calm immediately after the play ends. In between, that period of six to eight seconds or so while the play was in progress, my body, soul and heart were totally into the game. With every movement of the running back, I swayed and dodged. My sideline dancing confirmed that I could be very emotional, which a lot of people doubted. As soon

as the play was over, my mind was immediately back into the game and what we should do next. I was attuned to the situation. Then as soon as the ball was snapped again, I immediately went back into action. Since I never realized that I was doing all this moving and jumping around, I was often puzzled the next day, especially after a big game, about why I was so sore.

In the 1989 Gator Bowl there was one camera assigned to me by ESPN, and people seemed to enjoy my sideline performance. I am glad, however, it wasn't something that was discovered by television early in my career.

The players and coaches always had their fun with it, too, even Howard Beavers. But after I booted him in the seat of the pants when Alabama missed that late field goal between the hedges in 1965, he learned to stay away from me. Whichever end of the field I was on, you could bet that Howard would be on the other.

59

Big plays like the flea-flicker were typical of the 1965 team. It was a group with great potential if it had remained healthy, but after we upset Michigan in Ann Arbor, our enthusiasm was drained as we lost one player and then another until we were riddled with injuries. We could not field a team that wasn't bandaged from head to toe. Bob Taylor, pound-for-pound one of the toughest running backs we ever had, broke his leg against Florida State. Doug McFalls suffered a broken jaw, and Joe Burson's weak knees didn't hold up. They were all gone by mid-season, and those who remained were not in the best of health. Like quarterback Preston Ridlehuber, who got about gamely on badly bruised legs.

Atlanta. Surprising Tech with an unbalanced line, we upset them and finished 6-4. No bowl this time, but even with the frustration it was not a bad Christmas. Beating Alabama, Michigan and Tech had the state solidly behind the Bulldogs, and in the spring we would have that great freshman team to work with. We would be young in 1966, but we would finally have some material and depth at every position. Coaching was getting to be a lot of fun.

Those sophomores didn't disappoint us, either, losing only one game in 1966 by one point (7-6 at Miami). The turning point was beating Ole Miss in Athens 9-3, a very big upset for us. I remember how physically

PRESTON RIDLEHUBER — *"At Michigan in 1965, I was confident that we were going to win the game. We all felt pretty good, even though we were aware that Michigan was the defending Rose Bowl champs. I remember that a man named John Underwood, a writer for* Sports Illustrated, *sat at my table for breakfast the day of the game. I'm so happy that Vince wasn't there because he would have had a heart attack if he had heard the interview. I told Mr. Underwood that Michigan's big stadium didn't intimidate us. We had played in big stadiums before, like the Gator Bowl, which seated half as many as the stadium at Ann Arbor. I was positive we would win because Vince and his brother, Bill, and the coaching staff had instilled that in us. We had a good plan and we were in a positive frame of mind. When the sportswriter left, all my teammates said, 'We better win or they'll be after you.' I was not being boastful. I was just confident. There was a great change in attitude when the new staff came around. We believed."*

If Preston had been full speed, we would have beaten Auburn in Athens. He broke into the clear and was chased down at the thirty-seven yard line, and Ronnie Jenkins fumbled the ball to Auburn six plays later at the Auburn one-yard line.

We lost to FSU, Kentucky, Florida and Auburn, but we began to get some of our frontline players back by the Tech game in

imposing Ole Miss was. I had never seen a bigger college football team.

We whipped Auburn for the first time, at Auburn, and that was a great thrill to go back home and win against my old coach on the field where I had played. And we had to come from behind to do it. They jumped out front 13-0 and we came back on a muddy field to post our sixth conference victory and our first SEC title. Brad Johnson, our fullback, enjoyed one of his most successful Saturdays, gaining ninety-nine yards. Brad was a great mudder, the best we ever had.

Against Tech in Athens, it was to be Bobby Dodd's last regular season game. Tech had received the Orange Bowl invitation and was favored, but our players were really up. Two things in particular I remember about that game. One, Kent Lawrence ran onto the field with a play we had drawn up on the sideline. The diagram was for a sweep that gave us a first down inside the ten-yard line. The crowd saw what we had done and roared its approval. The other thing was that somebody from Columbus had brought a cannon to Athens to fire after we scored a touchdown, but it went off prematurely just as Bobby

Etter was lined up to kick the extra point. It caused him to miss and we fell behind as a result, 7-6. I was quite irritated, although we went on to dominate the game before winning 23-14. We emptied the bench the last five minutes, which enabled Tech to score late.

I'll never forget the next morning when I rode over to Atlanta to do my weekly television show. Both the Tech and Georgia shows were programmed by WSB-TV. Coach Dodd was coming out of the studio as I was headed in. He came up and said, "You were very kind to me yesterday, and I appreciate that." That last touchdown made the final score more respectable, and a coach appreciates it when another doesn't try to rub it in. I felt that Coach Dodd would have done the same for me. He was a very gracious man.

Former mentor Shug Jordan, gracious in defeat

Tech coach Bobby Dodd (R) never beat a Vince Dooley team

In Columbus the next week, they took that malfunctioning cannon and imbedded it in concrete, held a ceremony, and sank it in the Chattahoochee River. It would never go off prematurely again, and it would never, ever create problems between the hedges in a big game.

Beating SMU in the Cotton Bowl gave us a 10-1 record in '66 and optimism for 1967 with all those sophomores becoming juniors, especially with Jake Scott becoming eligible.

Before the 1966 season, Jake was ruled ineligible due to a lack of hours needed to become a sophomore academically. He was very bright, very capable as a student, but to put it bluntly, he never enjoyed going to class. He was too restless and hated the confinement. But on the football field, Jake was exemplary. Even in practice, Jake Scott loved football. He was a student of the game. As an

athlete, he was blessed with marvelous physical flexibility, speed and quickness and was likely to make the big play at any time.

When he was the SEC Player of the Year in 1968, we made up a highlight film of his big plays for the season. He made at least one big play — one that influenced the outcome of the game defensively — in every game. Jake, a maverick off the field, was one of the greatest players we had at Georgia. When the game began, nobody gave you a greater effort and performance than Jake Scott.

If Jake had decided to stay at Georgia in 1969 rather than sign with the Canadian league, it might have been a different season for us. He was that much of an impact player. It was players like Jake in those early years who made me take the thrill of victory for granted.

When Jake told me he was going to Canada, I didn't handle the situation very well. I should have made a greater effort in trying to talk him into remaining at Georgia. I might not have changed his mind, but I should have counseled him more.

When Don Shula reached a peak with his great Dolphin teams in the seventies, the offensive headliners were Larry Csonka, Jim Kiick and Paul Warfield, but who were his stars on defense? Jake Scott and Bill Stanfill, members of that great recruiting class at Georgia in 1965.

We didn't play that well as a team in 1967. We lost early to Ole Miss in Jackson, 29-20, and when we went to Houston for our seventh game, we had experienced discipline problems and left some players at home. Houston came from behind to beat us 15-14 on a two-point conversion. We were sloppy against Florida a week later, losing 17-16. At that point, I was beginning to believe my good friend Bill Hartman who always says that things have a way of evening out. If you win a bunch of close games one year, you'll find yourself on the other end sooner or later.

Looking back, I consider 1967 a case of missed opportunities, but we closed strong, whipping Auburn 17-0 in Athens on a windy day and edging Tech in a close game, 21-14, in Atlanta. Then we were very ineffective in losing to N. C. State, 14-7, in the Liberty Bowl. Our quarterback Kirby Moore took us from our one to the N. C. State one — a beautiful ninety-eight yard drive — but on fourth and one, the Wolfpack stopped Kent Lawrence on the sweep.

Then came 1968 which began on Tennessee's artificial turf in Knoxville, something we were not exactly pleased about. As a matter of fact, Coach Eaves was livid and called it a brillo pad. Having to play on that turf for

Jake Scott, a student of the game

the first time worried us, but there was a new rule which turned out to be more of a headache for us than the playing surface. That was the year they put in the rule that calls for the clock to stop after a first down. That new rule enabled Tennessee to tie us with a two-point conversion late after we had gone ahead of them, 17-9. From Knoxville, we began to grow and develop, becoming a very solid football team with excellent play on both offense and defense. Except against South Carolina, where we made enough mistakes to last for a season and got behind 20-0, we didn't give up more than two touchdowns all year to any team. After that game, in which we came back to defeat the Gamecocks 21-20, we averaged allowing 6.8 points per game for the rest of the season. On offense, we had that great balance, averaging 25.6 points per game. The highest total was against Florida when we won 51-0 in the rain.

In Jacksonville, with all the pre-game rain,

63

KENT LAWRENCE — "No question about it, after coming to Georgia and enjoying the thrill of playing between the hedges, the greatest stadium in the country, I still can't forget what happened to me at Clemson in 1967. Having grown up nearby in Central, South Carolina, you can't imagine the thrill of going back and playing against some of my old midget football buddies in the community. And then, late in the game, to get the call on a big play in which I scored what turned out to be the winning touchdown is unbelievable. I still think about it often. I remember too that before the stadium was expanded in 1967 how there were people everywhere. In trees, on top of buildings, the bridge. Coach Dooley was bringing a new excitement to Georgia football and I was part of it. It meant something special to me to put on that red jersey. While I had speed, I was still pretty small. But when I put on the red jersey, I felt big and strong."

the coaches met at the Gator Bowl thirty minutes before kickoff and actually devised a new game plan. We had originally planned to have Cavan throw the ball, but we considered eliminating the pass offense and concentrating on a ground attack. Fortunately, we stuck with the original play, a "damn-it-all-anyway" situation which Coach Jordan used to refer to.

That 1968 team could produce. We lost to Arkansas in the Sugar Bowl, but that's another story to be dealt with later.

We ran out of dominating football players after 1968, and that coupled with the thrill of victory wearing thin set us up for a new experience in 1969. There is an old saying that goes, "They always remember what you do in November." And that has a lot of do with how you are regarded in football. Winning early is nice, but it is best to send everybody home for the winter with a positive finish. We had the opposite in 1969. Although we lost to Ole Miss 25-17 after an injured Archie Manning came back taped together to lead them to victory, we nonetheless had three shutouts in our first six games while averaging 32.1 points on offense. Then we lost Dennis

Hughes, who was by far our best offensive player, and a few other key players. Suddenly we could not move the football. In our last five games we scored only nineteen points — three against Tennessee, thirteen against Florida, three against Auburn and none against Tech in Atlanta.

Tech had finally beaten us and that was hard to take, especially since they were not a very good team in 1969. I have never seen a team which started so strong struggle as much as our 1969 team did. It was a lonely weekend at the old Riviera Motel on Peachtree where we all gathered in my suite to lick our wounds.

Some of the Tech fans were calling my room and rubbing it in. I took all their calls and said nothing, realizing that giving them a piece of my mind would not be the proper thing to do. Nonetheless, it was a miserable experience, and we all sat around with long faces. Nobody said anything. It was like a morgue. We were used to enjoying a nice private party, rehashing our victories and listening to Erk tell his favorite stories. Erk could always make those post-game celebrations enjoyable. But not that day.

Finally through all the deafening silence,

Erk's wife, Jean, spoke up. She put things in perspective. "This is not the end of the world," she said. "Losing football games is not the worst thing that can happen to you. I once lost a child. This is not the end of the world."

Jean was right, but the agony of defeat was weighing heavily on us. We were ready to get back to the business of winning and thinking about bowl games. It is a lot more fun to spend the holidays on the road than at home watching other teams play on television.

But there was more to confront than losing to Tech and seeing our recruiting go downhill a bit. We were experiencing different attitudes with the young men we were bringing to our campus. I was the same as I had always been — rigid. My background included a family and teacher philosophy of never sparing the rod, and strict military discipline and training were fundamental.

The players we signed in the early seventies started asking a lot of questions and — in some ways — challenging our authority. I had to learn to respond, shifting from the rigidity of my training to a more sensitive appreciation of each individual's concerns. It was all part of a learning experience for me, but if I had not changed, I would not have made it much longer as a football coach.

One of the things that I have always appreciated about Coach Bear Bryant was his ability to adjust with the times. He was a winner over five decades from the forties through the eighties. He was the toughest of disciplinarians at one point, but he obviously learned from his players and kept Alabama atop the football world for many years. And on the field it was the same. He went from a conservative offense to complement his tenacious defense to a dropback passing game — with Joe Namath, Steve Sloan, Kenny Stabler and Scott Hunter — to the wishbone. He enjoyed success everywhere he went and in every decade of his long coaching career. There are many qualities about Coach Bryant I admired, but the one that I think was the most important was his flexibility, his ability to adjust to change.

I had to learn to change and adjust as we moved into the seventies, which was a decade of success for us with another championship down the road but also a decade of frustration and disappointment. The Georgia people had to adjust to a couple of disappointing campaigns, and they weren't very pleased about it.

Neither was I.

Nobody was more concerned about the mistakes that had been made than the Bulldog head coach, still three years shy of his fortieth birthday.

Mistakes can furrow a brow quicker than anything

CHAPTER 6
Playing The Percentages And Paying The Price

To err is human,
To forgive is divine,
But to forgive a football coach
is unheard of.

That paraphrasing of some traditional words of wisdom often sums up a football coach's life. When I started out in this business, I realized I would make mistakes. My objective was to learn from them. If that's the case, I'm a lot smarter now than when I started.

My worst mistake? I'm not sure, but a good place to begin is the Sun Bowl of 1969.

No question about it, we should never have gone to El Paso. A smart coach will never saddle his team with insurmountable odds. But that's exactly how it was when we lined up against Nebraska in the Sun Bowl on December 20, 1969.

When we agreed to play in El Paso, nobody had any idea we would be meeting Nebraska, a team that would wind up winning two national championships in a row and was in the fight to the finish for an unprecedented third straight title. To be honest, I was somewhat caught off guard when I agreed to play in the Sun Bowl in 1969 before bowl officials invited Nebraska.

Scheduling is so important in football, and within certain limitations you have some control over the non-conference teams on your schedule. It is best to give your team the advantage.

One year when Tennessee was enjoying a good start, Clemson went to Knoxville and played the Volunteers off their feet. At the time Clemson wasn't as competitive as it is now, and it was a clear case of the decided underdog putting the favorite on the mat. "You thought when you scheduled this game that Clemson was going to be a breather, didn't you?" somebody said to Tennessee athletic director Bob Woodruff. While he wasn't known for one-liners, Woodruff looked at his friend, Frank Howard, the retired Tiger coach who had just become ath-

Coach Frank Howard of Clemson

letic director, and wise-cracked, "When I scheduled this game, I thought Coach Howard was still going to be coaching."

Even Coach Howard got a laugh out of that, and the rotund Baron of Barlow Bend,

Alabama, would agree with the premise that to succeed in football you better know what you are doing when it comes to scheduling. That includes accepting bowl invitations.

None of us had any idea that the Sun Bowl was considering Nebraska, and had I been aware of that, our decision might have been to stay home. Frankly, we were without the resources to evaluate just how strong the Cornhuskers were in 1969. Fewer intersectional games were played then, and fewer national TV games. While I was aware that Nebraska had an impressive record, I had not yet become convinced, even after looking at film, that Nebraska was not typically Nebraska — meaning big and slow. That was the way the Cornhuskers had been traditionally, but after the 1966 Orange Bowl, Bob Devaney set out to change his program. He was happy with the size on his team but he wanted to add the dimension of speed.

Lightweight Alabama, which we had upset in Athens with the flea-flicker in September, was a decided underdog in Miami three months later, but the Tide whipped big, slow Nebraska 39-28 to win the National Champi-onship. A year later in the Sugar Bowl, Alabama's quickness embarrassed Nebraska's heft again, 34-7.

Those were bitter defeats for Bob Devaney, who immediately began developing speed in his team. He realized he could not win the national title without speed. Nebraska acquired the most elaborate weight-lifting facilities of any campus. They developed quickness, they recruited speed and were on the way to becoming the dominant team in college football when we met them in the Sun Bowl.

Devaney's sophomores of that year were the ones who led Nebraska to back-to-back national titles in their junior and senior seasons. Devaney later told me Nebraska was actually a better team at the end of the season in 1969 than two years later when the Huskers won that second national title.

I had lulled myself to sleep. When they took the field and I watched them warm-up, I was stunned by their quickness. I realized they were not just big. They were big and fast, just what Devaney wanted. Devaney would eventually get even with Bryant — in

BOBBY POSS — *When Georgia was thrashed by Nebraska 45-6 in the 1969 Sun Bowl, the Bulldogs scored their lone touchdown late.*

The placement snapping specialist was Bobby Poss, who went up to Coach Dooley on the sideline and said, "Coach, do you want to go for two?"

Poss recalls the Bulldog head coach saying, "Bobby, let's just get this damn thing over as quickly as we can."

When Poss took the field, the Cornhuskers All-America middle linebacker, Rich Glover, said, "No. 52, I'm gonna ram your head down to your shoe tops."

"Look a heah, Hot," Poss said. "Ain't no way we can score forty points with time running out. How 'bout takin' it easy on me." Glover grinned and stood up at the snap, while Poss leaned up against Glover and flailed his arms as he he were making the block of his life.

After the play, Glover patted him on the rear as he left the field, which prompted Dooley to later remark to Poss, "Where were you in the first quarter when they were scoring all those points?"

the Orange Bowl of 1971, winning 38-6, but no doubt there was some incentive in El Paso to show a team from the Southeastern Conference that the big and slow Nebraska teams of the past would soon be a distant memory.

Maybe I was not as experienced at the bowl decision-making business as I should have been. Maybe I was just a slow learner. Five years later I made an even worse decision by playing in the Tangerine Bowl after a poor season which ended with Georgia Tech beating us in the mud in Athens 34-14.

Actually, my bad judgment about bowls dates back to 1968 the week before the Auburn game, when we were undefeated (Tennessee and Houston had tied us) and ranked in the top ten.

First some background. In the late sixties, the prevailing view — and the man who set the trend was Coach Bear Bryant — was that it was best to make your bowl deal as early as possible. This was before the Southeastern Conference agreed to send its champion to the Sugar Bowl each year, which meant that you could be left out in the cold if you failed to deal early and quickly.

For example, in 1969 when we were bowling with a 5-4-1 record, LSU was 9-1 and stayed home. It was one of the saddest moments of Charlie McClendon's career. His Tigers scored 349 points, allowed only 91 and were ranked No. 7 in the country at the end of the season, yet they spent the holidays in Baton Rouge.

The Sugar Bowl was not that keen on LSU, only a short bus ride of ninety miles from New Orleans, and neither were Charlie Mac's players keen on the Sugar Bowl. The smaller bowls felt that LSU would wind up in a bigger bowl and scrambled to hook up with lesser teams. Like us. LSU and Nebraska would have been a great match-up in the Sun

Bowl, but LSU simply waited too late to make a deal and was by-passed for teams with poorer records.

The same thing nearly happened to us in 1978 when we had that surprising 9-1-1 season. We were still in contention for a trip to the Sugar Bowl, which took the SEC Champion, depending on the outcome of the Auburn-Alabama game which was played late that year. Most of the bowls had made their decision, so we could have been left in limbo. Fortunately, the Bluebonnet officials had not picked their teams and we were invited to Houston at the last minute. For a 9-1-1 team not to get a bowl bid would have been a tough break. That 1978 team deserved a bowl bid as much as any of my teams. Fortunately they got one.

But back to Alabama, which was a very dominant team in the sixties and seventies. And Coach Bryant was so influential that many bowl representatives would wait to see where he was going before they made a move. He was the bowl kingmaker if ever there was one. Therefore, early commitments became the norm for other schools.

When we rolled into Auburn on November 15, 1968, Sugar Bowl and Orange Bowl scouts were out in full force. The Miami delegation was there to invite us if we won the game. "We've got to have a winner," their representative, Bill Ward, told our sports information director Dan Magill at dinner the night before the game. They dined in Columbus at the Black Angus, a well-known steak place which was then the most prestigious restaurant in the area. The Sugar Bowl delegation, however, could have smirked in every direction because I had told them I would bring the Georgia team to New Orleans regardless of the outcome of the game. It was a done deal, although I was, out of necessity, coy with everyone.

Alabama Coach Bear Bryant set the trend for bowl selections

Since the Sugar officials had told us they would take us win or lose, I felt justified in making the decision. You know the old bird-in-the-hand theory! As was my custom, I played the percentages on that one, but it turned out to be the wrong decision.

The majority of our players preferred Miami. When the team jogged off the field a 17-3 winner, the Auburn student body hurled oranges in our direction. Up in the press box, Miami extended Coach Eaves the invitation. He came to me and said, "What do you want to do?" I told him that while I thought many of our players preferred Miami, we had made a commitment and should honor it. He said, "I agree with your decision to keep your word."

Nothing was said about the Sugar Bowl until Sunday when we convened the team for a meeting, but no question about it, visions of Miami Beach were dancing in their heads. If you talk to college football players today, they won't find anything wrong with New Orleans. The Crescent City now can hold its own, especially since the Superdome was built, with any city for a New Year's holiday bowl party. But with players in those years, the Orange Bowl had a more attractive image. Ours were no exception — the vast majority of them would have voted for Miami.

This was one of the most difficult times of my coaching career. How did I get myself into this?

Simple. I felt before the game that the Sugar Bowl's commitment to take us win or lose was best for our team and our program. As the decision maker, I was faced with either yielding to the preference of our players or going against my word. I have never forgotten the sound advice of my electrician father, a man who had to struggle to provide for his family all his life. He always told me, "Son, be a man of your word. A commitment is a commitment."

It might have been the best short-term decision for our football team to call the Sugar Bowl and renege, but you can imagine what that would have done to my credibility and that of the University of Georgia and its bowl relationships down the road. We had to go to New Orleans.

One thing about 1968 that is different from today is that then the head coach could be more dictatorial. He made the decision, no questions asked. That was never my style, although the final authority on any football decisions must ultimately rest with the head coach.

Even today, the head coach should make the final decisions, but not without input from his team. That is the mistake I made in 1968, but in those days there was too much behind-the-scenes bowl maneuvering to consult with the team. You had to deal in secret, which was bad business for the colleges and the bowls. I'm glad we got away from the old system.

What Coach Eaves and I appreciated about the Sugar Bowl was that it would give us a connection, an "in" with a major bowl we had not been to before, and there was a nagging concern that if — without commitment — we gambled and lost to Auburn, neither the Sugar nor the Orange would take us.

As a boy, I had gotten a ride over to New Orleans when Georgia played North Carolina in the Sugar Bowl in 1947, naively thinking I would be able to get a ticket. I sat outside old Tulane Stadium and listened to the roar of the crowd and promised myself that "someday I'll get in that stadium." Now here I was in New Orleans at the Sugar Bowl, a great place to be, but my team wanted to be in Miami.

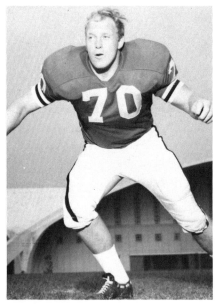

Brad Johnson   *David Rholetter*   *Dennis Hughes*

Maybe this contributed to the poor performance of the team — we lost 16-2 to Arkansas in old Tulane Stadium. I don't know, but I do know this — considering the times and circumstances, it was the percentage pre-game decision.

Since the players expressed their disappointment, we had to sell them on New Orleans, and we tried to make it the best trip possible. We stayed a full week while Arkansas came in two days before the game. The gossip was that we had no curfew, which was incorrect. We didn't play our best, but you must give Arkansas credit. They were a good football team and they were the underdogs, which is often the best posture in a bowl. But whether the players were up or not, whether there was too much leniency or not, it all boiled down to the breaks on the field. After struggling early, we moved into position to close the gap at the beginning of the second half. We recovered a fumble on their twenty after the kickoff and moved into scoring position at the one. At that point, there

was no question in my mind we were going to turn the game around. We were going to win. We were that kind of team. Up in the press box, with Arkansas leading 10-2, somebody said to Coach Eaves, "Do you think we ought to go for two?" Coach Eaves, never one to take anything for granted, replied, "Let's get the touchdown first." I can still see the play as if it were yesterday. Brad Johnson, our fullback, popped over the goal line, but suddenly the ball shot through the end zone. Touchback. Arkansas had the ball on its twenty.

We didn't know what happened at the time, but the films later told the story. One of our linemen, David Rholetter, blocked an Arkansas defender so powerfully that he flipped him. It was a heels-over-head block, the defender's leg swinging high in the air as he was upended. His foot hit Brad's arm and kicked the ball away, saving the day for the Arkansas defense. That fumble took the momentum away from us. As poorly as we played, I always felt that if we had scored, we would have won. They played outstanding, errorless football. We didn't, and we fumbled the game away. That's football. But never again did I make a bowl decision without consulting the team.

Our players were very enthusiastic about going to the Sun Bowl in 1969. They had heard the players from 1964 talk about how much they had enjoyed El Paso, and if we had beaten Georgia Tech in our final game we would have finished 6-3-1, the same as in 1964. The only difference is that this time around Tech upset us 6-0, and we went bowling at 5-4-1. That's not good. But the decision had to be made after the Auburn game. You have one game remaining with a shot at a post-season trip, so what do you do? You are faced with a guess about how you're going to come out against Tech. The time before it worked; this time it didn't. We had soured offensively. We had lost our best player, Dennis Hughes, and couldn't move the ball on offense. Even if we had beaten Tech, I don't think it would have been wise to take on Bob Devaney's team. There was a lot of wind that day in the Sun Bowl, but mainly Nebraska was a team of destiny. We should have been home by the fire watching Nebraska whip up on somebody else. What a miserable afternoon.

But history often repeats itself. We had a great team in 1971, we were respectable with seven victories for a couple of years, and then in 1974 we finished the Auburn game with a record of 6-4 and an option for the Tangerine Bowl in Orlando. This bowl later became the Citrus Bowl and had already begun to make its move into the big time. Orlando is a great place to take a family, and our coaches and players were excited about the trip. But Tech, our biggest rival, remained. Unlike 1969, we were playing in Athens. We felt that the per-

centages were in our favor, so we agreed to accept the bowl bid.

On the day of the Tech game, Athens was dowsed with the hardest sustained rain I can ever remember for a football game. Tech was the underdog, but they should have been the favorite. They were running the wishbone attack, ideal for a muddy field. And we ran the split-back veer, far from ideal for a muddy field. The wishbone was a power option, the veer a finesse option. What an advantage for them! It was even more miserable than playing Nebraska in the Texas winds at El Paso.

Through the years, we were fortunate against our main rival, Georgia Tech, with a 19-6 record in twenty-five years, but on that day they dominated us as much as we ever dominated any team. It was one of our most humiliating defeats.

From that experience came a sideline rule that was strictly enforced for the rest of my career. Tech was romping all over us, and on the sideline everybody was trying to cover up. The players were scrambling for rain gear, hunting for heavy parkas and gathering around a portable heater on the sideline. It was obvious they were more concerned about staying warm than being in the game. After that, the portable heater was gone forever. And nobody wore excessive, heavy clothing without approval from the head coach. We allowed air conditioning in the hot times of the year — you have to cool off — but it is never too cold to play football. Not at Georgia, anyway.

After Tech trampled us in the mud, we were 6-5 and going bowling. Win that last game and we finish 7-4, which is not bad for a bowl team. Many teams have enthusiastically accepted bowl invitations with a 6-5, record but I've never thought that was a good idea. The problem with 1974, just as in 1964 and 1969, was that we had to gamble on the

Tech game. In 1964 we were a solid football team; it was our first year at Georgia and there was an abundance of enthusiasm. We were playing Tech at home and got the breaks to come away a 7-0 winner. In 1969 we were having a tough year, but Tech had not won many games. They beat us 6-0, although in the fourth quarter we were in scoring position, poised to pull it out, but threw an interception into the Tech end zone. A day of sunshine might not have won for us in 1974, but it certainly should have made a difference.

Bowl games are important to your teams and your program, so you're willing to gamble. You take a chance. Fine if you win, but hell if you lose.

Naturally we caught hell after the Tangerine Bowl, in which we lost to a capable Miami of Ohio team, 21-10. One newspaperman suggested we had no class and that we needed a triple digit scoreboard to ring up all the points that were being scored on our defense.

Erk put a clipping of that derogatory article on the wall in his office and looked at it every day right on into the 1975 season, the year of the "Junkyard Dog" defense, which helped us rebound into a contender for the conference title before winning it a year later to break Alabama's hold on the annual invitation to New Orleans.

After the Tangerine Bowl, I decided to address the team. As I scouted the locker room to make sure there were only coaches and players inside, I was fuming inside. We had lost something. We had not done a good job coaching, and we didn't have the best attitude among some of our players. Our character and our fight were not typical of Georgia or what we had become recognized for.

I was embarrassed at what had happened to our program. This team did not need an explosive, verbal tongue lashing like the 1967 team did for getting into a fight after the Florida game, but the players coming back needed a lecture. It was a firm, deliberate message that left no doubt about my plans. They needed to know that things would be different. I told them I had let them down as a coach, that we all had let the University of Georgia down, but we were going to work like we had never worked before.

"If you think it's been tough, you don't know anything. Just wait until spring practice. You'll find out what toughness and hard work really is. We are going to become a football team again, one that will fight every play and be proud to wear the Bulldog colors."

Then I had to go out and meet the press and tell them that I was embarassed at what had happened to my program and that I was to blame. It all starts with the head coach, and right there underneath the stands at the Tangerine Bowl, I determined that there would be a new beginning at Georgia.

A coach makes many mistakes in his career. You learn from them, and I learned from gambling on bowl decisions. Fortunately we never faced the same circumstances in later years. We never again made a bowl decision unless we had seven wins already notched. We never decided on which bowl invitation to accept until we communicated with our players. The coaches first assessed our options and then we reviewed the situation and options with the players. After the conference made a deal with the Sugar Bowl to take our champion each year, the annual war cry on our practice field, just as I'm sure it was at every other SEC school with championship on its mind, was "New Orleans!"

Even after 1982, when we had won the SEC title three years in a row, it was important to our team to make a fourth trip. We lost to Auburn in 1983, which knocked us out of the conference championship, but our football players still fought hard in pursuit of Bourbon Street. We were invited to the Cotton Bowl, and there was much enthusiasm for playing a great Texas team and enjoying a change of scenery, but that was only rationalization. What we preferred was another New Year's in New Orleans for one simple reason: it meant championship.

After 1982, I remember a couple of fans saying, "Do we have to go to New Orleans, again?" It doesn't take long for people to become spoiled.

I remember an interview that a sportswriter had with some golfers about second chances with important putts. If you could take one over, which would it be? Naturally the golfers chose putts which either would have won a title for them or gotten them into a playoff for a major championship.

On the football field I've made countless decisions I would like to take back. And while you can't always isolate one call that later you can say definitely cost you a game, you remember many times when a successful play in a series could have been a turning point.

Of all the on-the-field decisions I would like to take back, one that particularly stands out came during the Cotton Bowl of 1976. We were playing Arkansas again and played them well for a quarter and a half. But midway of the second period, the game started to turn a little bit. You could feel it. I thought we needed something to regain the momentum, so I called for the infamous shoe string play.

Earlier in the season against Vanderbilt, our offensive coordinator Bill Pace noticed

that the Vandy defense always huddled tightly and held hands while getting the defensive call from the sideline. That created an ideal opportunity for the shoe string play. The previous play actually sets up the shoe string — you run a play to the sideline to get the ball on the hash marks. The offensive linemen never go back to the huddle, but instead they casually line up on the line of scrimmage to the wide side of the field. The quarterback, who then walks up to the ball, in essence becomes the center, and he puts the the ball in play as soon as the referee walks away. The quarterback has to be a good actor to make it work, and Ray Goff was perfect for the part. He knelt down to tie his shoe, suddenly picked up the ball and pitched it to Gene Washington, our sprinter-flanker who jogged into the end zone for a touchdown.

Ray Goff, a fine actor

Entering the Cotton Bowl, we knew Arkansas would be prepared for that play since they had seen it on film. We started strong, controlling the game with great momentum, but midway in the second quarter we lost it. You could sense the change. In an attempt to recapture the momentum, we called on the counter shoe string play, which was designed for Ray to flip to Gene who then would pull up and throw a pass to Ray, who actually was wide open on the back side of the field. It might have been a sensational play except for one thing: Arkansas, very alert, got in the backfield and forced a fumble. They recovered and scored, and we were never in the game after that. With our loss of momentum, it was as if we had poured fuel on their fire. The touchdown off the shoestring fumble only made it 10-10 at the half, but they never let us back into the game. I'd like to have that one back.

But doesn't everybody want more excitement? Doesn't everybody want more passing, more razzle-dazzle, more trick plays? Doesn't everybody like a coach who will gamble? Yep, they sure do . . . as long as it works. It had worked for us, a razzle-dazzle team that got to the Cotton Bowl on such plays as the end-around pass from Appleby to Washington in the Florida game, but in Dallas it was another story. You live by the sword, you die by the sword.

Incidentally, what made the difference in that game was the great play of the Arkansas defense, which was coached by Bill Lewis, who later joined our staff, and Jimmy Johnson, who went on to become the head coach at Oklahoma State and Miami and, more recently, the Dallas Cowboys.

In 1981 after beating Ole Miss in Oxford, I made one of my biggest coaching mistakes, something that normally would never have happened. It was a custom of mine that on game weekend I was constantly with the team. I rode with them, ate with them, met with them and went to the movie with them. Only when everybody bedded down at night did we go our separate ways, and even then

there was controlled supervision. I usually made the bed-check rounds with our trainer, Warren Morris, and our trainers and assistants were constantly in touch with our players to see that our weekend routine was followed up to the letter. Our objective was to make sure that there were no distractions, interruptions or interferences. We wanted everybody's mind and concentration focused on his Saturday assignment.

Over the years we may have had some players to slip out at night, but I don't remember too many major curfew problems. When there was one, we took strict disciplinary action. But any coach knows that with college-age adults, it is often a case of the caught and the uncaught.

Much of our success had to do with the fact that we always made it clear to our players what we expected of them and that we wanted them representing the University of Georgia in the best possible manner. Quite often we got letters from motel innkeepers and operators, complimenting our team on the good manners and gentlemanly conduct. We appreciated that and considered it a reflection on the program and the university.

But if a few players decide to take liberty with a situation, you can be sure that there is no better time than after a victory, and that is exactly what happened after the 1981 Ole Miss game which we won 37-7.

For years it was a challenge for us to produce our Sunday TV show when we played games in the Central Time Zone. We kick off an hour later, and editing can't begin until we return to Athens (the plane lands at the Atlanta Airport and the team is bussed on home). After the Ole Miss game, I thought it might help us to get an early start on the show if I flew directly into Athens on a charter plane available for that purpose.

Wouldn't you know it? I break the pattern and a discipline problem surfaces. Alcoholic beverages are never served on any of our flights, even to the administrative staff on board and Athletic Board members traveling with us. In fact, the airline generally does not stock any alcoholic beverages on our charters, but this time there apparently were some left over from an earlier flight, and a couple of players discovered that the compartment which contained the whiskey miniatures was unlocked. A few of our players had themselves a post-game victory cocktail or two.

This was very embarrassing. I had used poor judgment, and as a result of an investigation, I had to suspend a couple of players for the next game against Vanderbilt. After reviewing the situation with the airline, additional security precautions for future flights were instituted and the situation was corrected.

Naturally, this incident was a big item for the media. I felt I had to apologize for our conduct to Dave Garrett, then the Chairman of Delta Air Lines. Dave, one of the finest gentlemen I have ever been associated with, understood and in turn apologized for the airline's security breakdown on the trip.

It has always been my view that I should be with the team at all times, and this was the only time I made an exception. I was particularly upset because I have always tried to enforce strict rules of discipline when we travel. Up until the last few years, my wife Barbara never traveled with me. This was partially because she was usually at home with our children, who were involved with Friday night high school football, either playing or cheerleading. But mostly, my view came out of the Marine Corps experience. Marines never took wives on business trips or into combat, and I believed our travel party should not include wives (except for bowl

games and our annual trip to Jacksonville). I still think that is the best policy, aside from certain exceptions involving head coaches, the athletic director and the President. Those are the only ones I would consider, even after all these years.

It is only a game, they say. Okay, I can live with the ups and downs of a game or a season or an era, for all coaches must endure the difficult times which are as certain as death and taxes. If you stick your neck out there often enough, you are going to get it whacked off sooner or later. But a coach understands and accepts the fate of what takes place on the field as basic to the profession.

Sometimes it is developments off the field, however, that present the biggest challenge and frustration. Most people would say the infamous Jan Kemp trial would have to be considered a great mistake, and it was for the University of Georgia. But just like a failed decision on the football field, you can second-guess yourself till sundown and never receive a second chance. If we had it to do over again, I am sure the administration would choose another route, but at the time the decision was firm to fight it out in court. Nobody could have foreseen the adverse reaction and developments, and I didn't expect the worst myself.

To be frank, I was worried about the course of action we took, but I didn't voice my concern because the administration's legal advisors were so confident that going to court was the proper thing to do. Even if I had been overly uncomfortable with what was happening, it would have been difficult to offer unsolicited advice on a decision based on a researched legal position. I had always enjoyed a good relationship with university president Dr. Fred Davison, and I didn't feel that I should caution him about an issue that was outside my area of direct responsibility.

Many people have forgotten that the suit actually dealt with the First Amendment right of free speech. It involved Dr. Kemp's having been fired as a teacher in the Developmental Studies program. It was not a suit against the Athletic Association, although we were finally involved.

But the trial quickly got away from the First Amendment question and focused instead on the preferential treatment of athletes. There were charges, accusations and a rash of inaccurate and incomplete reporting. Dr. Kemp may have gotten a fair trial, but the Georgia Athletic Association did not.

To fully appreciate what took place, you have to recall what had developed with admissions policies of all colleges.

The best summation of what faced college athletic officials was outlined in a conversation David Davidson of *The Atlanta Journal* had with Walter Byers, long-time executive director of the NCAA. Byers was asked, "How do you assess the academic climate of college athletics? What do you think when you read in the newspaper that a kid who scores 470 on his SAT is admitted and is eligible?"

This was Byer's response: "Certainly I think the publicized cases would bother anyone who believes in the absolute necessity of high standards in higher education. I don't think it's only an athletic problem as such. Let me give you this thought: What happened during the 1960s was a matter of national policy. Minority groups and disadvantaged groups were going to be given access to higher education. Now, that was a national government policy implemented in a great many ways. It was designed to encourage institutions of higher education to open

doors and run remedial programs, if necessary, to give access not only to those who were disadvantaged financially, but disadvantaged from the standpoint of academic preparation."

Following through on the theme expressed by Mr. Byers, the local application of that national policy was the birth of "special studies" (later changed to developmental studies). This program was established as part of a desegregation plan mandated by the federal courts, overseen by the Office of Civil Rights, and carried out by the University System Board of Regents. That mandate insisted that the university provide disadvantaged students with the opportunity to attend college. The developmental studies program would enable them to acquire those fundamentals prior to going into the mainstream of academic college life.

The basic problem in athletics is that the NCAA and the educators of the institutions, as Mr. Byers pointed out, went further than necessary in lowering what was already a reasonable athletic eligibility standard. The lowering of the standards to a 2.0 overall average in all courses was, in essence, little or no standard at all. This, of course, opened the doors of opportunity to almost every athlete to earn a college scholarship regardless of his or her high school performance in college preparatory courses.

As we began drawing up guidelines for our program in accordance with these new NCAA regulations and in consideration of similar approaches by other institutions, we were placed in the position of offering scholarship aid to some student-athletes with very poor academic preparation.

The "1.6 Rule" required that a student predict a minimum grade point average of 1.6 for college work. This prediction was based on a standardized test score (ACT or SAT) combined with either his high school GPA or class standing. An instititution could determine a prospective student's prediction by using a table prepared by NCAA (or one prepared by the conference or institution and approved by NCAA).

The 1.6 formula, had it been maintained as an admission formula for athletes, would probably have kept us from the widespread abuses and problems of recent years. If an athlete scored poorly on the college boards but had applied himself in class, he still would have had an opportunity for admission.

Take today's minimum standards of 15 on the ACT (American College Testing) and 700 on the SAT (Scholastic Aptitude Test), for example. Under the 1.6 rule, a score of 15 on the ACT means that the athlete would have needed a 2.79 grade point average. A score of 700 on the SAT would have required a 2.85 grade point average for admission. Under the 1.6 formula, a 2.0 GPA would have meant that the athlete would have to score 959 on the SAT or a 21 on the ACT. The 1.6 rule was very practical, and it got kicked out.

Because of what transpired, colleges were soon taking high-risk students. The Georgia Athletic Association didn't admit the risk students; the University of Georgia did.

But we recommended them.

And that is where I, as Athletic Director, made a mistake. We simply recommended too many marginal or risk student-athletes. But even to this day, if you go back and look under every rock, you will find that we broke no NCAA or SEC rules. No university admission procedures or policies were violated.

I've been asked many times that if I had it to do over again, what would I change. I always said and still say that we should not have recommended so many risk students for admission. But two factors influenced our

eagerness in that regard. One is that we had documented evidence of many risk students who had applied themselves, persevered and earned their degrees. Even though the percentage of risk students who graduated was small, you always feel the one you are recruiting deserves a chance and that he would succeed.

Additionally, all schools were following a similar procedure with their recruiting policy. Most coaches I know prefer higher standards if they are enforced across the board. Then nobody has an unfair advantage. But a coach's bottom line is to win, and you want to have at least an equal chance with the competition.

It often boils down to this simple fact: if my opponent has a player who can run 9.5, I've got to have one who can catch him.

The most controversial statement of the Kemp trial came early when the university lawyer said that if risk students were admitted and were helped a little — enough for them to advance from "the garbage truck to the post office" — then they really hadn't been hurt in the process. That was a most unfortunate statement. In fact, the case was probably decided at that point.

Afterwards, new charges seemed to surface every day. Instead of trying to defend them all, we took the position that if our program was sound and based on integrity, which it was, we would survive. We might come away with a black eye, but we would remain on our feet. We would survive, and as a result, would become stronger.

We hunkered down. We turned the crisis into an opportunity. We recommended that the president hire Dr. Boyd McWhorter, former Dean of the College of Arts and Sciences and recently retired Commissioner of the Southeastern Conference, to join us as liaison officer with the faculty, answering directly to the President. We hired Dick Bestwick, former head football coach at Virginia, to direct our Student Athlete Services Department.

It was Dick's responsibility as head of this department to deal with all counseling, from academics to anything in our athletes' personal lives. After studying the situation, Dick told us was, "I am amazed. We have a lot of athletes who need counseling and directing, as it is with so many college athletes, but there is no scandal."

In the aftermath of the trial, in which Dr. Kemp won her lawsuit, including a big judgment and her job back, Dr. Fred Davison resigned after spending nineteen years building the University of Georgia into one of the South's most respected institutions. That was regrettable.

What was so ironic about the Kemp trial is that reforms were already in place before it started. Steps were being taken by a number of concerned college officials to raise standards. The trial simply expedited the reform movement, which has been good for college athletics. And I believe that what happened after the trial has been good. Too many problems had developed, and something had to be done which would result in improvements in college athletics. However, I would rather our program was not the one which had to suffer publicly to bring about a proper focus on the need for raising standards for athletes.

The reforms that were underway when the trial developed were in large measure spearheaded by Fred Davison. When you think of his concerns for standards and his sensitivity on the subject, it is actually incongruous that he became a fatal victim in such a controversy.

During the time of the minimum standard of a 2.0 average, which the NCAA adopted in 1974, the Southeastern Conference kept proposing to the NCAA that the 1.6 rule be reinstated but got nowhere.

Concerns over the lack of standards are what brought about Propositions 48 and 42, which have been in the news so much lately. And the man who had so much to do with Proposition 48 was Fred Davison. It began when Charles M. (Chuck) Neinas, Executive Director of the College Football Association, had a conversation with Homer Rice of Georgia Tech at the 1982 Atlantic Coast Conference basketball tournament. Homer kept reminding Chuck that something needed to be done about the image of college athletics. This motivated Chuck to visit Dr. Davison's old college office on Georgia's main campus before returning to his office in Denver.

Chuck had formulated a plan that would involve key college officials meeting and discussing ways to solve pressing collegiate athletic problems.

"Fred loved the idea of a meeting for such a purpose," Neinas says. "He was so bullish that he informed me immediately that the University of Georgia would underwrite the conference and host it at Sapelo Island." Fred also suggested to Chuck that we use the conference board format. This involves a meeting utilizing a circle of chairs with no table. Each person draws his speaking order from a hat. He then has five minutes to speak on any subject he chooses. If you want to respond or counter what has just been said, you have that option to speak immediately but you forfeit your original speaking position. You cannot speak twice. This format eliminated typically lengthy point and counterpoint discussions and allowed us to get to the heart of issues and accomplish a lot in a short period of time.

In a very productive session, everybody present agreed that if we were going to improve the image of college athletics, it had to begin with raising the academic standards. Those in attendance, in addition to Chuck Neinas, Dr. Davison and me, were: Donald B. Canham, Athletic Director, University of Michigan; DeLoss Dodds, Athletic Director, University of Texas; Jack Hartman, Basketball Coach, Kansas State University; Carl C. James, Commissioner, Big Eight Conference; Bob Knight, Basketball Coach, Indiana University; William E. Lavery, President, Virginia Tech University; Henry T. Lowe, Professor of Law, University of Missouri; Joseph V. Paterno, Football Coach, Pennsylvania State University; Homer Rice; James H. Wharton, Chancellor, Louisiana State University; James H. Zumberge, President, University of Southern California. Basketball coaches Dean Smith of North Carolina and John Thompson of Georgetown were invited but unable to participate.

It was remarkable that we were able to get that many people of that stature together at one time. Sapelo Island, one of Georgia's great natural treasures, offered an ideal setting for such a conference, and Dr. Davison was an enthusiastic and genial host, driving the guests around the island during our breaks and taking great pleasure in showing off one of the university's prestigious research outposts.

Everything was not smooth at the conference, as you can expect when you get that many men of strong wills and opinions together. In fact, in one session, Bobby Knight and Jim Zumberge got into a heated argument over an NCAA issue, and I thought at one point they were going to have to settle it with their fists. There were other heated disagreements, but everybody was committed to reaching conclusions that would be in the best interests of college athletics. Out of this meeting came a commitment to upgrade standards in college athletics, as outlined in the following excerpt from a press release dated May 9, 1982.

The group will recommend and encourage adoption of appropriate legislation at the 1983 NCAA Convention and will enlist the aid of others to support upgrading academic standards.

Should such legislation not be adopted by the NCAA membership, the group will recommend that the legislation be implemented by a coalition of institutions involved in the sponsorship of a major college athletic program with the understanding that such institu-

ETHICS COMMITTEE — *For ten years Coach Dooley was chairman of the American Football Coaches Association ethics committee.*

When he joined the committee, he immediately realized that sitting in judgment of his peers was a thankless job, but he was confident that a properly organized and well run committee could make a contribution to the profession.

In the late sixties, when the ethics committee met at the annual AFCA meetings, it was customary for members to search out coaches accused of misconduct, summoning them to the ethics council. This approach proved unworkable when a one-time chairman, Johnny Pont, who coached at Indiana and Northwestern, looked up Woody Hayes of Ohio State and asked him to appear before the ethics committee.

When he returned to the meeting room, he told the committee, "Woody said he wasn't coming."

Coach Dooley spearheaded a rewriting of the ethics code when he became chairman, putting some teeth into the policies and procedures and properly addressing due process.

After that, coaches and their schools were advised in advance in writing if they were to appear before the ethics committee. With the new procedures, the defiant Hayes later appeared before the ethics committee.

tions will coordinate their scheduling activities with those of similar inclination toward higher academic standards.

The proposal would require (1) satisfactory completion of substantive courses in at least three years of high school English and at least two years of high school mathematics with a minimum combined grade point average of 2.00 in these subjects that are basic for college preparation as well as maintenance of an overall high school grade point average of 2.00, and (2) achieve a score of 700 on an SAT exam or a 15 on an ACT exam.

The legislation is to be effective in the 1985-86 academic year and will enable the high schools and their students to adapt to the new academic requirements.

The group reviewed a number of other topics, foremost of which was the area of recruiting. The group believes that to maintain the integrity of intercollegiate athletics that penalties in connection with violations should be more stringent, consistent and equitable. In particular, the group recommends that penalties should be imposed upon coaches and athletes (or prospects) involved in violation of NCAA rules as well as recognizing the responsibility of an institution in the conduct of its athletic program.

This resolution led to Proposition 48, which was presented by Joe Paterno at the NCAA meetings in San Diego in January of 1983. Proposition 48 established new standards, including a core curriculum and minimum test scores of 700-SAT and 15-ACT. It became bylaw 5-1-j to be implemented with students matriculating after August of 1986. Then the NCAA adopted an indexing formula with some of the characteristics of the old 1.6 rules. With the new indexing procedure, a student-athlete, for example, with a test score of 680 could be admitted if he had a grade point average of 2.2 in the core curriculum. This was in effect for 1986. In 1987 it was changed to a 680 test score and 2.1 average in the core curriculum. Then in 1988 the original requirements went into effect.

"In addition to indexing there was a second modification to Proposition 48 involving the establishment of the partial qualifier category, which eroded the original intent of Proposition 48," says Dr. Bill Powell, our faculty Chairman of Athletics.

This loophole allows an athlete who does not qualify to enter school on scholarship, but he cannot compete (or practice) during his freshman year, and he loses that year of eligibility.

After the first year the partial qualifier becomes fully qualified, provided that he satisfies the institution's academic requirements.

Proposition 42, put on the NCAA books in January of 1989, eliminates all partial qualifiers. This legislation was, I am proud to say, sponsored by the Southeastern Conference. One of those who successfully lobbied for the SEC to pass this rule for conference institutions and subsequently sponsor it to the NCAA convention of 1989 was our president, Charles Knapp, who says:

It is my feeling that the academic qualifications of the student athlete should conform more to the academic qualifications of the other students on campus.

Proposition 42 is an effort to bring that conformity closer. If we don't support objectives such as Proposition 42, we are inviting the perception that athletes are being brought to the campus to perform athletically only and that there is no concern for their educational development.

We have a long way to go with making the academic qualifications of the student athlete conform to the academic qualifications of the general student body, but Proposition 42 is a step in the right direction.

To me it is clear that Proposition 42 will need some fine-tuning in the future which I welcome so long as we hold to the basic principles.

The problem remains one of some schools' searching for loopholes. In my opinion, we must standardize our admissions and raise them to a reasonable level if we are going to maintain the public's faith and trust.

Dr. Fred Davison saw this early on and fought for higher standards. He deserved a better fate than he got in the aftermath of the Kemp trial. He sincerely believed in intercollegiate athletics and wanted to raise standards to preserve the integrity of college athletes, but I doubt that many people are aware of his commitment and feelings. To convince people that he believed in standards, immediately after the Kemp trial he established a University of Georgia rule that no non-qualifiers would be admitted for athletic competition. None. I lobbied for a gradual move in that direction, feeling that instant implementation would leave us at a competitive disadvantage, which turned out to be correct. However, I supported his decision and concluded that in the long run, the University of Georgia would be better off by adhering to higher standards. Instead of complaining, we chose to become a leader. We were already in the process of establishing a mission statement on academic standards — before the Kemp trial took place — so we forged ahead.

Our Mission Statement, which we developed in association with the Atlanta public relations firm of Cohn and Wolfe, with input from everyone involved — from Dr. Davison to athletic board members like Dr. Alan Barber and Bob Bishop to almost the entire staff of the athletic association — is prominently displayed in our offices:

> *Our mission is to offer nationally competitive intercollegiate athletic programs which reflect the interests of our students and faculty, the Southeastern Conference, and the people of Georgia and of the nation who support our activities. These programs are a source of enthusiasm and loyalty. They enliven and enrich the life of our academic community; they keep our graduates in touch with the university long after they leave campus; and they serve as a common rallying point for people of all ages and backgrounds.*
>
> *We seek to enhance the academic endeavors of the university, by helping through our success to attract both promising students and the assistance of private philanthropy, and by providing direct financial support.*
>
> *Above all, we recognize that the university's obligation to the state of Georgia, and to the parents everywhere who send us their sons and daughters, is to provide our students with a level of quality education which leads to recognized academic achievement, contributing to their social development and preparing them for meaningful lives and careers. We are committed to the proposition that academic achievement is not and should not be a gift. Rather, it is a challenge that must be met by the individual students, as well as the university.*
>
> *Accordingly, all our efforts are guided by certain values we believe essential to the fulfillment of this task:*
>
> *PERSONAL DEVELOPMENT*
> *Our primary purpose is to promote the personal growth and physical well-being of our student athletes, to guide them to become in life the best they can be. It is our abiding goal to foster the ideals and standards which will enable them to grow spiritually, emotionally and intellectually, and to attain degrees in their chosen fields of endeavor.*
>
> *INTEGRITY*
> *By their very nature, athletics inevitably involve character development; for this reason, especially, we must conduct ourselves with utmost integrity. All our programs and the activities on our behalf by alumni and friends must be consistent with the policies of the university and the athletic bodies which govern us. We are to be at all times honest and forthright in our dealings with each other, the public and the media.*
>
> *TEAMWORK*
> *If there is one concept that drives us, it is our dedication to winning in the broadest possible sense. We compete to win — as individuals, as team members and as representatives of this great university. We clearly understand that the success of any one person is always the result of dedicated effort on the part of many people. So, while we are quick to recognize individual performance, we are even quicker to celebrate achievements of the team.*
>
> *EXCELLENCE*
> *Dedication to excellence should distinguish our efforts in every sport in which we compete, and should be*

reflected in the performance of all our teams and in the fiscal soundness of our programs. Individually and collectively, we strive always to give our all and, thereby, realize our best possibilities.

LEADERSHIP
Our goal is to maintain a model athletic program which other colleges and universities may wish to emulate. Beyond this, we shall continue to pioneer and promote policies which will enhance the quality of intercollegiate athletics throughout America.

Dedication to the personal development of our student athletes, unfailing integrity and excellence in our programs, teamwork and determination to play a leadership role nationally . . . these are the values which underlie our endeavors and the standards by which we measure ourselves.

In retrospect, there is no question that I made some mistakes in my twenty-five years — I unwisely left the team in Oxford; I gambled with my football team in going to bowls; I gambled on the field; I made judgments that were not as sound as I would have liked over the years — but that is football. Having an opportunity to replay those decisions would not necessarily mean that we would have won a bowl game in Miami that we lost in New Orleans, or that if we had made a first down in a certain game in a crucial situation we would have come away a winner. I always come back to the conclusion that if you play the percentages you have a better chance.

Mistakes are part of life, so when you make one, you have to be man enough to admit it. You must face up to it. But I must confess the furor involving the infamous Jan Kemp trial was the most difficult time in my coaching career. Unfortunately, too many out there still don't know the facts or the magnitude of the challenge. I have faith that we will eventually solve this problem. That will always be my philosophy.

CHAPTER 7
A Fundamental Approach To The Game Of Football

A *coaching philosophy does not develop overnight. It is coddled, nurtured, altered, adjusted and honed until it becomes second nature.*

It begins with the basics, which means that the coach's own instincts are important. He must know what he believes in, and he must employ sound judgment and adhere to fundamental principles.

Following are coaching principles which are certainly appropriate if you were describing Vince Dooley and his philosophy:

- *The head coach must remain a little aloof from the players and, to a certain extent, from the coaches.*

- *The first qualification of a head coach is to possess a cool head so that he may see things in their true relation to each other and so in their proper perspective. There are things in football of which the head coach alone can comprehend the importance.*

- *His first principle must be to calculate what he must do to win, and see if he has the necessary means to surmount the obstacles with which the enemy will oppose him. Once the decision is made, he must see that all do their respective parts to earn the victory.*

- *Football is composed of nothing but accidents: the great art is to profit from such accidents. This is the mark of genius.*

- *It follows that all plans must be made to minimize our own mistakes and to magnify the effect of the opponents' mistakes.*

- *In the struggle between equal teams, the difference is never physical but invariably mental.*

- *It is important to keep the squad eternally aware of the very nature of football so that they are not dismayed when things are going wrong.*

- *To defeat a weak opponent is not the problem: the problem is to win when he is as good or better than you.*

- *Almost all close games are lost by the losers, not won by the winners.*

- *Proper mental stance on game day stems almost entirely from attitudes built up over a considerable period of time. Pre-game harangues, as a rule, do more harm than good. Inspiration at zero hour is a poor thing to rely on.*

Now that you have read these principles, name the coach who authored them. If you quickly said Vince Dooley, you would be both right and wrong. Right in that each of those principles fits him perfectly, but he didn't author them. Those are the principles of the great Tennessee coach General Robert Neyland.

When Dooley went to Knoxville last spring to accept the Tennessee Hall of Fame Chapter's Gen. Robert R. Neyland Memorial Award, he discovered the Neyland football principles for the first time. When he read them, he said to himself, "This is exactly what I believe."

— L.S.

Every person has a philosophy. He might not sit down and outline a set of beliefs and viewpoints, but we all develop a philosophy of life. Every coach has a philosophy, too, and even if he doesn't proclaim one, the pattern of his career and the games his teams play will reveal, to a large degree, how he thinks.

My philosophy has always been to win the most games with the talent available. To me, that is what coaching is all about. What does that mean? It might mean 6-5, or 7-4, or 8-3. It could mean 11-0 and the national championship if all fell into place. What I always wanted most was to be a consistent winner. If you are consistent, you've got the chance to rise to a championship level. So how do you do that?

First by playing defense. If you are strong defensively, you've got a chance to be consistently good. You can win with defense.

Second, I think that good defense and a good running game go hand in hand, but you also must throw the ball effectively to complement your rushing attack.

And third, you must have a good kicking game.

You've got to do everything well, but you've got to play defense first.

It was Darrell Royal who said that when you throw the ball three things can happen, and two of them are bad. I never went around quoting Darrell, but from some of the things that were said about Georgia in recent years, you would think that I was the one who originated that statement.

Some of my reputation for not passing resulted from media analysis. Some of it had to do with the way things went for our teams. Give Darrell Royal the best passing quarterback around, and I suspect he would have taken a different approach with his offense.

Take Coach Bear Bryant, for example. He was a passing coach in the mid- and late

sixties when he had Joe Namath, Steve Sloan, and Ken Stabler, but check the record and you will discover that in those years Alabama also played great defense. When Coach Bryant had Scott Hunter at quarterback — and Scott was one of the best high school passing quarterbacks I ever tried to recruit — Alabama was weak on defense. They didn't win the conference title, let alone the national championship. In fact, Bryant became so disillusioned with the problems he was having on defense that after 6-5 and 6-5-1 seasons, in 1969-70 he moved completely away from the passing offense and installed the wishbone. The wishbone was good to Bryant, very good in fact, but at the time his teams were so effective at running the ball, they were also great on defense again.

The rules today have changed, and you must open your offense more to succeed. Despite my reputation, I would would be the first to admit that. But even with the liberal rule changes, you must maintain defensive efficiency to win. Ask Bobby Bowden, the acknowledged pass master among the longtime active college coaches. Bobby will tell you in a minute that when he has had his best teams, they have not only thrown the ball well but also played great defense and mastered the kicking game. Chances are his unsung hero was a running back who played in the shadow of the great passer.

It is interesting to note that when Bobby was at West Virginia, he was more of a running coach. When he got to Florida State, where the weather was good year-round and where, as an independent, he felt his program had to be more wide-open to attract players and sell tickets, he began to emphasize the pass.

The point about the weather is especially interesting. Barry Switzer preferred the wishbone when he was at Oklahoma, but maybe that's because in the Big Eight there are a lot of windy days when a passing team is at a distinct disadvantage. "It is a wind tunnel most of the season," says Bud Wilkinson, who had all those great teams and winning

gia). Like all national champions, those were complete teams.

In recent years in the SEC, Auburn has been the most consistent winner, and they have succeeded primarily with great defense.

> _FRANK BROYLES_ — _"Vince had a knack of leadership and rallying of support. He could pull the magic that was necessary for victory. He was deliberate. He knew in his own mind what he had to do to win. The only other coach I would compare him to in that regard is Bo Schembechler of Michigan. Trends would come and go but Vince and Bo would stick with what they believed was a winning formula that is very simple. You stop the run, you have a chance to win. You combine that with running the football and you have an even better chance._
>
> _"The best players do not necessarily make up the best team, but the best team always wins and Vince's teams made team effort. He did have Herschel Walker, who was a star, but most of his teams were what you might call "no-names" who played with great enthusiasm. They played for a cause, and he was able to get ordinary players to play like extraordinary players._
>
> _"Vince didn't chase fads and fantasies and go looking for a new way to win football games. He stayed with what he believed in and his players were grounded in those fundamentals and those principles._
>
> _"I remember a couple of years ago. It appeared there was no way he could win a certain game, but one of the announcers said, 'Well, somebody will make a mistake in the kicking game and Vince will win it.' That is what happened. He came from behind with no chance to win simply because his players always believed that defense and the kicking game would give them a chance at the end."_

streaks with the Sooners. "There are a lot of times when you just could not accomplish anything throwing the football." Look it up and you'll find that Wilkinson's great split-T offenses, the rage of his era, were complemented by defenses which yielded ground grudgingly.

The same is true of Miami, where Steve Walsh followed Vinny Testaverde who followed Bernie Kosar who followed Jim Kelley. What a run of quarterbacks! But talk to any coach in the business and he will agree that while they might envy some of the things Howard Schnellenberger and Jimmy Johnson accomplished with those Hurricane offenses, what they won with was defense. None of those Miami teams was one dimensional. They could throw the ball, and they won a national title with everybody singing the praises of Kosar and Walsh, but in critical situations they were often handing off to Alonzo Highsmith and Cleveland Gary (who incidentally transferred to Miami from Geor-

Even with Bo Jackson, they played excellent defense. They've been given credit in the last couple of years with developing passing efficiency, but when you get down to it, defense has been the key to their success.

Ask anybody about our 1980 National Championship team and they will bring up the running skills of Herschel Walker. No question, Herschel was the missing piece to the puzzle for that team, but we also were solid at every position on defense with stars like Jimmy Payne, Scott Woerner and Freddy Gilbert. And we were expert in all phases of the kicking game. That's the way it is when you are a champion.

It may have seemed that we handed the ball to Herschel play after play, but we were more than a running team. If you know anything about Georgia in the early eighties, you are aware that it was not unusual for us to call on Buck Belue to throw to Lindsay Scott in clutch situations. But with a tailback with the speed, power and durability of Herschel, you do what you do best, and that is run the football. Herschel kept the chains moving. Miami moved them with Walsh's controlled passing. If I had had Miami's personnel, a pass control game might have looked pretty good.

Balance is the key to a successful offense. In 1968 we averaged 198.8 yards a game running and 192.9 passing. Great balance. In the Herschel years, it was a few degrees more to the rush, but even then we displayed great balance. With few exceptions when you are consistently throwing for three hundred yards and rushing for one hundred, you are in for trouble. If you run for three hundred and pass for one hundred, you probably are okay. Nevertheless, you've got to be able to throw effectively to be a winner. Ideally, I feel that if you run sixty times out of a hundred and throw forty, you have the proper balance. But, of course, that can fluctuate in a given ball game.

When we started out at Georgia, limited substitution rules were still in effect. Because of our personnel, we ran a very basic offense, often lining up in a full house backfield. We were strong and we had a fighting attitude, but our early players lacked mobility.

We ran the option because the split-T offense had been so popular in the fifties and most coaches, including mine, were sold on option football. I had enjoyed some success as an option quarterback at Auburn, and one of our 1964 Georgia quarterbacks, Preston Ridlehuber, had excellent running ability. He was strong and ran with speed. Lynn Hughes, the other quarterback who switched to defense and made All-America, was not as strong as Preston, but his quickness made him an effective option runner.

Through the years, I have been partial to option football because it puts added pressure on the defense. When Erk Russell

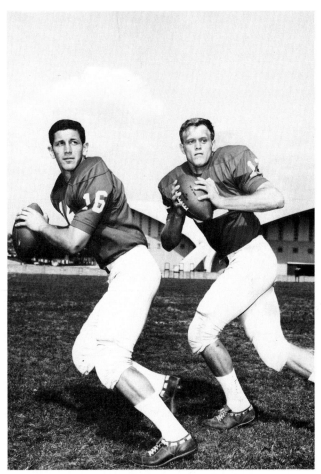

Winning option: Lynn Hughes (L), Ridlehuber

coached our defense, he spent most of his time concentrating on developing techniques to stop the option.

When Darrell Royal popularized the wishbone at Texas and Bill Yeoman developed the veer or split back set at Houston, their objective was the same as that of Don Faurot of Missouri when he invented the option in the spring of 1941 — to gain a two-on-one advantage at the point of attack. A former basketball coach, Faurot remembered that it was always the objective in basketball to create a two-on-one challenge for the defense. The offensive player either passed off the ball or faked the defender out of position and took the ball to the basket. Faurot concluded that the same thing could be done in football, and that is how option football came about. Nothing has influenced the game more in the last fifty years.

Looking back, there were times when we didn't throw very effectively, and that is obvious. But there were games when we didn't run it very well either, and afternoons when we didn't accomplish much on defense.

On the other hand, we were very consistent. If you average winning eight ball games a year for twenty-five years, you've got to be good at what you do.

We were good because we played good defense and had a solid running game, for the most part. We were a sound football team which minimized errors. And most of the time we were an aggressive, disciplined football team, and we played together and with spirit.

If there is one thing I always wanted people to say about my teams, it was, "When you play Georgia, you better buckle up your chinstrap because you've got a fight on your hands. When you play Georgia, they are going to battle you, and they're going to battle you for sixty minutes."

That reputation, which was a point of pride for us over the years, made us aware that opponents would always be ready to play, knowing the character of our football teams. We constantly reminded our players of this, which we considered a compliment. We were always reinforcing to them that the folks in the stands were aware when we fought hard. Likewise, they knew when it was not a good effort.

During my career, we minimized conversation about winning. What we talked about instead was playing the best that we could play and developing a pride that people in the stands would appreciate. I've said many

times that folks sitting out there watching don't always know as much football as they think. But it is their prerogative as fans to talk expertly about football, even about technical points on which they have no real appreciation or experience. One thing any serious fan or even a casual observer knows in a hurry, however, is whether a team is trying or not. Really trying, really fighting. Fans appreciate fighting effort.

It hurts to lose, and nobody feels worse than the coaches and players when it happens. But two games in particular stand out when I thought our fans hurt as much as the team: Florida State in Athens in 1964, and LSU between the hedges in 1987.

In 1964, Florida State had the great passing combination of Steve Tensi and Fred Biletnikoff, and on their last drive they moved down the field and scored on a sensational catch by Biletnikoff to win, 17-14. This was a game that our players to this day will tell you that Georgia really won, regardless of the scoreboard. That is how they feel in their hearts, even after all these years, having been underdogs and having played so well against a heavily favored team for four quarters.

After the game, the students came on the field and hugged the players and consoled them. The fans remained in the stands until the players went into the dressing room. They appreciated the effort and ached with us. A week later, Kentucky took the opening kickoff and drove for a touchdown, but the fans gave our defense a standing ovation when it came off the field. Our fans were hungry in those days. They were eager to console our players after a loss rather than criticize, and it made a difference.

In 1987 against LSU, we kept fighting back time and again and the crowd support was unbelievable. We finally took the lead in the fourth quarter, but then lost it back to LSU.

Then with one more chance, we drove back down the field, but a pass bounded off Rodney Hampton's fingertips into the arms of a Tiger defender, and we lost, 26-23.

The fans tried as hard in those two games as I can ever remember, and when it was over, they were as disappointed as our players. Why? Because they knew those teams gave all they had, and fortunately there were not many days in the last twenty-five years when the Georgia players didn't give a good effort.

"Who can ask more of a man than to give all within his span? For giving all it seems to me, is not too far from victory." Those words sum up my philosophy of football. That is a favorite poem of former UCLA basketball coach John Wooden, a coach I've always admired. I have, through the years, studied other coaches and their philosophies, and Wooden and the anonymous poet are right. You can't give more than you've got, which is the theme we always preached at Georgia: "Be the best that you can be." To give all you've got, to be the best you can be, is not going to guarantee that you will win the game, but it will give you a chance.

If you go out there and give it all you've got for sixty minutes, two things will happen: one, you'll be close to victory, you'll be in the game, you will have a chance; and two, if you should lose, you will have a pretty good feeling about yourself.

If a football coach is going to be successful over the long haul, he must develop a philosophy that is respectful of the percentages. Everybody gambles more today because of the rules, but if you review the record of the great coaches, you'll find that they all played the percentages. Never beat yourself. Let the other team make the mistake, just like General Neyland said. If you don't beat yourself, you have a chance of winning any game. That is how I approached football from the

beginning of my Georgia career. Research those 201 victories, and you will discover that playing percentage football influenced the outcome of many of those games.

Coach Jordan was a very good manager. He was able to assign priorities and emphasize the most important things to be done. He was very much the gentleman, but he could be very tough.

Shug Jordan, a tough gentleman

Although I have forgotten some of them, Coach Jordan used to operate with the "Seven D's" philosophy, which included points like (D)edication, (D)etermination, (D)rive, and so on. His last "D" was perhaps his best. He called that "D" the "(D)amn it all, we'll do it this way." That meant there is a lot of indecision and second-guessing in football, and there comes a time when you've got to be firm. You must make a decision and live with it. You can't beat around the bush and worry about what everybody else thinks. Make a decision, stick to it, and believe in what you are doing.

It was an early habit of mine to study other coaches, observing such things as fundamentals, game management and how they handled themselves, including their off-the-field habits. Scouting with Coach Eaves, there were two coaches in particular I was fortunate to observe closely each year — Coach Bear Bryant and Coach Bobby Dodd.

Bryant's teams always played hard. Historically, Alabama was outstanding on defense and was especially hard-nosed, which I liked. Dodd's Georgia Tech teams always played smart, and he seemed always to have a little finesse with his offense, a little twist for the right moment. Both coaches placed special emphasis on the kicking game.

I drew from the performances and philosophies of both coaches and incorporated into my coaching philosophy some of the things I picked up from watching Alabama and Georgia Tech play.

But above all, a successful coach emphasizes fundamentals and develops a sound, basic approach to the game. He may change with the times and trends, but as Darrell Royal once said about a certain big bowl game, "We are going to dance with what brung us," and that is fundamentals.

Following are some portions of my coaching philosophy:

DISCIPLINE

There are two disciplines for a football player. The first is team discipline, which is under the control of authority, where rules and regulations have been set forth. In football you must have order, rules and regimentation. The other discipline is an individual's self-discipline. This is the discipline an individual exerts on himself when team discipline is not in effect. One thing a coach strives to do is to help players learn to handle the second discipline when the decision is left up to them.

I have always tried to take a firm but fair approach. Discipline must not only be fair, there also must be the perception that it is fair. In every case, I always asked this question of myself: "Would I treat my own son the same way?" I can honestly say that I used that criterion in every case, and I have never second-guessed myself on that.

RULES

My philosophy is that it is important to have rules, but you must keep them reasonable and to a minimum. Above all, you must enforce those that you have.

ANDY JOHNSON — "I always wanted to be part of the Georgia tradition, dating back to the time when I scored a touchdown between the hedges for the Athens YMCA and the Redcoat band played a Bulldog fight song or two after I crossed the goal line.

"At Georgia I learned to appreciate discipline although I didn't always understand it. At the time, I didn't understand why I had to run laps at 6:30 in the morning for not making up my bed or if I didn't check in for breakfast or missed class. I didn't understand why hair had to be a certain length. How did those things relate to football? Now you sit back and reflect on it, and you say, 'That was Vince.' That is what he wanted and how he wanted his teams to be."

I have always believed in giving a player a second chance. Sometimes even a third one. You try to work with each person when he makes a mistake, as long as his behavior is not affecting the team behavior. One of the things that has always been important to me is not to brand a player who has made a mistake, but that seems to happen anyway. Mistakes should be forgiven and forgotten.

One of the toughest decisions I ever had to

Jiggy Smaha: a painful lesson

make was dismissing Jiggy Smaha from our team prior to the 1968 season. He was an outstanding athlete, playing right tackle on our defense opposite All-America George Patton.

But Jiggy, like I did to the brothers at Sacred Heart, wanted to test me. He should have outgrown all of that by college, but he had not, and when I felt his behavior was detrimental to the best interests of our team, I dismissed him.

It was a tough decision, a "(D)amn it all" type decision.

The suspension came the day before picture day in 1968. After a rules violation, Jiggy showed no remorse for his mistake. That kind of thing can spread over to the team, causing bad morale. It was his senior year, and he really could have helped us, but I told him right on the spot that he was through.

Two interesting developments resulted from that incident. First, that is when I began to appreciate that adage, "Necessity is the mother of invention." We took Lee Daniel, at 190 pounds, and made him our weak tackle and began swapping him and Bill Stanfill. We always lined Bill up on the strong side and Lee on the weak side. While Lee was at a disadvantage with lack of weight, he had brains and quickness. He was a big playmaker for us, one who had less ability but enough heart to give you a consistently winning performance Saturday after Saturday.

The other development, one which gives me great pleasure, has to do with Jiggy. I am sure he held the suspension against me for a while, but I am happy to say that today he is one of the staunchest supporters of our program. He has expressed great appreciation for having lettered at Georgia and is a proud Bulldog. It takes a big man to feel the way Jiggy feels, and I appreciate his attitude and support. He is an asset to his community, and I admire his courage and attitude.

ACADEMICS

My academic philosophy has always been that when we sign an athlete, we have the responsibility to help him help himself toward a degree. That is a philosophy, but let me cite the actual example of Chuck Jones, a wide receiver on our national championship team of 1980. One day in my office, we were discussing his status in regard to graduation, and he said, "Receiving my degree is very important."

I said, "Chuck, if that is to be—" Before I could finish, he interrupted and completed the sentence, ". . . it's up to me."

That became an important message and slogan in Georgia athletic circles the last few years. The first thing a recruiting prospect sees when he enters our building is that message: "If it is to be, it is up to me." That message is pointed out to every player and parent who shows an interest in our program.

You must help them all you can, and the number of athletes who do not take advantage of their opportunities is distressing. But in the final analysis, they have to get the job done themselves. Ultimately every individual controls his own destiny.

We provide tutors and counselors, and we believe our academic achievement center for our athletes is second to none in the country. We have the tools, but the athlete must respond. We constantly search for ways to improve our methods and to upgrade our tools, and we always strive to motivate our athletes. Over the entrance to our academic center are the words, "A sound mind and a sound body with a brave heart." That says a lot.

Sadly, our graduation percentage, which was high at one time, dropped off as the standards were lowered. I'm pleased now to see it rising again.

ADMINISTRATION

I have always believed that to be a successful athletic manager you must (1) employ good people, (2) provide necessary tools for them to work with, and (3) let 'em flap their wings.

You must praise their accomplishments and create a work atmosphere that people take pride in. If they are involved and feel part of the decision-making, you are likely to see a positive performance.

About ten years ago I became familiar with the Japanese buzz word of "wa," which means involvement. Japanese managers have gotten people involved, and their success is undeniable.

Everybody is important in any organization. That is why we have gone to great lengths to involve as many people as possible in the decision-making process. For example, our players make up committees on discipline, dormitory operations, the dining room, drugs, and so forth. These committees make very meaningful and valuable recommendations to me. We even carry this philosophy to the secretaries, who make suggestions to us on how we can better do our jobs in athletics. The department heads need to be involved, but so do the secretaries who have so much to do with determining our image with the public.

PEP TALKS

As I have said earlier, I have never had much use for the traditional Knute Rockne speeches. I believe it is more important to provide this type of encouragment all week and all season, not just prior to kickoff. You stress certain viewpoints in terms of general application, and you underscore certain values in everything you do.

We have always wanted our team to hear from different people as well as from our own coaches. Many former players have offered encouragement and inspiration to our teams, among them Frank Sinkwich, Horace King, Herschel Walker and Fran Tarkenton. When he was governor, Carl Sanders addressed our team. My last couple of years, columnist/humorist Lewis Grizzard spoke to the team on Thursday before we played Tech.

We were not asking these speakers to meet with our team in the hope that some comment might become a motivational factor for the upcoming game, but rather to make the team aware that the values we were teaching and stressing were important in life. We wanted the things we taught to carry over in life after football. We emphasized the importance of attitude, mental toughness, fair play, sticking to the rules and doing what is morally and ethically right.

All of our presidents, from Dr. O. C. Aderhold my first year to Dr. Charles Knapp in 1988, have met with our teams and offered something of value.

MEDIA

I have always had a good relationship with the media and have tried to be fair and honest and never lie to them. That approach hasn't always worked. Although I believe that ninety to ninety-five percent of the writers are good, hard-working people who are conscientious and do a fine job, there is no question that there are some "poison pen" journalists in the business. One of the major frustrations in dealing with the media is that they not only have a job to do, they are often faced with a challenging deadline. They don't have time to take a coaching clinic, and even if they did, a coach's perspective is seldom the same as a writer's. Also, a writer's personal mood can sometimes have a dramatic impact on what he writes.

My only complaint is that there are too many inaccuracies in today's journalism. An inexperienced writer can create an unfair misconception, and no number of corrections or amplifications can right that misconception. I would like for them to underscore fairness and truth in their daily chores.

Griffin Bell, when he was Attorney General under Jimmy Carter, once said that the Washington press corp didn't get the facts right all that often, but that it was better for our society to have it that way than for the press to be controlled. I agree.

DRUG AND ALCOHOL ABUSE

The problems with drugs and alcohol in our society are distressing. Like so many parents and professionals who deal with young people, I sometimes fear the worst. We must win the war on drugs.

As early as 1973, the NCAA announced that it would consider random testing for drugs. That bothered me at the time because I saw no indication that we were having serious drug problems. I said publicly, however, that if the problem had gotten as serious as the NCAA felt, the tests would have merit. I also noted that I felt it would be somewhat insulting to the athletes who did not indulge, and that this group would make up the largest percentage.

As time went by and we reached the end of the seventies, it became apparent that there was a problem and it was spreading. We heard more and more about drug abuse on campus. I began to hear that some of our athletes had experimented with drugs.

It wasn't long before I was convinced that drugs were a problem for our society. And if they were a problem for society, and a problem for college-age adults, then they had to be a problem for our football team. As I heard the rumors, I would tell our coaches that I wanted to find out what was going on. I wanted hard evidence. I would go to whatever lengths possible to find out, but we got nowhere.

We even went into the dorm rooms while the players were in class to see if we could find any evidence, but there was never a trace of drugs.

Finally in 1982 at the Sugar Bowl, when we were playing Penn State for the National Championship, one of our top reserves stumbled in at 4:00 A.M., obviously high on something. We assumed it was alcohol, and I suspended him from the bowl game. Later he began cashing bad checks, and it added up to his having a serious drug problem.

Then it came to my attention that one of our players had tested positive for drugs in a pro football screening test, so I launched a thorough investigation

In a meeting with our coaching staff, I pointed out to them that the reason we had not been able to respond to the drug problem was that none of us had come through the era of the drug culture. We didn't know anything about it. It was foreign to us. So we set out to educate ourselves on the drug situation. We brought in an expert from the National Football League. We brought in people from hospitals in Athens and Atlanta who could tell us more about what was going on in the real world with young people. We also visited alcohol and drug rehabilitation hospitals.

After six months, we instituted a two-point drug plan: One, we began testing, which we were absolutely convinced was the only way to find out what was happening, and two, we tried to educate and counsel our players about drugs.

We knew this would lead to some bad publicity, but we had to do it. We suspended the players who tested positive for drug use, and the media jumped on the story. Then, as we knew would happen, opposing recruiters started saying, "Georgia's got a drug problem; you don't want to go there."

Not only did we believe we were right, we knew that we would be ahead of everybody else. We operated with the confidence that if it is society's problem, then it is our problem. We wanted to take a leadership role in trying to control the problem and help the kids in our program understand the consequences and ill effects of drugs. It was more than discipline for our team. We sincerely wanted to help.

Every year we have improved our program, and many colleges have consulted with us to learn what we are doing and have modeled their drug programs after ours.

And now the NCAA has adopted a drug policy. We may not be solving every problem that comes up, but we are addressing the situation. As drug abuse seems to be waning, we are going to have to place greater emphasis on the problem with alcohol.

We've always had rules against drinking during the season, but I think we have to reassess this issue and give some thought to what should be done about a problem that society tends to accept.

And, of course, we must continue to work to eliminate steroids. The desire among all athletes to play professionally has too many of them willing to take risks. I hope what I hear is way off base, but some suggest that as many as seventy-five to eighty percent of NFL players on many teams are using steroids. We test for steroids at Georgia. While there might be some rare exceptions, steroids have not been a problem for us.

It is our objective to identify every player with a drug association and then try to help him. We don't ignore the fact that he needs help, so our program is designed to help, not to sentence. Of course, in order to maintain proper morale, consistent abuse has to result in serious disciplinary action.

We will always have critics of our drug program, but my answer is that when you are in a structured situation as we are in football where one player depends upon another player, a player who can't function to the best of his ability is letting the team down. Also, it is our objective to send productive citizens and proper role models into society.

What will this person be like in life, if he doesn't deal with his problem? What about pilots, doctors? How much damage can they do if they become negligent from drug abuse? A lot of lives are at stake, and drug abuse cannot be condoned. A pilot high on drugs or an intoxicated ship's captain should be warning enough to our society that we must take strict measures for alcohol and drug abuse. Testing has to be a part of any success we have toward winning the war on drugs.

When we have a drug problem with an athlete, the first requirement is that the athlete call his parents. We put a coach on the phone with them and the coach helps explain what is happening, but the athlete must tell his parents that he is to undergo counseling. That is a difficult thing for an athlete to do, but addressing the problem with the parents is an important first step.

We have never had a parent to complain; all we have received is positive feedback. What is heart-warming is to hear from an athlete who tested positive, straightened himself out, and later thanked us for what we did toward helping him solve a problem and a crisis in his life.

That is one of the truly special rewards of coaching — helping out a kid in need.

The Seventies — a time for the tough to get going

CHAPTER 8
A Roller-Coaster Through A Turbulent Decade

As my friend John "Kid" Terrell, one of Georgia's greatest fans, says, the seventies were a time when the real Bulldogs stuck together until Herschel came along. There is a lot of truth to that. Those were up and down years for us. We were inconsistent. We had not yet developed the maturity and consistency which would characterize our teams of the eighties.

One year we had 'em laughing and telling jokes, the next they were dining on the sour grapes of losing more games than they thought we should, and their teeth were set on edge.

The seventies were a time when I learned something about coaching, and learned much about myself. All the philosophy I had been exposed to and the things I truly believed became important. It boiled down to an old sports adage — when the going gets tough, the tough get going. I chose to hang tough and survive. The only thing was that it took longer than I anticipated to reach that consistency level we aspired to obtain.

> *JOHN TERRELL — In the seventies when Dooley's reserved personality was a frequent topic in Athens, banker John Terrell, one of Georgia's most ardent fans, quipped, "If he will make that chapel bell ring on Saturday night, I can find somebody else to drink with."*

There were problems, but there were some rewarding successes. Although we experienced off years, we fielded four of our most exciting teams. What was so warming about the '71, '75, '76 and '78 teams was the element of surprise. We were not supposed to accom-

plish much but were contenders and finished strong. Maybe it also was because each of the teams that preceded them, except in the case of 1976, were such disappointments.

> *JIMMY POULOS — "When I scored against Tech in 1971, I didn't think about it being something that people would remember for a long time. I just wanted to win the game. But now, it is something that comes up everywhere I go. People remember the play, they remember the game, and it makes me proud that something I did means so much to so many people in this state."*

In 1970 we were erratic, losing to Tulane in New Orleans, 17-14, to Mississippi State in Jackson, 7-6, to Ole Miss in Athens, 31-21, when Archie Manning picked us apart, to Florida in Jacksonville, 24-17, and finally to Georgia Tech for the second year in a row — this time between the hedges, 17-7. We averaged 24.2 points per game, scoring thirty-eight against Clemson, thirty-seven versus Vandy, fifty-two on South Carolina and thirty-one at Auburn, but against Tech in the big game we failed miserably. Defensively we shut out Clemson but allowed thirty-one points to Ole Miss, thirty-four to South Carolina and twenty-four to Florida. The only bright day was when we put it together against Auburn, when Pat Sullivan and Terry Beasley were juniors, upsetting them 31-17. That was one of the biggest upsets in college foorball that year and one of the biggest of my career.

In 1972 and 1973, we were 7-4 and 7-4-1, respectively. We beat Tech both seasons but again inconsistency plagued us. We didn't complement ourselves like we seemed to do in the past. When the offense was having an off day for whatever reason, the defense was not effective at taking up the slack. And when the defense went through a bad afternoon, the offense couldn't carry them. The schedule then included Tennessee before the annual Florida game, giving us four tough games in a row, and that increased our challenge considerably.

There are many places where seven victories are roundly appreciated, but not in Athens once you get your program established.

But if 1970 enhanced every success of the 1971 team, which was led by sophomore quarterback Andy Johnson of Athens, then 1974 made the 1975 team one that could own the town by winning a few games, which it did.

I don't believe there was a more depressing time for our fans than the winter of 1974, when we lost to Auburn, 17-13, Georgia Tech, 34-14, and Miami of Ohio in the Tangerine Bowl, 21-10. "We are going to get Dooley," a prominent state legislator told offensive coach Frank Inman. I was hung in effigy. There had been a time when I could walk down the streets of Athens and nobody knew me. After 1974 I could have walked down the street and many people would probably have felt like crossing to the other side to avoid me. My popularity had reached its nadir.

In December of 1965, when I was considered and ultimately offered the Oklahoma job, there was a song to the tune of "Hang Down Your Head, Tom Dooley," begging me not to leave Athens. It was cleverly written by Elmo Ellis, vice president and general manager of WSB Radio and sung by Sherrie Johnson. I was happy they didn't come out with a new version of that song with the problems I was enduring after 1974, when they literally wanted to hang me. I didn't hang my head, but those were dark, difficult times.

Never have I experienced such complaining and bickering. I was enough of a historian to understand that these things can and will happen to anybody in the profession. As a matter of fact, it had just happened to Coach Bryant at Alabama, following back-to-back seasons of 6-5 and 6-5-1. The Tide ran up big scoring totals but were losing too often, and the Alabama people were complaining that the Bear was too old and had lost his touch.

They were saying that I was too conservative, that I didn't know my players' names and was stuck up and wouldn't speak to anybody. Realizing that I was misunderstood, I told my good friends that I couldn't change my personality. But the truth of the matter was this: when they don't win enough football games, they are going to find something wrong with you and the way you coach, no matter what. It may be your offense or your personality or the way you dress. And if you don't turn it around, they will get you, indeed.

MIXON ROBINSON —
"That Tech victory in 1971 was the most exciting thing I had ever been involved with. But my brother was on the Tech team. When the game was over, we rushed on the field and were whooping and hollering and going crazy. I started slapping my brother on the back and said something like, 'This is amazing. Isn't it great?'
"He said, 'Well, no, it really isn't.'"

What people didn't understand was that I was unhappiest of all. No group of dissatisfied alumni could have put more pressure on me than I placed on myself. I was determined to keep my mouth shut and work until things were resolved. If I couldn't get the job done, they wouldn't have to run me off. I would have left myself, on my own, if I ever concluded I couldn't have delivered.

You must remember that these were changing times. We had campus protests, stimulated primarily by the Vietnam war. Attitudes had changed all across the country, even in the conservative South. With my military background, I was, perhaps, too rigid. I had to change and adjust. I became a better communicator and learned to be more sensitive to what players were saying and asking. Still, what takes place on the field sums up your abilities to the public.

If you compare the records of our 1974 team and our 1980 national champions, you can quickly determine that I was a better communicator in 1980. But it wasn't just that I was ten years older and wiser.

There was another more important factor. During the down times of the seventies, we usually had teams of lesser talent. One thing

The seventies brought many changes — even in Vince Dooley's look

*"Pepper Power"
worried many
Bulldog supporters*

I learned early in my career is that winning has a definite impact on communication. When you win everybody relates, everybody communicates. When the record is bad, the rumors abound and the perceptions become skewed to unbelievable proportions. I remember that at a certain Atlantic Coast Conference school, a basketball coach was fired and it was whispered that he was having an affair with a cheerleader. You hear zillions of those kinds of unfounded stories all the time, but the situation was put into proper perspective by the athletic director who scoffed at such innuendo and gossip. "That is a bunch of hogwash," he said. "If he had won the ACC tournament, he could have been dating a vice presidents's wife and nobody would have said anything."

Unfortunately, that is often the way it is with some of the more vocal fans. The winners are telling jokes and the losers are screaming for a new deal.

A head coach's job can get lonely in the tough times. When you win, everybody shares the victories. But when you lose, only one person must shoulder the blame. As President John Kennedy said after the Bay of Pigs disaster, "Victory has a thousand fathers; defeat is an orphan."

Never had I been more ready for a new season than in 1975. I had to take the heat for 1974. Only I could shoulder the blame. There was no reason for excuse-making, as people in the state were preparing for my demise. Pepper Rodgers, who had come back to Georgia Tech, leaving UCLA for his alma mater, was drawing a positive reaction with his wishbone offense. He had gained some concessions from the Tech administration and was building a winning program. After he beat us in the mud in Athens, the soothsayers generally agreed that he would bring the state back to Georgia Tech again, like it once

had been with Bobby Dodd. Even some of our most loyal supporters, including an athletic board member, said, "We'll never beat Tech again." I couldn't concern myself with the complaints and rumors. It was a matter of working hard and resolving to straighten things out.

Prior to the Georgia-Oregon State game, September 14, 1974, Beaver Coach Dee Andros brought his team to Atlanta for a week of practice in the Georgia heat. The colorful Andros, who weighed three hundred pounds and was known as the

Pepper Rodgers

Great Pumpkin because of his size and OSU's orange colors, entertained the Athens Touchdown Club on Wednesday night before the game.

One of his funny lines was that he had a variety of nicknames and that the Oregon people took delight in calling him the Great Squash. "I don't care what they call me," Andros said, "as long as they call me to eat."

But Andros was not just funny. He made a couple of insightful comments, one of them having to do with Pepper Rodgers leaving UCLA and the PAC 10 Conference and taking over Georgia Tech.

"Pepper," Andros told the Touchdowners, "will make Vince Dooley a better football coach."

To tell the truth, Pepper, whom I enjoy and whose son, Kelly, wound up transferring to Georgia, had a very smart plan. It was his theory that the wishbone simplified recruiting because it does not require as many skilled players. Running backs like the wishbone. For quarterback, all you need is an athlete, one with speed and quickness. They are much easier to find than those with passing

103

skills. If you don't pass out of the wishbone, then you don't need to recruit skilled recievers. Get some beef at tight end, linemen who can knock people off the line of scrimmage, and then control the ball, play defense, and chances are that you will win more than your share.

While I never was that keen on the wishbone offense for us, I did respect the fundamental strengths of the formation and realized that Pepper was right about his recruiting philosophy. I used to kid Pepper that his non-passing wishbone made me look like a pro-style coach.

While the wishbone would not remain the dominant offense in college football—rule changes liberalized offensive opportunity as time went by—it was a propitious offense for those years.

No question about it, Pepper initially represented the cohesion that Tech had been seeking since Coach Dodd's retirement, and he would be a tough opponent to contend with both on the field and in recruiting.

As time went by, some internal conflicts developed at Tech, and I don't think Pepper, a free-spirit style, was willing to compromise, but that wasn't any of my business. I was too concerned about trying to compete with him on the field.

In the rain and mud in 1974, he embarrassed our team in Sanford Stadium. I've never been so embarrassed. Not even when Nebraska blew us out in the Sun Bowl in 1969. Tasting that thrill of victory was more desired than ever, which is one reason why the '75 Bulldog team will always be a favorite.

Before we could rebound in 1975, which solved a lot of problems and eliminated all rumors about lack of rapport with players and the like, there was a personal matter of great concern that had to be addressed. Not only was I bothered about the potential con-

sequences if we didn't field a competitive team in 1975 with my contract running out, I wanted to eliminate any distractions and also give us an opportunity to recruit.

My sense of security has never made me worry about contracts, personally. I could live with a one-year contract like the faculty and everybody else on campus, except for one thing—recruiting.

It is not what the facts are, it's the perception that has weight. The perception in the summer of 1975 was that Vince Dooley was in trouble, that he was in the last year of his contract, and that a new coach might be moving in at 755 Milledge Circle toward the end of the year. Those kinds of rumors are often just that, rumors and nothing more, but it is unsettling to high school prospects and their parents.

Sometimes when changes come about, the successor often does well, but people are dubious about change, especially high school athletes and their advisors. If you want to put yourself in recruiting jail, give your competition a chance to talk about the fact that your contract is running out and there soon may be a new coach on the scene.

At the time, I generally had been given multi-year contracts that would be renewed or extended when there was a big year that warranted it. A reward incentive. I had gotten an extension after the 1971 season, but based on that general policy, the '72, '73 and '74 seasons did not fit the unwritten procedure for contract renewal or extension.

However, I felt that we had demonstrated in ten years that we had developed a sound program that had never embarassed the university, and that there had been enough success and tradition established that it was reasonable to ask for a renewal. A new contract would stop all rumors, keep our recruiting on track and most of all keep our football team from reading in the papers every day that 1975 could be my last year as the Bulldog head coach.

I went to Dr. Fred C. Davison and reviewed all this with him. Fred was a president whose contributions have meant a lot to the University of Georgia. He always believed strongly in the value of intercollegiate athletics. He loved the Bulldogs and understood what I was saying. He did not hesitate; he and the Athletic Board awarded me a new four-year contract in late summer.

The announcement of the new contract took place the day the Sky Writers tour hit town. Writers from newspapers in the Southeastern Conference states toured SEC schools each August and arrived in Athens right after the Athletic Board had met. This resulted in a lot of positive publicity nationally for the university and Dr. Davison for the stand he had taken.

Suddenly a lot of cynics and yappers were shut up. We could go about the business of coaching and winning football games which we did with the Junkyard Dogs, who went from giving up twenty-four points per game to fifteen, quite a difference. Erk Russell had experimented in 1974 with some fifty defensive schemes, but he returned to the eight-man front in 1975. He believed in the 60 and felt that was what he knew best and decided to stick with it.

Sam Mitchell had joined our staff as defensive backfield coach for 1975, and we went to a four-four scheme there. It was a 60 scheme originated by John Ray, an assistant at Notre Dame who later became the head coach at Kentucky. With this variation, we were back with the eight-man front concept. This turned out to be a very sound and important defensive decision. The four-four featured two down linemen and six standing up, which was an effective defense versus the

option that most teams had gone to — either the wishbone or veer.

Even though we opened with a loss to Pittsburgh in a game in which we made costly mistakes, it was a happy year for us. Of all the teams I've ever been associated with, that 1975 group was really special. It justified Dr. Davison's decision at the only time in my career when there was reasonable opposition mounting. The good thing is that we followed that season with an even better one in 1976, when we won the conference title and the Bulldog faithful formed a sea of red in the French Quarter. Nobody had any problems with the decision to play in the Sugar Bowl. In fact, I don't remember hearing Miami mentioned at all in those days.

Hugh Hendrix

We had one of the best offensive lines ever in 1976, although we tragically lost one of our outstanding linesmen in the summer when Hugh Hendrix died of a rare blood infection. The season was dedicated to his memory, and we were derailed only once—at Ole Miss, which won, 21-17.

I could have almost predicted that loss after what had happened the week before in

105

Athens. We whipped Alabama, 21-0, controlling the game from start to finish. They were never in it. Alabama had been so dominant in the SEC (five straight conference titles) that our victory set off a celebration which almost never ended. Our students celebrated and partied into the next week. Classes had to be called off. On the weekend of the game, you could not drive down Milledge Avenue, a sorority and fraternity thoroughfare, for the mass of humanity. To dominate Alabama like

After Alabama, the players shaved receiver Coach Pat Hodgson's head, having already gotten to Jimmy Vickers earlier in the season. And they were anxious to trim others, including you-know-who.

The shaved head craze for our players began before our first practice. It spread to most of the team, including quarterbacks Matt Robinson and Ray Goff.

At a team meeting that first week in August, I walked in and looked at the

MATT ROBINSON — *Georgia's second touchdown in the 21-0 defeat of Alabama in Athens in 1976 came just before the half on a quarterback option into the strong side of the Alabama line — "the worst percentage call in football in that situation," Dooley was to say later.*

With seconds left on the clock, Dooley and offensive coordinator Bill Pace talked on the phone and agreed to run a sprint out to the wide side of the field, and if no receivers were open, to throw the ball away and kick a field goal to make sure that the Bulldogs went in at the half with something on the board. When the signal from the sideline was made, quarterback Matt Robinson misread it and ran the option to the short side of the field into the strength of the Alabama defense, which meant there was no room to option. The offensive line nonetheless blew the Tide off the line, and Robinson walked in for the TD. "That's what you call coaching," Dooley cracked afterwards.

that in those days was unheard of.

We should have remembered that a few years later when, after our run of six straight wins in Jacksonville, Florida defeated us in 1984, 27-0, and their students and fans almost demolished the Gator Bowl. Great victories against certain teams in certain years just naturally lend themselves to euphoric reaction.

skinned heads that begged for acknowledgement. "Okay," I said, "if we win the Southeastern Conference title and beat Tech, I'll shave my head." I thought my promise was probably safe.

With each conference victory and each assistant coach greeting the razor, the team kept reminding me of my promise. Finally, after we wrapped up the title against

RAY GOFF — *"In 1975-76, the veer was great for us, but I believe any offense would have been successful with the line we had in those years: Steve Wilson, Randy Johnson, Joe Tereshinski, Ken Helms, Mike Wilson and Joel Parrish. You would get to the line of scrimmage and all you would see was running room. If it hadn't been for those guys, I wouldn't have made all-conference, we wouldn't have won the championship and nobody would have heard of me, especially the Georgia Athletic Board, in December of 1988."*

106

Auburn, 28-0, on the road and defeated Tech in Athens, 13-10, with a late field goal, I knew that I had to schedule a date with my barber. A commitment is a commitment. I avoided the impromptu shearing in the locker room, which was the fate of our assistants, but I knew that I had to join the bald brigade.

I decided that I would shave my head and wear a wig called "the hugger," which I got from my barber John Salvadori, to the coronation party (crowning of the SEC champs) hosted by the Athens Touchdown Club in early December. When I walked in, it was obvious that something was up. I ignored all the comments, keeping the straightest of faces, but I did look different. There was a lot of buzzing throughout the room.

When I got up to speak, I reminded the team that a commitment is a commitment and ripped off the wig to an explosion of applause by the players and touchdown clubbers.

Unfortunately, I pulled my act too quickly. I should have waited until the day of the game. That surge of emotion might not have been enough for us to whip Tony Dorsett and Pitt, but we could have used an extra incentive in that game, which we lost, 27-3, when they shut down Ray Goff and our veer.

Erk's comment after the Touchdown Club banquet was that I had set bald heads back fifty years.

After 1976, it was déjà vu in 1977 when we couldn't maintain any consistency. We had lost a lot of football players like Goff, Matt Robinson, Joel Parrish and Mike "Moonpie" Wilson. The coaches knew 1977 would be tough, but for our fans it was just three years earlier that we had gone through the dismal 6-6 campaign. They were not prepared for a losing season. They never are at Georgia, and to be frank with you, I wasn't prepared for it either. Except for Kentucky and Auburn, which scored thirty-three points each on us

A shaved-head Dooley congratulates Pitt Coach Johnny Majors

BEN ZAMBIASI — *Bulldog linebacker Ben Zambiasi, 1974-77, was always up for a game. He nervously started to peak on Friday afternoons, and by Saturday he was so emotionally fired up that he would throw up before the kickoff without fail.*

As the team spent those final moments in the locker room, Ben made his trip to the bathroom to calm his nervous stomach. The team ultimately became superstitious, not wanting to take the field until Ben had thrown up, and on one or two occasions they were nearly late for kickoff, waiting for Ben to do his thing.

and Florida with twenty-two, our defense played respectably most of the year, never giving up more than two touchdowns in any of the other games. But we were without quarterback stability. We went through six quarterbacks before the season ended, perhaps an intercollegiate record.

Davy Sawyer, a freshman, played in the Thanksgiving Day Scottish Rite Junior Varsity game and then, after Chris Welton was hurt, played all of the second half of the varsity game on Saturday. That probably is the only time that has ever happened, a quarterback playing the entire junior varsity game and half of the varsity game in the space of three days.

Clemson beat us 7-6 in Athens for their first

Davy Sawyer: double duty

win between the hedges in sixty-three years, and we played Alabama a great game in Tuscaloosa before losing, 18-10. But 1977 was the year we set the Georgia fumble record. We became an unsound football team. We lost four of our last five games, including Florida, Auburn and Tech. It was one of only two times in my career when we lost all three of the last games to our big rivals, Florida, Auburn and Tech. It happened to us again in 1984 when we had another of those years when we didn't complement ourselves very well.

Unlike 1974, when we lost in the Tangerine Bowl and prolonged our agony, we stayed home for the bowls when we were 5-6 in 1977, but it was almost as dismal an off-season because we had so few talented players coming along in 1978. While we were blessed with great spirit and team leadership in 1976, we had a lot more talent to work with. In 1978, the team that become the Wonder Dogs probably won more games on heart and guts than any team I had at Georgia. That was our year to finish on top in the close games. We won six games by a total of twenty-five points, four by a total of six. Compared to 1975, 1978 was happiness intensified.

That was the year we beat Kentucky in Lexington, 17-16, on Rex Robinson's late field goal, after upsetting LSU in Baton Rouge the

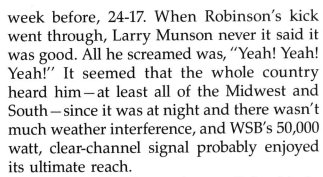

WILLIE McCLENDON — *"I'll never forget the first time I met Coach Dooley. My mom and my dad were with me. He said, 'If you come to the University of Georgia, we'll teach you how to be a man. We won't give you anything but an opportunity. We'll try to instill in you how to strive to be the best.' My parents liked what they were hearing.*

When I came to Georgia, I expected things to be good, and they were in 1975 and 1976. But then they weren't so good in 1977, and everybody expected the worst for 1978. That is when Coach Dooley is at his best. The fans were down on us, the media was critical, even Coach Dooley said we were the worst group of seniors he had ever had. That provided a lot of emotion for us. We were determined to be a different team. In our hearts we knew we were better than what people thought, and when an athlete has it in his heart that he expects to do well, he usually can find a way. We may not have been the most talented team in 1978, but no team had more heart.

"You don't come from behind like we did at LSU and Kentucky and against Tech in Athens if you don't have heart. We began the season knowing that we could make the chapel bell ring on Saturdays and we did."

week before, 24-17. When Robinson's kick went through, Larry Munson never it said it was good. All he screamed was, "Yeah! Yeah! Yeah!" It seemed that the whole country heard him—at least all of the Midwest and South—since it was at night and there wasn't much weather interference, and WSB's 50,000 watt, clear-channel signal probably enjoyed its ultimate reach.

We lost to South Carolina at Columbia in 1978, and George Rogers, their great runner, was eager to come over and shake my hand. It was the same when they whipped us in Athens the next year, the only time we ever lost back to back games with the Gamecocks. But in 1980, I never saw George when the game was over. For some reason, George didn't come around that last time. The loss to South Carolina was our only regular season defeat in 1978, but we were tied by Auburn at Auburn, and when it was over I apologized to the team for not going for two points after our last touchdown.

There was 5:35 left when we scored our final touchdown, and I felt there was too much time on the clock to go for two, especially when we had the momentum

Yeah! Yeah! Yeah! Rex Robinson

TIM MORRISION — *One of the most famous and exciting plays in the Dooley era was the Rex Robinson field goal that defeated Kentucky, 17-16, at Lexington in 1978.*

When the field goal team took the field with seconds remaining, there were only ten players in the lineup, which could have resulted in a penalty. The player missing from the lineup was tackle Tim Morrison. Fortunately for the Bulldogs, Kentucky called time out in an effort to put more pressure on Robinson the kicker, enabling the coaches to find Morrison and get him into the game. Morrison confessed to an irritated Coach Dooley that he was on his knees praying for a successful kick.

"Well," Coach Dooley responded, "Coach (Fran) Curci has just answered your prayers by calling time out."

REX ROBINSON — *"Against Kentucky in 1978, as we began to make that last drive downfield, I stood over by myself on the sideline and prayed that whatever happened, I would be able to handle the situation. If I made it, I didn't want to get the big head or become too filled with the pride of success; and if I missed, I didn't want to let it later get to me in similar situations.*

"Mentally, I just wanted to prepare myself to do the best I could and to live with whatever happened. I had done it a million times, so just do it one more time and try not to think about it. It wasn't my greatest kick and I didn't immediately know if it was good. There are pictures of me looking at the official to see what the call was. Every now and then, I break out the audiotape of Larry Munson's voice. I can tell you everything he said. It is a moment that will stick in my mind forever."

going. If it is under two minutes, you should unquestionably go for two, but at five? That's too much time remaining. What hurt us was that we were unable to contain the great Auburn backfield of William Andrews, James Brooks and Joe Cribbs, which we had to do to get the ball back.

The two-point decision was a good percentage decision, but it didn't work out. Two weeks later we faced a similar situation against Tech, but in that game, there was no decision to make. With 2:24 left, it was a foregone conclusion that we would go for two, the worst percentage play in football, but one that has helped make college football more exciting.

In 1979 we were pretty good at winning the conference games until we faced Auburn, which pounded us 33-13 with that trio of great backs. That was the year we rededicated Sanford Stadium, which was fifty years old, but a 6-5 season is not the best record for celebrating a milestone birthday of what I think is the prettiest college football stadium in the country (although in the rededication game against LSU on October 13, we won, 21-14).

We beat Ole Miss, LSU, Vandy, Kentucky and Florida but lost to Wake Forest, Clemson, South Carolina and Virginia, entering the Auburn game with a 5-4 record. Whip Auburn and our record would have been 6-4, undefeated in the conference with a game to play against Tech. You think the Sugar Bowl scouts were nervous? They came to town wearing their light blue sport coats, but

110

underneath everything they had on was orange. If we had won the game, that blue would have turned green. Gangrene, as a matter of fact.

The contract between the Sugar Bowl and the Southeastern Conference stipulated that in case of a tie for the conference title, the last appearance rule would go into effect. The team that had played most recently would yield.

What made it tough on the Sugar Bowl,

"Yes." With the bad bowl experiences of 1969 and 1974, why would I have agreed to play in New Orleans? One simple reason — our team felt that was what the contract called for and we should not break the contract. I was not very comfortable with what might happen and was happy that the worst scenario for the Sugar Bowl never came about.

With Alabama having defeated Auburn and headed to New Orleans, Sugar Bowl officials breathed a sigh of relief and set about

ANTHONY ARNOLD — "The big touchdown in the Tech game in 1978 was something. When I lined up, I saw the defense was going man-to-man, which meant that with my quickness I would have a chance to get open. The defender grabbed me as I went to break by him, and we both ran for the sideline and ran out of room. I looked back and Buck [Belue] was in trouble. The defensive man let up and I turned up field. I looked up and here came the ball. All I had to do was catch it and cruise."

even after we lost, was that with our 5-1 record in the conference, we still could have been designated the host school if Auburn had defeated Alabama a week later, and with those great backs, nobody would count the War Eagles out.

Since the week after Auburn is always an open date for us, prior to our game with Tech I drove over for the Auburn-Alabama game and wound up sitting with the Sugar Bowl officials, who were pulling hard for Alabama. When Auburn rallied late, I found myself consoling the Sugar Bowl scouts who were in misery, fearing the worst. They could see Auburn winning and then us losing to Tech and hosting the Sugar Bowl with a 5-6 record.

The week of the Auburn game in Athens, there was the question of whether we would have gone to the Sugar Bowl or not. I said,

preparing for a big New Year's celebration, but when the new year got underway they were busy lobbying to get the "last appearance" clause out of the contract with the conference. They succeeded, and I was one of the Athletic Directors who supported their objective. In 1980, '81 and '82 the Sugar Bowl was very pleased the last apprearance rule was not a problem for Georgia playing in New Orleans three straight times.

With one week left in the 1979 season, I certainly was not celebrating. We had Tech to play, and I didn't want to post my second losing season in three years. If Tech had beaten us it would have been 5-6 again as we had been in 1977.

Buck Belue's ankle was broken in the Auburn game, but we had enough to get by Tech 16-3 at Grant Field. Jeff Pyburn took over the offense, playing outstandingly in his final game as a Bulldog, and it was a great thrill for me and the coaches to see him finish on such a high note, since he was the subject of a lot of criticism when things went poorly for us. Steve Kelley had a great game at tailback, his best and only game on offense. When Herschel came along, Steve went to defense and was one of those solid players who helped us win the national title.

When I shook hands with Pepper Rodgers afterwards, I knew he might not be around much longer. You could see it in his face. I thought about the fact that I was castigated many times in my career for not being a Georgia man, which I could do nothing about. Here was Pepper, a Tech man, and the Tech people had soured on him.

Jim Brosnan, the baseball pitcher/author, once suggested his sport would take murderer Charles Manson if he could hit .300. Sometimes I believe some college football fans would accept the devil as head coach if he could go 11-0.

With the Sugar Bowl decision having been made by Alabama's victory over Auburn and our 6-5 record, there was nowhere to go for our team. There was no longer any controversial decision for us to make.

It was simple. Nobody wanted us.

Except Herschel Walker.

Jeff Pyburn, finishing on a high note

CHAPTER 9

"Old Man River," He Just Keeps Moving The Chains

My first memory of the little town of Wrightsville, Georgia, named for state senator James B. Wright, is of the summer of 1965 following my first season as Georgia's head football coach.

My wife, Barbara, and our kids Deanna, Daniel and Denise (Derek was not yet born) headed to the beach for a much needed vacation. George Fesperman, one of Georgia's grandest Bulldogs, had graciously offered us his beach cottage. We drove down Georgia 15, one of the state's most traveled north-south corridors, passing through Wrightsville, which is the seat of Johnson County, and which for many years fielded nondescript Class C high school teams.

Prior to that time, a few Wrightsville athletes had gained scholarship assistance here and there — Freddie Layton and Herb Norris at Georgia, Roy Thompson, Jr., at Florida State, Al Chamlee at LSU, Jim Jordan at Arizona and William Scott at Clemson — but you could safely say Wrightsville was not a recruiting hotbed.

That summer when we passed through this community of twenty-five hundred, little did I know that less than five miles from the center of town was a three-year-old black kid by the name of Herschel Walker who would leave such an important stamp on Georgia football and on my coaching career.

At the time, the high schools of Georgia did not field integrated teams, and a black football player in a Bulldog uniform was about as far from anyone's mind as the moon.

When we journeyed to Ann Arbor that fall for a game with the University of Michigan, the few black players on the Wolverine team drew considerable attention and piqued our curiosity. My own experience with black ath-

The Dooley family at the beach

letes at the time was limited, except for having coached several outstanding blacks at Parris Island during my military duty. This experience, plus my conviction that integration of our teams was imminent and for the best, made it easy for me to adjust to the presence of blacks on our team a few years later. But in the summer of 1965, you would have had me shaking my head if you had told me that a black freshman running back fifteen years later would lead a team of mine to the national championship and later win the Heisman trophy.

I'm happy to say that Herschel came our way. I learned a lot from him and consider him one of the most remarkable people that I have ever been associated with — not just an exceptional athlete, but an exceptional person.

In my opinion, he is the greatest college football player ever, and if he had remained at Georgia for his final season, most experts

Terry Hoage: A diamond that was almost overlooked

would probably agree with me. There is one snag — Tony Dorsett gained 6,082 career yards and Herschel's total was 5,259. No doubt he would have "rushed" past Dorsett by the fourth or fifth game in 1983 had he not signed with the New Jersey Generals.

The first time I met Herschel was in 1978, Willie McClendon's great senior year. Willie was a big back with speed who could make that tough yard inside, and he could sprint to the corners on the sweeps. We also used him to go over the top in critical short-yardage situations. Willie was an exceptional back, one of our truly great players, but Herschel could do everything Willie could do and with more pounds and greater speed. Herschel

Facing Page: Herschel was plenty to smile about

took our offense to a new level, but I think he was impressed with Willie's class as a runner and as a person.

One thing that was important to Herschel's success, and he would be the first to agree, is that we signed several outstanding football players the year he made his decision to become a Bulldog. We felt that his signature would be "icing on the cake," but we had already enjoyed a prosperous recruiting campaign when he made his choice.

It is quite interesting that while we were waiting for Herschel to make up his mind about Georgia, we were vacillating on whether or not to offer a scholarship to Terry Hoage of Huntsville, Texas.

Fortunately for us, nobody else was anxious to sign Terry. They were probably as

115

concerned as we were about reports that indicated he lacked speed. On top of that, he had been hurt his senior year, suffering a leg injury, and there was no way to properly evaluate his ability. Bill Lewis went out to Texas on a late recruiting swing and reported back that he liked Hoage's attitude but really didn't have much to go on. When we perused his grade transcript, we recognized right away he was a player whose academic ability would never concern us. In fact, his superior ability as a student was the determining factor in offering him a scholarship. I was not sold on him as a player, based on what we knew, but was aware that he was head and shoulders above everybody else academically. In fact, Terry had to work at football, but the classroom was a snap for him.

So in the early months of 1980, we signed the two athletes who would turn out to be the greatest offensive and greatest defensive players I ever coached, one the object of a nationwide recruiting rush and the other enjoying no attention at all. Quite a contrast.

The way we got Hoage was that an Athens native Dr. Dick Payne had joined the faculty at Sam Houston State and was an associate of Terry's father, Dr. Terrell Hoage. Dick Payne called us and recommended Terry. Otherwise, Terry probably would have enrolled at a small college or walked on at a Southwest Conference school and would have never roamed between Sanford's hedges.

Little did we know that Hoage would become such a great player, but after he blocked a Notre Dame field goal early in the national championship game, we should have had creative historian Dan Magill originate an alliterative nick-name for Terry right on the spot. When it came to the big play, no defensive player we ever had could match Hoage's overall ability and performance,

even though he was not the great natural athlete. Jake Scott made many great plays, but he was the natural athlete. Terry was an over-achiever if there ever was one. His play-action timing was extraordinary. There has never been a smarter defender to wear the Red and Black.

With Herschel, we were not sure what to expect either. We knew he was big and fast, which is a great place to start, but we were not certain how he would fare in major league competition, having come out of a Class A program. I believed that he would achieve greatness, but I never dreamed his initial impact would be so sensational.

Even in pre-season practice, while he was making the adjustment to a higher level of competition, he did not display the skills that would suddenly blossom in the Tennessee game on September 6, 1980. Before our opener in Knoxville, I had made the remark that I was worried that he might be just a big, stiff back. He seemed a little tentative.

That goes to show that you can never be certain in recruiting. It is not an exact science. Recruiting is the lifeblood of your program. It can be a very rewarding experience or it can become the worst of experiences. I have fond memories of certain recruiting episodes, but nightmares from others.

My first year off the sidelines will probably cause me to agree with what Coach Frank Howard said when asked upon retirement at Clemson what he would miss about coaching. He said that he would probably miss the games and the fun that comes with working with young athletes on the field. "But there is one thing I won't miss," Coach Howard said, "and that is some smart alec seventeen-year-old kid telling me he ain't quite made up his mind where he's going to school." That expresses the sentiment of most long-time head coaches.

116

What is so frustrating about recruiting is the breaking of the rules. We have made great improvements through the years, but we have a long way to go. What you have to accept first off is that coaches are extreme competitors. They will go to great lengths in order to win, and some will even break rules to achieve their objective.

Some of the things that have been done in recent years in recruiting which have made a difference are:

• The calendar has been restricted. There was a time when you could contact as many players as often as you liked, the year round. Now there is a limited period when there can be contact (between the time the prospect's season has ended, including playoff games, and signing date, which is the second Tuesday in February). During this time you may contact a prospect three times at home and three at school.

• The eliminating of all alumni and boosters in recruiting has been a good rule. It was bad for the loyal alumnus who was sincere and wanted to help without breaking rules, but as it is in every case, there are the two percent who spoil the system. It is better for college athletics that this rule was enacted.

• Head coaches cannot leave the campus on signing date. If you go to one home to sign a prospect, you feel you should go to all the others, but obviously that was not possible.

• Coaches cannot leave the campus for recruiting after signing date except for the month of May. In the month of May, you can evaluate prospects, but you cannot contact them. You can visit spring practices and look at film, but that is it. You are allowed to begin evaluating again in November, but no contacts can be made until after the prospect's season has ended.

These are good rules and have improved the recruiting situation, but there are additional rules which I would like to see added to the books, rules that in my view would make further improvement. We need to continue tightening the rules, and to intensify the punishment for both coaches and athletes who break them.

A factor that helps with coaches is that if an assistant is involved with any violation, especially where there is a pattern of abuse, you can call the NCAA offices in Kansas City and check on his record. The NCAA does not disclose details but will inform you if there is any previous association with rules breaking. Most schools, when hiring a coach now, call Kansas City to learn if the coach's record is clean. It used to be that a coach could cheat and bail out. Now his probation follows him.

This is why I support investigative reporting. Nothing embarrasses like public confirmation of illegal conduct. Most head coaches believe bad publicity is a deterrent.

We also need to hold athletes more accountable. The NCAA is trying to establish a punishment program for the athletes as well as penalizing the coach and the school.

In my twenty-five years at Georgia, we were investigated several times, but there was never a major penalty. There were no bowl or television sanctions levied against us, but I was upset that we had any problem.

In the first instance, involving a player from Douglas, Georgia, by the name of George Smith, we had an assistant coach, Wayne McDuffie, who was accused of making an extra recruiting visit. But the biggest damage was that after Wayne took a job with the Atlanta Falcons, he went to say good-bye to George and left him a Georgia sweatsuit.

The University of Georgia had to pay for that violation. The assistant was no longer an employee when he violated a rule, but the school, nonetheless, was held liable. That was tough to take, but I am in agreement with the NCAA position. Holding the school responsible for immediate past sins is the only way we can exercise any control and provide any deterrent to violations.

In the other case, involving a player named Tyrone Sorrells, an unthinking alumnus feeling sorry for a needy kid arranged a bank loan to help him buy a used car.

We were greatly upset about all this, but we uncovered seventy-five percent of the violations ourselves and reported them to the NCAA.

After these two instances, we came down hard on our coaches. We reminded them that they would be fired, no questions asked, if there were serious violations. We expected them to abide by the rules and to inform careless and insensitive alumni that we expected them to follow the rules.

Since the NCAA pursued us pretty hard during this time, many felt that it had a vendetta against Georgia because of the court case involving television, when Georgia and Oklahoma, representing the College Football Association, successfully sued to take away the NCAA's granting of exclusive television rights.

Even the respected Dean Rusk, former Secretary of State and then a member of the university faculty, suggested that we would need to watch our every move. I don't think that the NCAA had a vendetta against us, but since they were so dedicated in their investigation, what I am pleased about is that they found no pattern of abuse. Looking the other way was not my style of operating, and while I never soap-boxed, I was serious about our following the rules.

As we improve the recruiting rules and the policing of them, there are at least three other items of legislation which I hope are inked on the books soon:

(1) Telephone restriction. It is legal to call prospects day and night, any time of the year. You call a kid, and he has call waiting on his phone. He puts you on hold while he talks to another coach from another school. This goes on all night. Coaches call frequently because they don't want players to keep box scores — coach so and so has called ten times and you have called only twice, so he must be more interested in me than you are. Maybe we should set up a telephone calendar, making it permissible to call only on certain nights of the week during a certain time period.

(2) There should be no recruiting until a player has finished his junior year. This means that if he comes to your campus on his own, he would not even be given tickets. Eliminate all contact with juniors across the board.

(3) Void the freshman eligibility rules. This would solve many problems, not only with allowing the player to adjust to the campus and college life, but to eliminate the area where athletes are most often misled. "Come with us and play early," is a pitch more and more kids hear every year. It causes many problems.

While I believe that eliminating freshman eligibility is best for the game — it would allow athletes the opportunity to adjust academically, socially and athletically before facing the demands and pressures of big-time competition — many coaches, understandably, disagree.

It would provide class unity and pride while giving the players four years in which to complete their eligibility and five years to earn their degree. Five years is the average time it takes most players to graduate, anyway.

Statistically, only four or five freshmen each year make the traveling squad, and only one or two of those make a significant contribution.

Defensive back Tony Flack is the only player we ever recruited who started the first game of his first year. Not even Herschel Walker and Lindsey Scott started in their first games.

We've had some pretty good teams since the freshman eligibility rules went into effect in 1972, but very few players have been good enough to start and make an impact their freshman year. Yet, practically every athlete you recruit thinks that he will start right away.

Eliminating freshmen from competition in football and basketball, while allowing them to practice and play a limited number of junior varsity games would solve many problems in recruiting.

One of the reasons that the public assumes there is more cheating than there really is has to do with the competitive aspect of recruiting. When a coach, competitive by nature, loses a prospect to another school, he always complains that the playing field was not level.

They invariably accuse their competitor and cry "foul." There had to be an under-the-table deal. Part of that is stung pride and some of it has to do with the personal feelings you have for your school. If you are a coach at the University of Georgia, where there is a winning tradition and where the facilities are so outstanding — none any better anywhere — and where there is a great university with a broad field of study to choose from, where the campus is pretty and the girls are attractive, then you wonder how an athlete could possibly consider going anywhere else, especially if he is from the state of Georgia.

Tony Flack, the only freshman to start

We believe we have everything a young man would want in Athens, so why would he not sign with us? It is sometimes hard to accept, but some kids, for whatever reasons, are attracted to other institutions, and it doesn't mean that the competition is guilty of anything underhanded in recruiting.

It is unfortunate that recruiting has gained

so much attention in recent years. The publicity makes it tough for everybody — most of all the athlete — but we have to make the best of it. Too much attention for high school seniors is not a good thing. Some have difficulty living up to their reputation which, in many cases, may even be exaggerated or distorted in today's media world. Because of early publicity on a prospect, some are mis-evaluated and overrecruited.

You are not allowed to time them for a sprint, and you cannot work them out. You evaluate them in games, in practice and on film. You talk to their coach and coaches who play against them. But nothing is foolproof in recruiting. Mistakes are easily made. It is easy to be misled. It is easy to mislead yourself. False impressions too often cloud a recruiter's thinking. Then, too, some players are difficult to evaluate, especially quarterbacks. That is why you have so many fourth-round draft choices, like Joe Montana, becoming so successful professionally.

We always liked to say that we sought the athlete who would rise above the coaching, like Jake Scott or Terry Hoage or Herschel Walker, one who during the course of a game will do something that will drastically change the outcome of the game, something he was not taught.

Another important recruiting circumstance is that change brings on promise. If you stay in one place for a long period of time, it means that there often will be change taking place at the schools around you, which brings on new enthusiasm, new opportunities and gives your opponents a recruiting shot in the arm.

During the past twenty-five years, there have been six coaching changes at Georgia Tech; five at Clemson, South Carolina and Florida State; four at Florida; and three at Auburn, Alabama and Tennessee. With so

many new beginnings, it made the recruiting challenge tougher.

Too often in recruiting, once you make up your mind, there's no turning back. It's like fraternity rush — you pull out all the stops and sometimes you make two mistakes in the process. First, you spend all your time recruiting one player and let one of lesser reputation slip by right under your nose, and he is the one who turns out great. If recruiting were a science, you would never miss a Terry Hoage or a Jimmy Orr, who walked on at Georgia and later became one of the NFL's greatest receivers. Nobody offered Wayne Peace a scholarship, so he walked on at Florida and started for four years for the Gators; he was a marvelous college quarterback.

Second, if you make a commitment on a player, you do your best to recruit him. Even if you feel he is not a great athlete but suddenly the competition gives him a lot of attention, you are required to step up your efforts. If an opponent tells a kid he is great, you must follow suit.

And the problem with the truly great ones is the preposterous lengths you often have to go through to get their signature. Some of them must keep tallies on attention. Who could blame the kids if they expect to ride into town on a white horse?

The excessive attention and the pressure to sign top players often leads to a lot of misunderstanding, too. The worst problem is that recruits are promised too much, and I am not talking about anything illegal. They are promised too much in the way of their football future, which is why the freshman eligibility rule needs changing.

Regardless of what you do, often players and/or their parents believe they are misled anyway. My feeling was always that we should be up front with the way we ran our program and never sidestep any issue or

120

question. Also, I believe strongly that if we make a commitment to a young man, then we must provide the atmosphere and opportunity for him to utilize his skills both athletically and academically. These points were always underscored:

- Inform the player and his parents what kind of program you run. Tell them that it is a regimented program with strong rules and regulations. Rules violations would be met with strict disciplinary action.
- It is a team-oriented program with very little room for prima donnas.
- While we strive to develop the best possible run-pass balance on offense, we fundamentally were going to run the football.

If you average winning eight games a year for over twenty-five years, you not only are good at what you do on the field, you are good at recruiting. Sometimes we were even great, but generally speaking we recruited well most of the time, especially given that we emphasized recruiting within the rules.

You are never going to do as well as you like in recruiting. When you sign what the various analysts suggest is an outstanding crop, you look back over your recruiting classes and realize they are not always as good as their pre-freshman rating. Except for the classes of 1965 and 1980, most of our groups were not as good as their reputation.

When I am asked who influences recruiting the most, I always reply that, generally speaking, it is the mother. It is mom who has spent the most time with the athlete in his young life. She is the one who has had that special relationship with him. She knows him best and she is the one who has had the patience to deal with his questions and problems. That is not always the case, but in most instances, the hand that rocks the cradle is the most influential.

There was a popular story at one time about an assistant coach who had determined that the mother was the key to prospects. He chose to recruit the mother and succeeded. "The mother enrolled at our campus and the player signed with our competitor," is the way the story goes. Usually, if mama is sold on your program, chances are you are going to wind up with the prospect.

Although I don't think Mrs. Christine Walker tried to influence Herschel on a particular school, I felt we had a chance with him because she wanted him to stay close to home. It was important to her to be able to see him play. The family was close, and she obviously didn't want him to sign with a school like Southern Cal, even though the Trojans apparently wound up in the finals. But even if we had known in the beginning for sure that he would remain close to home, there were plenty of schools to worry about other than those located as far away as the West Coast.

Recruiters came from everywhere to sell Herschel on their school. Coaches like John Robinson of Southern Cal and Earle Bruce of Ohio State felt it was worth their time to travel to Wrightsville to meet with the Walkers and make a recruiting pitch.

Give Mike Cavan credit. He made the supreme sacrifice and effort on our behalf. The recruiting rules were different then, which meant that about the first of the year, Mike took up residence in Wrightsville. He should have paid local taxes.

We had been advised that Herschel was not going to sign right away, that he would take his time, but none of us expected it would last as long as it did. He finally made up his mind Easter Sunday, April 6, 1980.

Barbara had spent considerable time working out all the details of a family vacation to New York and Boston, and naturally she

Mike Cavan was instrumental in signing Herschel Walker

expected me to come along. I told her no problem, if Herschel had made his decision by that time. When spring holidays came around and the family headed north, I remained home, much to Barbara's annoyance. She didn't understand why one player could be so important. It didn't take her long to appreciate what it meant. She was there in Knoxville when Herschel displayed his remarkable talents for the first time.

But on that Easter Sunday she was off several states away with the kids and pouting about my decision. I knew that I had to be ready to go to Wrightsville, just a hundred miles South of Athens, on short notice — provided that the news was good, that Herschel would become a Bulldog. Although I

realized he might not enroll at our campus, I tried to think positive. At least privately. For sure, I had to stay close to the fire until he made a decision.

After attending early morning mass on Easter Sunday, I went to my office in the Coliseum to catch up on some work when Steve Greer, who had played for me and then served as defensive assistant and recruiting coordinator, showed up in my office as excited as he could be. He was trying to act calm, but it was impossible. He began talking in rambling, almost incoherent fashion. I couldn't make sense out of what he was saying, but I soon gathered that he had gotten a call from Mike Cavan who had said that Herschel was going to sign with Georgia that afternoon. By the time I figured that out, I was as excited as Steve and took off with him to join Mike in Wrightsville.

When we arrived a couple of hours later, Mike reminded me that we had used up our official visits and that none of us could actually sign Herschel. I'll never forget driving up that little dirt road, five miles out of town, that led from the pavement to where the Walker's lived. It was a very modest house with humble rural surroundings. Not unlike Jackson Street in many respects. We were dealing with good, honest hard-working people. An education meant something to families like the Walkers, and so I was doubly glad that we were signing Herschel. He had already demonstrated an appreciation for the educational process.

We had already signed his sister Veronica to a track scholarship. We were expanding our women's athletic program across the board, and Veronica was our first full scholarship athlete in women's track. Naturally, that caused a lot of comment, but I thought it was a smart decision. We knew that as a little boy, Herschel's first ambition was to be able to outrun his sister. I felt that if she were that good, then she ought to be worth a scholarship and would make a contribution to our lady Bulldog track team. I was right.

As it turned out, our scholarship investment in the Walker family brought us a right nice return. In addition to leading us to the national championship and three SEC titles, Herschel made a $100,000 contribution to the Butts-Mehre campaign.

The signing of Herschel actually was handled by his father, Willis, who took the grant-in-aid form inside while we remained outside. Mike and Steve, who have always enjoyed hunting and playing golf together, were beside themselves. They were about to explode but kept a rein on their emotions

until the document had been executed and we could go in the house and congratulate everybody.

Inside, there was a six-by-six trophy case with dozens of trophies which Herschel, his sister Veronica and his brother Renneth had collected. Most of them belonged to Herschel, but his mother was quick to point out that her other children had won some of the trophies on display.

Herschel didn't seem interested in showing off his awards, but he took great pleasure in sharing his poems with me. I read with interest what he had penned, learning right away that this great athletic talent had some intellectual depth and understanding. He was different.

And that is the first thing his mother said about him. "Herschel was always different." Different in that he never lacked self-motivation. When he came home from school, she never had to fuss at him about his homework. He studied his lessons automatically.

When he enrolled at Georgia, he needed some support work in a couple of subjects and was placed in developmental studies. But Herschel didn't stay there long. He was in class every day, sitting on the front row, applying himself and becoming totally committed to his school work. That commitment paid off.

After the Tennessee game his freshman year, we played Texas A&M in Athens the next week, and Herschel was the talk of the town. Against the Aggies he rushed for 145 yards and scored three touchdowns. When somebody asked him later what he did Saturday night after the A&M game, he replied that he went home and studied. While the campus was partying, with the Bulldogs record 2-0, the star of the team was back in

Herschel: Heavyweight durability with the agility of a flyweight

his room with the books. Yes, Herschel was different.

From the first game, Herschel was something to behold on the football field. After he got off to the great start at Knoxville and was settled into our system, he displayed remarkable talent, developing into the most dominating player in college football. With the capable supporting cast, Herschel became the centerpiece of the national championship team.

It is easy for me to talk about Herschel because I admired not only his ability to play but his enormous self-discipline. He trained hard to get the maximum from his ability. When someone asked him about alcohol and drugs, he said, "This is my body, and I would never put anything in my body that would harm it."

After his mother's pronouncement that he was different, the coaches came to expect the unusual from him. On reporting day in August of 1980, I arrived at my office around 5:30 A.M. and saw Herschel riding around the Coliseum. He must have arisen at 3:00 A.M. to arrive in Athens that early.

Naturally, his teammates were anxious to meet him. They were aware of the enormous publicity he had received, and the varsity was curious to learn if they had a hotshot prima donna in their midst. Immediately Herschel charmed everybody and was soon called, "Humble Herschel." It is traditional for the freshmen to carry the varsity's bags to their rooms on reporting day at McWhorter Hall. Herschel fit right in, grabbing bags and carrying out his assignment. He had no interest in breaking with tradition. With his great attitude, he defused any potential irritation on and off the field. But he always did that.

Herschel was never a fancy runner with a unique style. He had speed and power. He could stop and start. He was strength personified. I used to describe him as "old man river" — he just kept rolling along, right into the fourth quarter when the defense was tired and he seemed fresh and unstoppable. During his three years, in which we won the SEC title each year, there were a lot of linebackers who enjoyed taking a breather in the final quarter. With Herschel, that was costly. His performances were not always spectacular, although as a freshman he seemed to break a long run every game. He was more like a heavyweight boxer who kept coming at you. When you get into the thirteenth, fourteenth and fifteenth rounds, you separate the champion from the rest. That was Herschel Walker. His durability was unmatched. There has never been a back to carry the ball that often in every game, week after week. On top of that, he very seldom fumbled.

He was a coach's dream because of his attitude. First of all, he believed in the team concept. You never saw him putting himself first. His attitude was to please his coaches and his teammates. His offensive linemen loved him because he made them feel that he truly appreciated their efforts.

Herschel promoted team morale. It was fun to be around him because of his attitude. He was always in peak condition. He was self-disciplined, and he was blessed with extraordinary concentration.

Although we were capable of throwing the ball during his time, we realized that with our defense being as effective as it was, all we had to do was keep giving the ball to Herschel and he would keep the chains moving and we would wear everybody down.

With Herschel it was three basic plays. Herschel right, Herschel left, Herschel up the middle. You didn't have to design anything special for him, just hand him the ball.

We did try to develop more ways to get him the football, which is why we began using him more in passing situations his last year. After his freshman year, when defenders learned how to tackle him (chop his legs rather than come at him high, where the result was always disastrous), he did not have as many spectacular runs, but in many respects he showed more running ability. He would make those tough four, five, eight, ten and twelve yard runs that moved us down the field. Since he got the ball four out of five plays, it didn't look like much was happening, then all of a sudden he would pop out of there for twenty yards or so.

Whether he was grinding out first downs or popping a long one, he belonged in the elite category. It is difficult to imagine all of that size and speed and mental toughness in one package. But his durability was equally impressive. I always come back to that.

Don Leebern, starting tackle on Georgia's 1959 Orange Bowl team and one of my closest friends, was a teammate of Pat Dye's at Georgia. He also played with Frank Orgel, who joined Ray Goff's staff in the spring of 1989 but coached with Pat when Bo Jackson was at Auburn.

The Auburn coaches knew they had a remarkable back with comparable size and speed to Herschel's, but Don's friends confided in him that they were disappointed that Bo would not shoulder the Auburn offensive load like Herschel did. (With the wishbone, Bo did not get the ball as often as he would have in an I-formation. That's why Coach Dye switched to the I for Bo's final year.)

It is ironic that these two great athletes came along about the same time. Bo had a

Herschel gets an assist from his coach on the sidelines

fancier step than Herschel, a better change of pace, but I believe Herschel was a fraction faster. Herschel was a little stiffer than Bo, but no athlete ever surpassed Herschel in getting the maximum out of his ability and hunkering down with eagerness to be the workhorse of the offense.

Herschel's performance in the Sugar Bowl against Notre Dame tells you so much about him. When he came out after the second play, Dr. Butch Mulherin came over and told me that Herschel's shoulder had been dislocated but that he and Dr. Mixon Robinson and our trainer, Warren Morris, had gotten it back into place. I thought to myself, "That's it. If we win, we'll have to win without Herschel." But on the next series when we got the ball back, he suddenly jogged on the field. He could play hurt because he could set his mind to do whatever he wanted to do. He was the best you'll ever see at that. He gained 150 yards against one of the toughest defensive teams Georgia has ever faced, one that had never given up a hundred yards to any back. And with an injured shoulder.

That was the happiest day of my life, winning that national championship, and Herschel's performance was vital to the outcome. After the game, the Canadian League began making overtures to Herschel, but he declined, saying, "It doesn't make sense growing up in one country and playing football in another."

A year later when the new professional United States Football League was formed, the talk of Herschel turning pro heated up. There was also a lot of conversation about his challenging the NFL's policy of not signing underclassmen, which led to a funny story involving the late John Luck of Enigma, Georgia. John told Bobby Rowan, now a Georgia Public Service Commissioner, "Why don't they leave that boy alone? Let him do whatever he wants to do. If he plays for the Bulldogs on Saturday, we don't care what he does on Sunday."

Little did I know that Herschel would later wind up becoming entrapped by the new league following the Sugar Bowl in 1983. It was a sad day for Georgia, although I could not blame Herschel and his family for being interested in a million dollar offer. I have never believed that he truly wanted to sign with the Generals. It was a tough situation for him, however. He was hearing the arguments that he had made All-America, that he had already won the Heisman trophy, and that there was always the possibility that he might become the victim of a career-threatening injury. Finally, there was the suggestion late at night that he should sign, and then if he changed his mind the next morning the contracts would be torn up. In Herschel's mind, although he had put his signature on paper, it was not valid until he said, "Yes, that is my signature and I am turning professional." He was too trusting in that situation, because copies were made of the contract. All of them were not torn up.

We kept hearing rumors that he had signed, but Herschel told us he hadn't. Even though you could say he was naive and that he may have been given to immature rationalization, in Herschel's mind it was not a valid signature until he said it was. He was tricked. He was burned, but I am sure it was a mistake he learned from and will never repeat.

Legally, however, it was a different matter, and when a member of the new league showed Mike Cavan the contract with Herschel's name on it, he called me with the news. We had no choice. We made it easy for the USFL. In the saddest day of my coaching career, we declared Herschel Walker ineligible.

I'll always believe Herschel wanted to stay and become college football's all-time leading rusher, setting a record that might never have been broken. He wanted to lead Georgia to one more championship and to spend that senior year on campus with his friends. Herschel really enjoyed college.

But he couldn't change what had been done, so he, in typical fashion, made the best of it. He didn't look back. With that great self-discipline, he moved forward, viewed the situation from a positive standpoint and became a dominating player in professional football, just like he was at Georgia.

In my conversations with Tom Landry, before he was let go by the Cowboys, he was enthusiastic about Herschel as a running back. I think Coach Landry had reached a point where he was about ready to get out, but I also think he wanted to stay around and develop an offensive line and watch Herschel really dominate the NFL. He said last December, "If we can ever get to where we can get Herschel in the secondary, there is no telling how dominant a football player he will be."

You spend your life in football for the opportunities to coach young men like Herschel Walker—special not just for the courage to pop a shoulder back in place and challenge America's toughest defense or to blast off tackle for seventy-five yards. You appreciate his modesty — a reluctant super-star, we called him — his regard for his team and his school.

I keep in touch with Herschel and appreciate his continued support of our program. Whenever I am in Dallas, I try to meet with him and am always pleased to find him in peak physical condition, upbeat and positive — just like he was on picture day in 1980.

When I think of his attributes, I remember his quiet-spoken mother saying he was different. Christine Walker may not have tried to influence Herschel in his final decision, but that warm mother's touch is very evident in his background. Even if we had not had a ban against spiking the football in college, I believe Herschel Walker still would have turned and handed the ball to the official. He enjoyed a very sensitive and stable upbringing, and I don't think Herschel, if he lives to be a hundred years old, will ever embarrass his modest and gentle mother.

CHAPTER 10
A Wing And A Prayer For A Team Of Destiny

Every coach dreams of an undefeated season after which his team is voted the national champion, but it becomes a reality for very few. Although there is still time left, neither Bo Schembechler of Michigan nor Tom Osborne of Nebraska has enjoyed that undefeated national championship season. It hasn't happened to Bobby Bowden of FSU either. Here are three outstanding football coaches who deserve the best in their profession, but that ultimate season has not come their way. It doesn't take anything away from them as coaches, but they have paid their dues, and I hope that someday it happens to them as it did for me in 1980.

After I resigned, I was asked on a television special if I would have considered my career incomplete without winning a national title. Without hesitation, I said, "Yes," but later I began to think about my coaching friends and concluded that if it had not happened to me, I really would not have had any regrets.

You think about all the people who never win a Super Bowl or a World Series, and you rationalize for them that it is not that important. Look at those who have never even played in a Super Bowl. Merlin Olsen, for example, never got there. Ted Williams never played on a World Series championship team. Ernie Banks of the Chicago Cubs never even played in a World Series. Archie Manning, the most versatile and dominating quarterback I ever saw and who has become a good friend, never got close to a playoff game — never even played on a winning team while with the Saints. Sam Snead never won the U. S. Open, Arnold Palmer never won the PGA title. One of the toughest breaks in Fran Tarkenton's remarkable career is that he played in three Super Bowls and lost every time. Fran shared some poignant thoughts about his unfortunate experience:

It is something that lives with me every day. There is not a day that goes by that I don't think about not winning the Super Bowl — the failure of those three days that I had a chance to play in that game, the ultimate game in pro football. I haven't learned how to deal with it, frankly.

I've heard people say they accept it as life, but I can't. I wish that I could. It absolutely bothers me that I've never been able to live it down. And the sad part is that there is no tomorrow. I can't go back at age fifty and play again, but I've had dreams at fifty, forty-eight, forty-four, forty-two and in the back of my mind, I still think I could if somebody would give me the chance. And that's sick, but that is how much it bothers me. I wish I could cope with it and deal with it, but I really haven't been able to do that.

I don't know how I would feel if I had not experienced that undefeated, national championship season, but I do know that I consider myself very fortunate to be in the company of the Bear Bryants, the Bud Wilkinsons, the Joe Paternos, the Shug Jordans, the Ara Paraseghians. I will always be grateful that everything fell into place in 1980, the year Mount St. Helens blew its top in Cougar, Washington; Shirley Temple became a grandmother; our rescue mission for the hostages in Iran was aborted in an Iranian desert; and Ronald Reagan became our President.

Most of all, I am grateful that Herschel Walker came our way to lead us to that championship. But actually we won because we were more than Herschel Walker. We were defense and kicking. We could kickoff, and we could cover kickoffs. We could punt, and we could cover punts. We could return punts, and we could keep opponents from returning much of anything on us. We could make third down conversions on offense, and our defense could keep the other side from converting. We were an outstanding team with a few great players and one super player at tailback. Most of the team, however, were average or above players who believed in themselves and had the ability to rise to the occasion. We could make the big play, and we always found a way to win.

Perhaps we were a team of destiny. I have never really known what to say about such notions, but I now realize that when it came to winning football games, we were a team that had more than its share of breaks. We fought hard, we earned our way, but things broke just right for us in the big games, starting with Tennessee.

We had numerous question marks when we opened in Knoxville on a hot September night, one of them being at tailback where Donnie McMickins was the starter and Car-

Lindsay Scott leaves behind a trail of Tennessee tacklers

nie Norris the backup. Next in line was Herschel Walker. We had agreed that we would let each of them play two series. Donnie and Carnie did a good job, but there was something electrifying about Herschel's entering the lineup for our team.

After that game, I often said that Herschel didn't know exactly where he was going, but wherever it was, it would be in a hurry. That's why he excited not only the fans but our team as well. For three years, every time he got the ball there was anticipation that something spectacular might take place. Often, it did.

He was the difference in our team, but he was no island. We were a team, and what was so pleasing about Herschel Walker was that he enjoyed being part of the team.

In that first game, however, the team was a little unsettled at the start. Tennessee scored first — on a safety — and then took Rex Robinson's placement kick and drove for a touchdown to go ahead 9-0, which was the halftime score. On the Vols' second possession in the second half, they threw a thirty-six yard touchdown pass for a 15-0 lead.

That was the point where developments that got us off to a start began taking place. Tennessee went for two and didn't make it. It didn't seem like much of a factor at that point, but it was to be very significant later.

After the kickoff, we couldn't move the ball and punted to their safety Bill Bates, who fumbled. A mad scramble ensued, but nobody was able to gain control of the ball until it had squirted through the end zone, giving us a safety.

Things were beginning to pick up. We were gaining some momentum. After Tennessee's kick, we drove for a touchdown, Herschel getting the final sixteen yards on that memorable run over and through the Volunteer defense. Interestingly, one of the

players Herschel ran over, Bill Bates, is now a teammate on the Cowboys and good friend.

On our next possession we drove for our second touchdown. This time Herschel got the last nine yards and we were ahead 16-15. But Tennessee was not through. The Vols later drove to our five-yard line. On Tennessee's next play, first and five, Nate Taylor, the Tifton Termite, put his helmet on the ball and it flew out and into the hands of our backside end, Pat McShea. Another big break for the Bulldogs. But we were backed up. The clock reminded Tennessee that there was still enough time.

Our last break came when Jim Broadway, not our strongest punter but one of our most consistent (he became the first-team punter the week before the game when regular punter Mark Malkawicz broke his shoulder in practice), booted the greatest kick of his career — forty-seven yards from the end zone. I bet he never kicked a forty-seven yarder before or since, but that was typical of our national championship team. When the game was on the line, the Nate Taylors and the Jim Broadways came through for us. Herschel was great, but our team complemented his remarkable ability.

Two weeks later, Clemson arrived in Athens, expecting to show Herschel up. They tried diligently to recruit him and were disappointed that he did not become a Tiger. It was a point of pride with them that they stop Herschel.

Give them credit. They always played well against Herschel, but Clemson considers Georgia one of its biggest rivals and always comes to play. They had some success slowing Herschel down, but again we had the right stuff to win the ball game. Scott Woerner, one of the best all-around performers we ever had, returned a punt sixty-seven yards for a touchdown. He later returned an interception ninety-eight yards to the Clemson two to set up our only offensive touchdown.

And in one of those fitting endings to a big game story, Jeff Hipp of Columbia, South Carolina, intercepted a pass at our one-yard line that clinched the victory for us, getting an assist from his roommate, Frank Ros. The pass skipped off Ros' helmet and into Hipp's hands — two South Carolina boys teaming up on the play that won the game.

Each week we continued to find a way to win. And it was different every time. That was the characteristic of that team. Even though Herschel was the star, he did not look on himself as a star. He proudly wore the big TEAM, little ME tee-shirt and sincerely believed that slogan was important to our success. Although we averaged 27.7 points per game offensively, we did not score that many points in the critical games: sixteen vs. Tennessee; twenty vs. Clemson; thirteen vs. South Carolina; twenty-six vs. Florida; and seventeen vs. Notre Dame. But we managed to score enough to win, which championship teams will do.

In a close, hard fought game against South Carolina, we took a 13-0 lead on our first possession in the third quarter. Herschel popped through the right side for seventy-six yards, displaying that stunning speed. Three defenders had an angle on him, but he simply outran the angle. ABC televised the game nationally, and Herschel's run caused a lot of comment around the country the following week because of that great burst of speed, but the game was not over by any means following that impressive dash.

The Gamecocks scored a field goal and a touchdown in the third quarter to narrow the gap to 13-10. George Rogers, who won the Heisman trophy that year, was to their offense what Herschel was to ours. A power

runner with excellent speed, Rogers liked to get the ball often in a big drive, and Coach Jimmy Carlen and his staff naturally agreed that the ball should go to George. With 7:20 left in the fourth quarter, the Gamecocks began operating at the Georgia forty-seven following a punt, and it was Rogers for nine, Rogers for three, Rogers for eight, Rogers for seven. They were driving and we were beginning to feel the pressure of a powerful back's thrusts and a ticking clock. Then after a time out, South Carolina called on Carl West and a play later came back to Rogers, who swept to his right when Dale Carver hit him hard and ripped the ball out. Tim Parks recovered. Our defense saved the day at our seventeen.

The clock wouldn't tick fast enough as we called on Herschel ten times in an eleven-play drive that ended at the Carolina one. They took over with forty-five seconds left, and Jeff Hipp intercepted a pass three plays later. Add the names of Dale Carver and Tim Parks to the honor roll of players without whom we would not have won the national championship.

Beating South Carolina set off a celebration with everybody except our coaching staff, who knew that it would not be easy to come back from a tough, physical game with Carolina and regain our sharpness for the Florida game the next week in Jacksonville.

Through the years we have tried to schedule a game before Florida that would not be that demanding of our team. You want to be as fresh as you can when you play the Gators. By this time of the year, you are positioning for the SEC title. At least you hope that is the case, and it was for us many times during the last twenty-five years. Not only do you want to be up for the game, you want to head to Jacksonville in the best possible physical condition.

South Carolina took a lot out of us emotionally. You just can't count on that little edge when you play big games back to back. In the second game, you may lack that crispness in blocking and tackling. You are just a little off, and it can make a big difference.

That is why with three such tough finishing games — our three greatest rivalries, Florida, Auburn and Tech — we want to schedule a nonconference team at home the week before Florida, when we have a better than even chance of winning the game. But that doesn't mean you can take a team lightly.

In one of the few times in my life after Coach Eaves "educated" me about respecting your opponent, I made such a mistake in 1975 in this so-called "breather- before-Florida" situation. In the year of the Junkyard Dog, we had a defense that always kept us in the game, but we were not that talented nor did we have much depth. Florida that year was running what they called the "broken bone." Doug Dickey had added to his wishbone offense several passing variations that were ripping everybody's defenses apart. Except for an off day in the second game against N. C. State, when they scored only seven points, the Gators were cracking defenses for three touchdowns or more every outing. When we got to Jacksonville, the "broken bone" offense was averaging twenty-nine points per game.

During the season, coaches have enough to worry about week to week, but they keep an eye out for what is happening down the road with future opponents, even if they are smart enough not to say anything publicly.

After we defeated Kentucky 21-13 in Athens in 1975 with Richmond coming up, our coaches began talking among themselves about what we could do to stop Florida. The consensus was that it would be the most difficult assignment a Georgia defense had ever had in Jacksonville. So they began hinting to me that we ought to take advantage of the Richmond game to begin working to stop the "broken bone." Interestingly, Erk was against the idea, but Sam Mitchell, who had scouted the Gators offense, offered some convincing arguments in favor of early work for Florida. I went along with it, and we had to fight for our lives against Richmond, a team we edged 28-24. To beat the Spiders we had to come up with a fumble on their last drive late in the fourth quarter.

You think I didn't privately feel stupid? How could I go against my long-standing principle of not ever looking ahead? But since we were not upset by Richmond, we did have the advantage of getting our players' attention the next week, and I am sure it was hard for Doug Dickey to get his players ready for us. They warmed up for us by swamping Auburn 31-14 and then had to watch films of us struggling against lowly Richmond. That was one tough coaching assignment. Even so, we had to fight our tails off to win against a truly great Florida team, 10-7, when Richard Appleby threw the end around pass to Gene Washington late in the fourth quarter.

When a member of our TV crew asked Richard after the game if he was nervous when we sent the play in, he responded with a classic comment: "Well," he said, grinning from ear to ear, "I guess you could say I was a little nervous, but you can say that I rose to the occasion." After that experience, you can be sure that I would never be caught looking ahead again under any circumstances. That was the first and only time in my career that I allowed myself to look ahead. Fortunately, we got away with it.

For our football team in 1980, there was no question about our being up and ready to play Florida. That was a foregone conclusion. But having that tough, emotional game with South Carolina was a drain on our emotions, and the bumps and bruises of a jaw-to-jaw physical confrontation don't heal overnight.

Over the years we enjoyed some great afternoons in the Gator Bowl, and one of the reasons was the fact that before they played us each year, Florida had to face Auburn. Of course, we had the same situation the next week when we had to play Auburn. That was one of Gen. Bob Neyland's keys to winning at Tennessee. He worked hard at the business of scheduling and never played two tough opponents back to back. And it was Bobby Dodd who perfected that pattern at Georgia Tech. I always felt that one of the reasons Coach Dodd wanted Tech to leave the SEC was that in the sixties he had to play LSU and Alabama back to back and right at bowl selection time.

With our 1980 team we had to play not two tough opponents back to back, but three in a row. Tech is always a tough one for us, it being our biggest rival, but we do have an open date before our last game of the season with the Yellow Jackets.

When we got to Jacksonville in 1980, we were ranked No. 2 in the country, right behind Notre Dame, which was even more incentive for Florida to knock us off. We were undefeated in the conference, and I am sure that the Gator players wanted to do what we had done several times to them — play the spoiler's role. But there was more to it than that. If they had beaten us, they would have remained in the conference race since they had lost only one game, to LSU earlier in the season, 24-7.

Before the game, George Haffner's basic but to the point scouting report on Florida said, "Florida has excellent runners on defense. They run to the ball well. They blitz very effectively. Their defense is designed to make you go the long way, a lot like Georgia's. We need the best passing game of the

year in order to beat them, and Buck's play will be vital. We must not make mistakes and we must make third down conversions if we are going to win."

Erk Russell simply told his defense to concentrate on every play. "The best way to win," he said, "is not to lose. Concentrate. One little five-yard slant could result in a touchdown. Lock your arms, make the tackle. Make the play. When you see the ball, break to it. Eleven red hats on the ball, every play."

Again the game was on television and it turned out to be a classic, like so many Georgia-Florida games seemed to be. On our first possession, after our initial first down, Herschel blasted for seventy-two yards and the Gator Bowl began to rock. Naturally I was worried. I didn't want our team to relax and think that it might be easy. I stalked the sideline, barking out my message not to let up. We scored on a thirteen-yard pass from Belue to Ronnie Stewart in the second quarter, but Florida scored too, and with their first quarter field goal it was 14-10 at the half. Both teams in it, both teams fighting for victory, and a national television audience not about to leave their sets.

We shut Florida out in the third quarter while adding two field goals by Rex Robinson to take a 20-10 lead with fifteen minutes left. But in the last quarter, Florida scored and went for two to close it to 20-18, then added a field goal to overtake us, 21-20. With time running out, they punted out of bounds on our seven-yard line, and in many sections of the Gator Bowl, the celebrating began.

But as I looked up at the ticking clock, I was thinking, "It's not over. Maybe we can find a way to win one more time. If we can get a first down and move the ball, there is time for us to win it with a field goal." But after two incomplete passes, the knot in my stomach was tightening. As Buck dropped back on third down, I was thinking, hoping, praying for that first down. The pass was in the air and Lindsay Scott went up for it. My first reaction was, He has the first down! He hit the ground and started running, and I was thinking, He's got more! Suddenly he cut to the sideline, and I picked him up about the Georgia forty and began running with him. I outran him for about five yards, and then he bolted into the clear. I could see that it is a footrace, and with his speed I realized that he could go all the way. But even as he crossed the goal line, I was reacting to the inevitable. I knew there would be a mad rush for the end zone, and I wanted us to avoid the delay of the game penalty which comes when you do all that celebrating on the field. But how can you expect your team to be that disciplined? There was too much emotion and too much enthusiasm. Every player on the team rushed out to mob Lindsay. Also joining the fun was sportswriter Freddy Jones, who later became our ticket manager. I always kidded Freddy that if the fifteen-yard penalty which resulted had cost us the game, he never would have gotten a job with us. With the help of that penalty and a twenty-one yard kickoff return, Florida put the ball in play at the Florida thirty-six. The clock continued to reflect frustration. There were fifty-nine seconds left, which meant that they had time to score. Fortunately, Mike Fisher, a Jacksonville boy, intercepted a pass on first down and returned it to the Gator thirty-eight. We had done it again. We had found a new way to win.

On the flight home, realizing that Georgia Tech had done us a favor by tying Notre Dame, 3-3, we were aware we likely would take over the top spot in the polls. Naturally, that bothered me since I was well aware of the history of what often happens to No. 1-ranked teams before the end of the season.

Lindsay Scott stuns Florida

BUCK BELUE — *"When the pass to Lindsay turned into the winning touchdown, my mother [Mrs. Sandra Belue of Valdosta] missed it. When Florida got ahead, she was on the way down to the dressing room to console her oldest son. She heard the roar of the crowd and had no idea what was happening. Some say it was the greatest play in Georgia history, and my mother misses it. But you come to appreciate how mothers feel. I was her son and if I felt bad, she was there to console me. That is one time I am glad it was different from what she expected when she got to the locker room."*

A winning combination — Buck Belue and Lindsay Scott

LINDSAY SCOTT — *"The pass that won the Florida game was a matter of doing what you were supposed to do. For years I had been drilled to react just like that — catch the ball, tuck it and get up field as quickly as possible. At the moment I didn't expect to go all the way, but it was a situation that I was familiar with. It was something I had done for years in practice and games, so doing what I was supposed to and reacting from all those drills enabled me to score the biggest touchdown of my life."*

With our No. 1 ranking, Auburn had plenty of incentive when we arrived there on November 15, 1980. They obviously were ready, taking the lead in the first quarter with a thirty-four-yard touchdown pass. They were leading 7-3 when another hero showed us another way to win. Greg Bell broke through and blocked a punt in the second quarter, and Freddie Gilbert picked the ball up and sprinted twenty-seven yards for a touchdown. That propelled us to a 31-21 victory. We were Southeastern Conference champions, and after beating Georgia Tech 38-20 in Athens, we would play Notre Dame in the Sugar Bowl for the national championship.

The state of Georgia was overcome with excitement after the Tech game. The undefeated season and No. 1 ranking had Bulldog fans intoxicated with our success. But they became nervous and upset — some were immediately embittered — when they dis-covered that I would soon interview for the athletic director and head football coach positions at Auburn, my alma mater.

Naturally, I would have preferred that we wait until the season was over, but I couldn't dictate the timing. Auburn was making a change in coaches and would also offer the athletic directorship to me.

That was something that I felt needed to be addressed at Georgia, which I will explain later, but Auburn was my alma mater. I felt that with Coach Bryant about to retire at Alabama, the timing was perfect for Auburn to regain a position of dominance in the SEC (and as it turned out, I was right, with Pat Dye doing such a fine job in recent years). On the other hand, we had had a good run at Georgia and the timing might not be as good down the road as it had been in the past.

The thing that I wanted people to understand was that Auburn was my alma mater and that it was only the second time I had

Bud Wilkinson recommended Dooley for the Oklahoma coaching job

considered another opportunity.

When Oklahoma offered me the head coaching position in 1965, I was thirty-three years old and the considerations they laid out for me were very tempting to say the least. I had admired Bud Wilkinson, who had become impressed with the job we were doing when he was in Athens for the Alabama/flea-flicker game as a color analyst for NBC. In fact, he was on the sideline when we scored the flea-flicker TD and were making a decision on whether or not to go for two. After deciding to go for two, I turned to Bud and enthusiastically said, "We're going for it!" Then Bud, just as enthusiastically, said, "We've got to!" Bud gave me a terrific recommendation to the president of Oklahoma after his long-time assistant, Gomer Jones, resigned under pressure.

My head was swimming pretty good when I returned to Athens following the interview at Oklahoma, but there was such a genuine outpouring of emotion at home that I realized it would be difficult to leave. It boiled down to a couple of basic points: Barbara really didn't want to go, and Georgia gave me a better contract, which included a nice raise and more responsibility in that I became assistant athletic director.

The feelings of the administration and people in the state were important, too. If I had felt they didn't want me, I probably would have left. Bill Pace, one of the outstanding assistants we had at Georgia, was offered the Texas Tech job when he was head coach at Vandy, and the same emotional pull by the Vandy alumni and friends kept him from going to Lubbock (which he said was his worst mistake). Bill says the same thing happened later to Steve Sloan, his successor, who also was offered the Texas Tech job. "He returned to Nashville to a giant welcome home party and said he was staying," Bill

says. "Then his coach, Bear Bryant, called and told him he was crazy and to take the Tech offer where he had a better chance to win. That is when Sloan reversed his decision."

At the time most analysts would have suggested Oklahoma had greater potential than Georgia, but I felt we could win at Georgia, and when everybody made me feel that I was wanted, I turned Oklahoma down.

From that time until the Auburn thing came up in 1980, I never even discussed another job with anybody. When I got calls, I told them that I was not interested in leaving Georgia. But in 1980, it was different because it was Auburn and because we were still unsettled on the athletic director relationship in Athens.

After the Gator Bowl in 1971, I became more involved as assistant athletic director and began attending athletic board meetings on a regular basis. As time went by and Coach Eaves began to consider retiring at age sixty-five, I let it be known that I was interested in becoming athletic director. Coach Eaves and I worked closely on many matters involving the athletic program at Georgia, and he recommended me for the job when he retired.

Dr. Davison was bothered by the demands that would be placed on my time, and he believed philosophically that the two jobs should be separated. While I agreed with him that in most cases the two jobs should be separate, I honestly believed that I was an exception to the rule. I felt that I had demonstrated a broad interest in athletics, had played basketball and considered it at one time my favorite sport, and had managed all phases of the football program to where I had a solid base in administration. On top of that, I was familiar with the Georgia program from top to bottom.

When I applied for the athletic director position, I told the committee that I felt that I

138

was qualified and outlined two projects which I felt needed to be undertaken: (1) enlarging the stadium, and (2) developing an athletic museum and football team complex, which eventually became the Butts-Mehre Building.

Don Leebern, a member of the search committee, was my strongest supporter. The committee originally voted 5-1 to recommend as athletic director Reid Parker, who had been our faculty chairman of athletics to the athletic board. Don voted against the recommendation, strongly believing that I should be the athletic director.

When Dr. Davison asked Don to meet with him in Athens to discuss the issue, he advised Don that he wanted a unanimous vote on the recommendation. Don told him he could not go along with a unanimous vote.

I could see a disastrous split coming about with the athletic interests wanting an athletic man as AD and the administration wanting an academic man as director. Real problems that could have ruined an outstanding setup were about to develop.

Eventually I went to Dr. Davison and suggested a co-athletic director setup. Dr. Davison liked the idea, and I became AD for sports, and our faculty chairman of athletics, Reid Parker, was named AD for administration.

Auburn made me a very attractive offer, and I was very interested in the job. However, after I returned to Athens, I realized that my roots were more recent and deeper where I was than where I had gone to school. My children had all grown up in Athens, and they were Georgia through and through. As a matter of fact, when we went to the airport to fly over for the interview at Auburn, Derek, our youngest was crying. He was only twelve at the time and kept saying, "I hate Auburn."

That was an emotional reaction at an immature age, but it was a reflection on what had taken place with my children. They had never known anything but Georgia.

Two factors important in my final decision were the purchase arrangement for my house and the athletic directorship. The Georgia Student Educational Fund, our scholarship support organization, had purchased the house we live in from Johnny Griffith when he moved out of town in early 1964. GSEF first offered it to Coach Eaves on a rental basis, but he declined. When they offered it to Barbara and me to rent, we decided to accept. Over the years GSEF had improved and maintained the house, but we felt that since it was the only home we ever knew in Athens that we should have an opportunity to purchase it, and a very favorable agreement was struck on that in late December 1980. We had lived there for seventeen years, and Barbara felt that if something should happen to me, ownership would provide some security.

On the AD question, I told Dr. Davison that while the co-athletic directorship had worked well for the interim, I felt that down the road there should be only one athletic director. By that time, he had become comfortable with the job that was being done and felt that I could manage my time and schedule well enough to handle both jobs. After things settled down, Reid Parker, a loyal alumnus whom I had a great working relationship with, retired to his old job with the Forestry School.

One of the reasons I was so keen on serving as athletic director was the cadre of long-time Georgia-trained and Bulldog-bred associates whose ability and loyalty I could count on — Bill Hartman, Dan Magill and Virginia Whitehead. With this trio of rare talents and dedicated friends, I knew we could get the job done. With Dan's growing responsibilities in tennis, we brought in Claude Felton, a Georgia graduate who was then a public relations executive for Georgia Southern, to serve as sports information director. Claude, like Bill and Dan and Virginia, became a valuable and trusted advisor. Since then, we have added such capable administrators as John Schafer and Lee Hayley, who have meant a lot to me and to Georgia. Hayley, a former teammate, has been associate AD since 1981. I can defer to him without worrying about the store when I'm away, and there has never been a more loyal friend and associate.

Saying no to Auburn and working out the details of a few points at Georgia took a few days. While it was going on, there was a general feeling that I would take the Auburn opportunity. If I had been younger, I might have had more difficulty turning it down, but I am very pleased with my decision. I appreciate my alma mater, but by 1980 I had really become a Bulldog, much to Derek's great pleasure.

When it was over and I announced that I was staying, everybody then refocused on the Sugar Bowl and the Irish of Notre Dame.

Notre Dame, what a tradition — the one truly national team in college football, playing in New Orleans where there is a great Catholic flavor. There was so much sentiment for the Irish even though our fans outnumbered them almost two to one. Everywhere we went, it was "How 'Bout Them Dawgs!" I said many times that I wasn't sure about the team, but for sure I knew that the fans would be ready.

At one of the pre-game dinner parties, Barbara went up to Father Theodore Hesburgh, the eminent president of Notre Dame, and told him that she assumed that he and Notre Dame's legion of fans would be praying for the Irish. She seemed to catch him a little off guard and he responded, "Barbara, my God doesn't have time to concern Himself with such matters as a football game." Barbara replied, "Good, because mine does."

We had to play a peak game against Notre Dame's tough defense, and a few prayers here and there didn't hurt. With us leading 14-7 and Notre Dame with one last chance, I did a little praying myself, but Scott Woerner's interception with 2:56 remaining enabled us to stop their last threat and run out the clock. I had no quarrel with Herschel Walker winning the MVP. After all, he scored two touchdowns and gained 150 yards with a dislocated shoulder. But I thought there should have been two MVP awards. If there had been, and had it been up to me, I would have also given one to Scott Woerner. He really played a sensational game on defense.

FRANK ROS — *"I can vividly remember the last seconds of the Notre Dame game in the Sugar Bowl. I was the captain of the team, a thrill that ranks right up there with being granted American citizenship. I was born in Spain but grew up in Greenville, South Carolina, and on the sideline in the Sugar Bowl, I thought about how great it was to be an American. My eyes were filled with tears. We were down under a minute, and we're very excited on the sideline. But you know how serious Coach Dooley is — it's never over till it's over. I said how happy I was that we had won the game, and I can't repeat what he said. Then I realized he was not aware that they had no more time outs. I said, 'Coach Dooley, they can't win. No more time outs.' He cracked a little smile, but he was still in control. He wouldn't celebrate until the clock said zero."*

Scott Woerner (19): His defensive play in Sugar Bowl was worthy of MVP

Our defense set up Herschel's two scores, first when the Irish failed to field a kickoff at their one (recovered by Bob Kelly) and later forcing an Irish fumble at the Notre Dame twenty-two.

One of the players we took on the trip was Terry Hoage, only a freshman at the time, and there is an interesting story of how he made the traveling squad. During our pre-bowl practice in December, he kept blocking field goals. In one particular practice session after he had blocked a third kick, I stopped practice and awarded him a battlefield promotion. "You have just made the traveling squad for the Sugar Bowl," I told him and the team. It turned out to be a smart move. Early in the game, he blocked a Notre Dame field goal attempt which set up our field goal in the first quarter.

Georgia was voted the national champion by every poll in the days following the game. Nothing can compare with that moment in New Orleans, and I was pleased to celebrate in the French Quarter with the thousands of Georgia fans who were delirious.

I couldn't help but think about what they were thinking — three more years of Herschel.

He would lead us to two more conference championships, and we would be in the hunt for the national title the next two years. In 1981 we were a much better team offensively as we averaged 165 yards passing and 282 yards rushing per game. The only off day we had was at Clemson — the eventual national champions — when we turned the ball over nine times. That was a season total for us in 1980, but I had feared the worst after we waltzed over Tennessee 44-0 in that first game. It would have been good for us to have struggled and won. Maybe we could have gotten the players' attention two weeks later. After Clemson, we really developed into an outstanding team. The big game again was Florida in Jacksonville, where we won by the same score as in 1980, 26-21. Florida jumped off to a 14-0 lead in the first half, but with 1:10 left, we went sixty-eight yards for a touchdown, hitting Herschel over the middle for the last twenty-four yards as the clock ticked down to less than a minute to play.

In the third quarter, Buck Belue hit

Herschel, the dominator

Herschel again, this time for a sixteen-yard touchdown pass to make it 14-14 when the final quarter began. We scored on the fourth play of the fourth quarter but missed the extra point and Florida went ahead 21-20 on their next drive.

Then THE drive began. With 10:16 left, after being penalized on the kickoff, we began at our own five-yard line. We ran Belue a couple of times, and Buck threw a key seventeen-yard pass to Lindsay Scott, but this is where Herschel was unbeatable. He carried the ball eleven times in a seventeen-play drive that brought us the winning touchdown and ate up most of the clock. Herschel indeed could be a dominating player, and he was at his best with the game on the line. He got a valuable assist from fullback Ronnie

Stewart, who had seventeen knockdowns while leading interference for Herschel.

A late defensive mistake enabled Pitt to whip us in the Sugar Bowl, but in 1982, we went right back to work winning every game and ending up undefeated and ranked No. 1 when we played Penn State, which had come so close but had never won a national title. Joe Paterno had posted perfect records but had missed out on being voted No. 1.

We got behind 20-3 but made a gallant comeback only to suffer a bitter loss, 27-23. It

Penn State's late touchdown in the '83 Sugar Bowl broke Georgia's spirits

John Lastinger, a competitor

would have been nice to have won that national title one more time.

It would have been nice, too, if we had known that Herschel would be with us in the fall, but unfortunately we not only lost him to the USFL, we lost him after the signing date, which meant that we would play the 1983 season without a running back. It is tough to sign good backs when you have a Herschel Walker around, and we suddenly went from a dominating team at tailback to one which was without the speed and power that had made us such a feared team for the previous three years. But we were determined to show that we were not a one-man team. Not only did our team resolve to prove that, our coaches worked as hard and as effectively as ever. In fact, that may have been the best coaching job of any of my staffs at Georgia. To get the mileage out of that 1983 team that we did was remarkable. We were tied by Clemson at Clemson and lost to Auburn in Athens, 13-7, even though we recovered an onside kick late and were hoping that that magic of the past would carry us through one last time. Unfortunately it did not, and we were denied a fourth straight conference title.

But there was some magic left with this team which upset No. 1 Texas in the Cotton Bowl for the 10-9 victory that ranks as one of the greatest upsets by our team. Interestingly, we contended for the SEC title and got to the Cotton Bowl by upsetting Florida in the Gator Bowl by the same score, 10-9. The key to our success was the competitive play of our quarterback John Lastinger, who was not the most gifted quarterback we ever had. In fact, John would have been happy remaining at wide receiver when we moved him to quar-

Facing page: Celebration after upsetting No. 1 Texas in the Cotton Bowl

144

terback after Belue graduated in 1981. John was not a great runner and neither was he a great passer, but he was a winner. He took a lot of criticism when things didn't go right, but one of the happiest moments of my career was seeing him score that winning touchdown against Texas in Dallas. I'll never forget his comments when he hit the pylon and rolled over and saw the official's upraised hands, signaling touchdown. "Glory, Glory to ole Georgia!" John said.

When we started fall practice in 1984, we had been the class of college football the previous four years with a record of 43-4-1. It was a new beginning. We were not the football team we had been. We did not have the players we once had, and we began a down cycle. This is not an ungrateful coach talking because I know how hard it is to win seven games.

But in Athens, Georgia, *only* seven wins represents a down cycle.

JOHN LASTINGER — "I didn't come to Georgia to play the glamorous position of quarterback. I just wanted to play. It can be tough out there for a quarterback, and I had my tough days. After I had a bad afternoon at Clemson in 1983, Coach Dooley called me into his office on Monday for a meeting. He said, "John, do you want to start Saturday?" I said, 'Well coach, I'll have to play a perfect game or the crowd will want my head on a platter.' He said, 'Todd Williams is really playing better than you, but if you want to start, we'll start you.' I felt Todd deserved to start, and that is what we agreed on. Thirty minutes later, he called my parents and explained it to them. I've never forgotten that. He is a busy man, and he didn't have to do that."

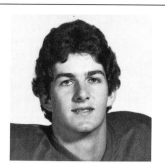

CHAPTER 11

Seven Wins . . . Again . . . And A Brush With Politics

In 1984 we finished 7-4-1, but we felt we had not played well and believed we should be better in 1985. We obviously had entered an era of lesser talent, and we learned something about ourselves in the first game in 1985 against Alabama.

When we finally got ahead late in the game on a blocked punt, Alabama took over at its twenty-nine with :50 left on the clock. They promptly made one of those five-play drives that brings on sleepless nights for a coach. First of all, our team celebrated too quickly after we scored on a blocked punt and took the lead. We were hit with a fifteen-yard penalty although I was beside myself on the sideline trying to restore order. Mike Shula, the Tide quarterback and also the son of Don Shula of the Dolphins, picked our defense apart, scoring with fifteen seconds left on the clock. So instead of a come-from-behind winner, we were a disappointed 20-16 loser. Those are the drives we traditionally made, not the kind that were made against us. "What is going on here?" I thought.

From that point on, we were an inconsistent football team, particularly in the big games. We did not have the talent on defense to stop the opposition in critical situations. For years we were a bend-but-don't-break defensive team, but we had trouble maintaining that style of play. In addition to losing a lot of outstanding football players after 1983 and not recruiting as well as we would have liked, the offensive rules were changing, which put more pressure on defenses. Many traditionalists in the business felt that the rules virtually legalized holding.

I am a traditionalist, but I feel the rule changes have generally been good for the game. The offensive emphasis has added

"What is going on here?"

147

more excitement to college football, and I am for that.

There was excessive holding for a while, but the officials, coaches and players are now much closer to being on the same wavelength. We are getting more consistency in the calls on the field, which stems from the understanding that an offensive lineman cannot allow his arms and hands to venture outside the frame of the defender's body. If you keep your hands inside, it generally will not be called unless a lineman is guilty of blatant holding. Outside the body becomes holding almost every time.

To move the football in today's game, you must have speed and quickness and be able to throw the football. On defense, you simply must have exceptional athletic ability, especially with the rush and in the defensive backfield. We lacked big-play capability. We went through a period from 1984-88 when we did not have enough pure talent on defense, as we had in the four previous years. That made a big difference in our record.

What we discovered in 1984 was that we could hold our own against the lesser teams on our schedule — we even scored sixty-two points against Vandy, the most ever by any of our teams — but in the big games we were not consistent enough nor did we complement ourselves well enough to achieve the production we sought. We were not a complete team. We were not competitive enough

in all phases of the game.

Yet we were mature enough and could maintain a level of play that would bring us seven victories, eliminating any possible bowl controversy before that last game was played. We lost to Georgia Tech in 1984 and 1985, but before those games were played we had seven wins already locked up when the bowl invitations were issued.

What troubled us about 1984 was that it would not go away. We found ourselves unable to win more than seven games the following season. Then in 1986, we got it up to eight and subsequently nine my last two years. What I had hoped for in my last season was to make it back to ten victories, but we were one game shy.

During this time, we experienced the side effects of the Kemp trial. The bad publicity no doubt made it tough for us with a lot of people who really didn't know the facts. We didn't enjoy the best image, which is important in recruiting, but the most difficult thing is that we had to endure the fear and reality that high school athletes out there would listen when our opponents and critics told them that they would not be able to pass at Georgia where the standards were higher.

In the aftermath of the Kemp trial, as has already been pointed out, Dr. Fred Davison decided that we would not take any partial qualifiers. To receive a grant-in-aid from the University of Georgia, you had to make a

---

ALF VAN HOOSE — *Alf Van Hoose, long-time columnist for the* Birmingham News, *was a Dooley watcher for all of the Bulldog head coach's twenty-five years.*

"The thing that impressed me," Van Hoose says, "was that Coach Dooley always beat the teams he was supposed to beat. He might have lost a few games when he was favored, but very seldom did he lose a game he was really supposed to win, and that is the mark of a great coach."

minimum of seven hundred on the SAT or fifteen on the ACT, no exceptions.

The problem this created in recruiting was that a borderline player was often scared away. If he made 680 or 690, it wasn't worth the effort to go through the frustration of taking the exam over and over again while there was a scholarship waiting for him at another major school.

For those athletes who genuinely were interested in the University of Georgia, the competition could put some very interesting thoughts in their heads. Like, if you choose to go to a junior college, what are the guarantees Georgia will take you? Or, so you go to junior college and get hurt. Ask Georgia what they will do then?

The problem was that we could not put anything in writing about what our position was, which made it difficult for a lot of kids who truly wanted to enroll in Athens. Let me underscore again that while all this put us at a disavantage, we did not complain about the administration's position. We supported it, but had to broaden our geographical recruiting base and work a little harder.

In 1986 we made a decision to hire a full-time departmental recruiter, understanding that we could not meet the challenges of this job without a person who did nothing but work in the recruiting process every day. We hired Bob Pittard as our recruiter. In 1986 we brought in the best class since 1982, and I believe the full-time recruiting setup, along with a better job by me and the assistant coaches, has been more productive.

And now that the SEC and subsequently the NCAA have adopted the rule that partial qualifiers will no longer be admitted, I believe that Georgia's recruiting will improve appreciably. Ray Goff is an excellent recruiter, which is important, but when he goes into a home to talk about the University of Georgia

and the question of the academic qualifications comes up, he won't need to address the "less than seven hundred test score issue" any differently from any other coach. That is a significant break for him and for Georgia.

The problems of the mid-eighties — the Kemp trial and the recruiting adjustments that ensued — were difficult for us, but when you are faced with challenge, you find a way to survive and compete. Like the German philosopher Nietzsche said, "That which does not destroy me strengthens me." After the trial ended, I was determined to stick it out until we got back on our feet. But before the Kemp trial came about, a potential opportunity surfaced which caused a massive reaction in the summer of 1985.

Since 1977, first through the Bulldog Clubs and subsequently through Hallmark Travel of Atlanta and its Bulldog travel agent Pat Williams, I have been a member of the host team for an overseas trip, primarily to Europe. Most of the time we take these trips in April and May, following the G-Day game, but because of the birth of my first grandchild, Patrick Dooley Lindsey Cook, in May, and the fact that our destination was Scandanavia, we chose to travel in July.

Two days before leaving, the news surfaced that I was interested in offering for the U. S. Senate race in the fall of 1986, and for the twenty-four hour period leading up to our departure for Brussels on Saturday, June 29, I was hounded by both sports and political newsmen from every direction. When Sabena Flight 562 departed Atlanta for Brussels, the Atlanta newspapers even sent a reporter along. While I am not naive about the fact that the head football coach of the University of Georgia for more than two decades is a newsmaker of sorts, I can truthfully tell you that I was overwhelmed by the media response. It was not anything that I had

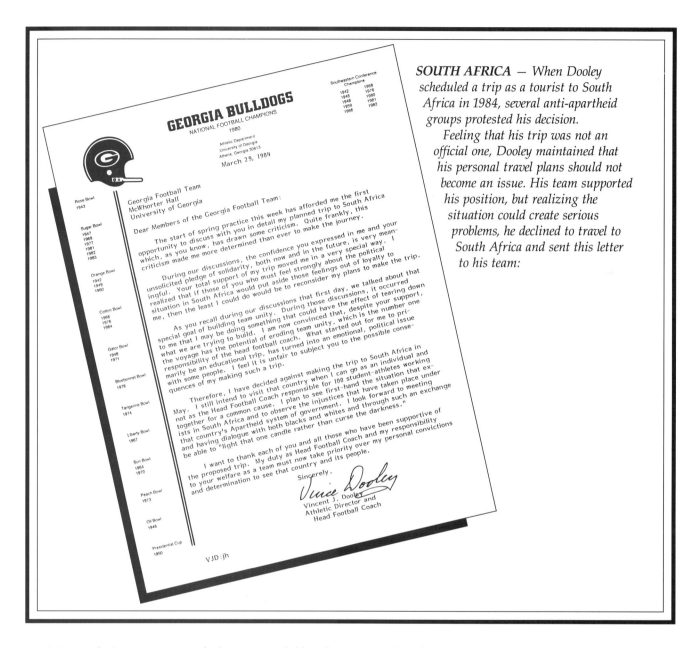

GEORGIA BULLDOGS
NATIONAL FOOTBALL CHAMPIONS
1980

Southeastern Conference
Champions

1942	1968
1946	1976
1948	1980
1959	1981
1966	1982

Athletic Department
University of Georgia
Athens, Georgia 30613

March 29, 1984

Rose Bowl
1943

Sugar Bowl
1947
1969
1977
1981
1982
1983

Orange Bowl
1942
1949
1960

Cotton Bowl
1966
1976
1984

Gator Bowl
1948
1971

Bluebonnet Bowl
1978

Tangerine Bowl
1974

Liberty Bowl
1967

Sun Bowl
1964
1970

Peach Bowl
1973

Oil Bowl
1946

Presidential Cup
1950

Georgia Football Team
McWhorter Hall
University of Georgia

Dear Members of the Georgia Football Team:

The start of spring practice this week has afforded me the first opportunity to discuss with you in detail my planned trip to South Africa which, as you know, has drawn some criticism. Quite frankly, this criticism made me more determined than ever to make the journey.

During our discussions, the confidence you expressed in me and your unsolicited pledge of solidarity, both now and in the future, is very meaningful. Your total support of my trip moved me in a very special way. I realized that if those of you who must feel strongly about the political situation in South Africa would put aside those feelings out of loyalty to me, then the least I could do would be to reconsider my plans to make the trip.

As you recall during our discussions that first day, we talked about that special goal of building team unity. During those discussions, it occurred to me that I may be doing something that could have the effect of tearing down what we are trying to build. I am now convinced that, despite your support, the voyage has the potential of eroding team unity, which is the number one responsibility of the head football coach. What started out for me to primarily be an educational trip, has turned into an emotional, political issue with some people. I feel it is unfair to subject you to the possible consequences of my making such a trip.

Therefore, I have decided against making the trip to South Africa in May. I still intend to visit that country when I can go as an individual and not as the Head Football Coach responsible for 100 student-athletes working together for a common cause. I plan to see first-hand the situation that exists in South Africa and to observe the injustices that have taken place under that country's Apartheid system of government. I look forward to meeting and having dialogue with both blacks and whites and through such an exchange be able to "light that one candle rather than curse the darkness."

I want to thank each of you and all those who have been supportive of the proposed trip. My duty as Head Football Coach and my responsibility to your welfare as a team must now take priority over my personal convictions and determination to see that country and its people.

Sincerely,

Vince Dooley

Vincent J. Dooley
Athletic Director and
Head Football Coach

VJD:jh

SOUTH AFRICA — *When Dooley scheduled a trip as a tourist to South Africa in 1984, several anti-apartheid groups protested his decision.*

Feeling that his trip was not an official one, Dooley maintained that his personal travel plans should not become an issue. His team supported his position, but realizing the situation could create serious problems, he declined to travel to South Africa and sent this letter to his team:

anticipated. It was one of the most difficult experiences I've ever encountered. But first some background.

Dating back to my graduate work at Auburn, where I obtained a master's degree in history, I have always had a serious interest in politics. The title of my master's thesis was *United States Senator James Thomas Heflin and the Democratic Party Revolt in Alabama*. All of my graduate papers were on elections involving Southern demagogues like Huey Long of Louisiana, Kissin' Jim Folsom of Alabama and Pitchfork Ben Tillman of South Carolina.

As the head coach at Georgia, I was often in the company of governors and U. S. senators and was always very curious about their jobs and the political process. Spending time with Senator Richard B. Russell and Senator Herman Talmadge in Washington was always a highlight of any trip to the nation's capital. Political books and political columns were a priority on my reading lists each year, but no thought was ever given to offering for political office.

But my exposure to politicans because of my longevity at Georgia broadened and grew, and I became privy to more and more political activity. My lawyer and good friend, Nick Chilivis, became revenue commissioner when George Busbee was elected governor of Georgia in 1974. Then in 1979, one of my college teammates, Fob James, was elected governor of Alabama. That really got my attention, since Fob had had no prior political experience.

About that time my brother Billy and I bought a duplex at Gulf Shores, south of Mobile near a beach where we used to sleep out at night. (We couldn't afford lodging then, so we slept on the beach.) We both wanted a place to go that was near our roots, since the Jackson Street neighborhood had been bulldozed away to make room for the Mobile City Auditorium. Fob built a home in the area, and we wound up meeting a couple of times a year to fish.

On those fishing trips, with my interest in politics, I made Fob aware that my political curiosity was more than cursory. He enjoyed sharing with me some of the experiences he had in both getting elected governor and running the state government.

What had happened with Fob was that he had enjoyed considerable business success, creating the firm Diversified Products, which became a major sporting goods distributor and which he later sold for over $47 million. When he sold out, he was still a young man and was far from retirement. He considered politics an opportunity to serve his state and looked on it as a higher calling. As a political newcomer, he knew that it would be a consid-

A taste for politics: Dooley with Hubert Humphrey (above) and Barry Goldwater

In the stacks with Porter Kellam

FRANK HOWARD/LIBRARY — *In his last three years at Georgia, Coach Dooley made a contribution of $100,000 to the university library, a gift which naturally received favorable review with the media.*

It was not the first time that his interest in libraries had made headlines. In his first year at Georgia, he spent much of his spare time browsing about the university library. His interest surprised Director Porter Kellam who remarked that he had "never heard of a football coach hanging out in the campus library."

A member of the sports information staff, after talking with Kellam, wrote a story about Dooley's library interest, and it was picked up by the wire services.

When Frank Howard, the colorful coach at Clemson, read the wire story, he said, "Tell Dooley that makes good reading, but he better spend his time coaching the football team. On the other hand, he's pretty smart. The library will be a nice, cool place to hide out when the alumni are mad with him after he loses a couple of games."

erable challenge for him to run a successful campaign for governor.

Fob was then introduced to a political pollster, DeLoss Walker of Memphis, who had gained notable credibility with his directing of Dale Bumpers' campaign for the U.S. Senate in Arkansas. Fob hired Walker to run his gubernatorial campaign, and after finishing second in the primary, he won in a runoff. After he was elected Governor of Alabama and I made one of those trips to Gulf Shores to fish with him, he invited DeLoss down to join us.

It was nothing more than a friendly fishing outing, but I think by that time Fob realized that down the road I might have serious interests in a political campaign. During that fishing weekend in the spring of 1985, DeLoss, who had also worked in the campaign of Joe Frank Harris when he was elected Georgia governor in 1982, reviewed the two political opportunities he saw in Georgia, which were the senatorial campaign of 1986 and the campaign for governor in 1989.

His opinion was that the senate race offered the best opportunity because he considered Senator Mack Mattingly vulnerable politically and there likely would be fewer candidates joining the race. As it turned out, there were only a couple of challengers, Hamilton Jordan and Wyche Fowler, who won.

Following that weekend with DeLoss and Fob, I spent considerable time evaluating the possibility of a statewide campaign. Naturally I had been advised by Fob and DeLoss of the natural assets I had, including name recognition and familiarity with the state, its key leaders and media. But it was not a decision to be made without serious reflection. And time was short.

Success in one field does not mean that it will translate in another. But while I had no prior political experience, why not consider a second career, especially one on a different level than that of a football coach at the state university? In my view, we need more successful people to consider political opportunities rather than leaving it the domain of the professional politicians. I was intrigued with the idea of the senate race and had always been fascinated by this distinguished body and some of its notorious characters and colorful statesmen.

In order to make a decision as the summer began and my European trip was approaching, there was a need for further counsel. I called on Jim Minter, then executive editor of the Atlanta newspapers. I have always enjoyed my friendship with Minter and respected him not only for his highly regarded professional qualities, but also for his knowledge of the state and its political history. Jim naturally kept an ear to the ground and had been amused that the Democratic party had not been able to produce a candidate with enough appeal and political moxie to challenge Mattingly, the Republican candidate who had upset Talmadge just prior to our defeating Florida in 1980 and remaining in the hunt for the national championship.

When I told Minter why I had come to see him, he became very excited and offered immediate encouragement. He called in his political editor, Bill Shipp, a long-time political observer and a sage and knowledgeable reporter. Bill, too, was encouraging. Much of this I understood. While the encouragement was sincere, they, as newspapermen, enjoyed the prospect of a Democractic challenger who might make it interesting in the summer. Newspapers don't particularly enjoy a political campaign in which there are no fireworks. It is a little akin to a Georgia running over a VMI in a mismatched football game. They, naturally, suggested that a story of my interest should be written, and I had no problem with that.

But when the news hit, I was deluged with phone calls. Not only from the media but from countless Georgia friends and fans with a variety of questions and comments. Claude Felton, Georgia's very able sports information director, was swamped with calls and requests.

At the time, I said that I was interested in the senate race but I had not made a decision. I had talked with Dr. Davison, our president, informing him of my interest, but was not prepared for the uproar and overwhelming reaction.

We scheduled a press conference the morn-

BOBBY ROWAN — *In the fall of 1985, after Dooley had decided against running for the Senate, there still was a lot of speculation and indecision in regard to who would carry the Democratic banner.*

A few weeks after Dooley's decision and before Wyche Fowler made his commitment, Bobby Rowan, who later was to become publice service commissioner, called a friend of Dooley's and said, "If the coach wants to get back in this thing after the first of the year, there still would be plenty of time for him to enter the race and get elected."

The friend said, "No, he is not interested anymore. Besides, after having said no, changing his mind and then running would mean that the voters would not respect his attitude and would hold that against him."

Rowan quipped, "No, you're wrong. You are looking at it like honorable men. The electorate don't expect that of you."

ing of the departure for the European trip, and one of the interesting comments that resulted was that since former Senator Talmadge and his wife, Lynda, were along, that the Senator was making the trip to offer advice and insight into the campaign. He was as amused by that suggestion as I was, since he first learned of my possible interest when he read it in the morning paper that day.

However, since he was in our traveling party, I naturally took every opportunity to hear what he had to say on any subject. Whether you like his politics or not, one thing you must concede is that Herman Talmadge is enormously well read, and his diverse historical and political knowledge and insights are impressive. His memory is remarkable and his bank of facts inexhaustible.

Even if I had had no interest in the U. S. Senate at the time, you would have found me keen on listening to the senator talk on whatever subject was topical or convenient. On a train ride of about six hours from Stockholm to Oslo, we discussed numerous subjects, and it was one of the most enjoyable days of our trip.

We all settled into a compartment which would accommodate at least three couples. When the senator pulled out one of the huge cigars he smokes one right after the other, my wife and her friend Myrna Smith immediately eased out of sight. It didn't bother me, an old cigar smoker, but on top of that, I was eager to hear what he had to say. Soon I was engulfed in heavy cigar smoke and endless facts.

Nothing about my campaign plans came up on that train ride. I suspect Senator Talmadge was a little like I might be with another football coach — not presumptuous enough to offer unsolicited advice. But there was a private moment later on the trip when I asked him for his thoughts. He, too, was very

encouraging, but was quick to advise that there was no need to hurry, that I did not need to announce my plans for several months.

Senator Talmadge was viewing it from a practical political standpoint, which made eminent political sense. No question, at that point I was assuming — even with the mass of microphones and questions at the pre-trip press conference — that I would have the fall to assess my plans and then announce my intentions after the football season had ended. I had no plans to become involved with any organized political activity while coaching the Georgia football team. Even if there had been no outside pressure, I would not have intentionally saddled myself with any sort of conflict of interest. I would like to have coached the team as an unannounced candidate, but when I got home, I realized that was unrealistic.

When our plane from Europe arrived at the Atlanta airport, I was almost attacked by news people, just like you see in the movies. Even though I was prepared for a media reception upon returning, I did not think my situation would command that kind of attention. Not only were there writers everywhere when I cleared customs, they dogged my every step for days.

Some people were curious, some supportive of the idea and some emotionally upset. There are a lot of people out there who are concerned about who is elected U. S. Senator, but not as concerned as they are about the welfare of the Georgia football program. Even those with a balanced view did not care for any wavering that would affect the Bulldog football team. They felt that I needed to make an immediate decision, and Dr. Davison said that I would have to choose between the senate race and coaching the football team. He was right, and while I agreed with him, I felt that I should have reasonable time to make a decision. Any other political candidate could have gotten away with waiting, but not the head football coach at the University of Georgia, especially with the season's start a little more than a month away.

On the one hand, I was bothered about the prospect of abruptly severing a relationship that had been in existence for so many years. I did care about the University of Georgia and its athletic program, particularly the foot-ball team. On the other hand, I realized that the senatorial positon was of that higher level of service, and in that regard I felt justified in severing the relationship.

Barbara was bothered by the prospect of ending our relationship with Georgia more than I. She felt that there was not time and the proper atmosphere for us to make the kind of change that reflected our feelings about our years with the university.

During this time, there were many phone calls and letters. You expect that, but you

A FAMILY AFFAIR — A stable family situation is a great source of confidence and strength for a football coach, and it begins with the wife. I am very fortunate to have had someone like Barbara to look after things at home when I have had to be away so much.

In addition to being a wonderful wife and mother, she has often had to serve as a surrogate father. Without her conscientious devotion to family, my four kids Deanna (now Mrs. Lindsey Cook), Daniel (married to the former Suzanne Maher), Denise and Derek would not have had the proper influence and stability that they have had.

It is difficult when you have the commitments a coach and athletic director has to give the family the time it deserves. It is hard to achieve a balance in doing what you expect of yourself in the job and finding time for the family. As a consequence, they suffer, but not nearly as much because of a totally dedicated wife and mother.

Once when we were leaving the Municipal Auditorium after the induction ceremonies of the Alabama Hall of Fame, a circus performance had just concluded and parents and their kids were joyfully leaving the circus,

The Dooley Family: (Front) Daniel and Suzanne, Patrick (Cook), and Denise. (Middle) Derek, Deanna (Cook), and Barbara. (Back) Lindsey (Cook), and Vince.

spilling happily into the streets.

Recalling one of my favorite childhood memories when my daddy took me to a circus, I said to Barbara, "Why didn't we ever take our children to a circus? That is one of the greatest memories of my life."

She turned and said, "I did."

don't anticipate a random letter's helping you make up your mind. That is, however, what happened to me.

One particularly interesting letter suggested that I had come too far to leave Georgia at the time. The writer noted that we had begun the Butts-Mehre building, and that I needed to see its completion and stay around long enough to win two hundred games and another championship. That letter started me to thinking. I had not considered the two hundred wins, a prestigious milestone for a college football coach, one that had been earned by only seven coaches previously.

As I talked with political experts and advisors and the major Democratic politicans themselves, I began to see that there was not enough time for me to make an orderly decision in regard to the Senate race. Too little time, with newspeople following your every move, brings about pressure from which you cannot relax and think clearly. It became obvious to me that the timing was right politically but was not right athletically. Soon I concluded that I would put off any political aspirations until a later time.

One of the things that bothered me about leaving Georgia at that particular time was the fact that the Kemp trial was coming up. While I had no inkling that it would be the bombshell it became, I did not want to appear to be running out when Georgia was facing a controversy of any kind that related to our football program.

On July 25, 1985, I stood before the microphones and the countless reporters and announced that I would not seek political office and that I was ready to go about the business of coaching the Bulldog football team. When the last question was asked and the last interviewer left the room and I was free to move about without interruption, it was one of the happiest days of my life. But deep down, I think I knew the bug would bite again.

I left my office late that afternoon and rode by Woodruff Field, where our teams practice, and I surveyed that beautiful complex and scanned the incomplete construction of the Butts-Mehre building and reflected on the great success and fun of the past twenty-two years. "I really couldn't leave all this," I said to myself. But the potential for that internal tug of war remained. When I evaluated the Oklahoma offer, the state literally asked me not to go, and I stayed. When I considered an opportunity with my alma mater, I realized that my roots were far deeper at Georgia than at Auburn. And now that I had tested the pull toward another field, I found myself feeling as I had before — that Georgia, the University of Georgia, was where I belonged.

But I also realized that regardless of my commitment to Georgia, I was reaching the age and the point in my career when I would soon need to step aside as a coach. While I might not be sure of my future in terms of non-coaching options, it was evident to me that I would not be coaching much longer.

This left the door open for the political idea to continue to nag me, and it would right on into the summer of 1988 when I made up my mind that my twenty-fifth year in coaching would be my last.

CHAPTER 12
There's More Than One Way to Measure Success

Like most people, when a football coach moves into his later years, he leans more toward sentimentality, and I enjoyed becoming something of an elder statesman in the Southeastern Conference in the eighties.

When Coach Bryant retired, I became the dean of SEC coaches and had reached a certain comfort zone — comfortable with the program at Georgia in terms of stability, resources, potential and an opportunity to succeed in all levels of competition.

After we expanded Sanford Stadium following the 1980 season to accommodate 82,000 and moved into the Butts-Mehre Building in the spring of 1987, I felt that we had the finest facilities of any school in the country. We needed a new baseball stadium, and that project is underway and will be completed in 1990. In addition, the university plans to build a new student physical athletic center to which the Athletic Association will contribute $5.5 million. This will upgrade facilities for our men's and women's swimming programs, as well as provide an auxiliary basketball gym and a permanent gym for sports like volleyball and gymnastics.

As we settled into a consistent level with our football program — even though we did not get back to that championship level the last six years as I had wanted — we all could take great pride in the enviable position that we had reached.

Under Liz Murphey's leadership, we were competitive in women's athletics across the board. We had shown much improvement in basketball under Hugh Durham (including a trip to the Final Four) and other men's sports. We had won the men's SEC's all-sports trophy, annually awarded to the team with the best overall program in the league. And we won the trophy for the best overall women's program four out of five years. In fact, in the decade of the eighties, the combined men's and women's program had the best overall record in the SEC. I am very proud of that.

We were selling out of season tickets as we had since the late sixties, counting student and faculty tickets. We may have had some single game tickets for sale over the years, but we generally sold out of season tickets. In some years, there was a waiting list.

After that first season in 1964, when we enjoyed a jump in season ticket sales from 5,662 to 8,171, we had gradually sold more and more season tickets until we reached our optimum the last eight years when we sold over 48,000 (including students and faculty, over 68,000). In annual contributions to the Georgia Student Educational Fund, we advanced from $76,488 (1,749 contributors) in 1964 to $4,764,236 (12,136 contributors) in 1989. Of course, a huge budget is required to fund a successful men's and women's athletic program.

But even our tangible success could be traced to the fact that we were in a positive leadership role. We had aligned ourselves with excellent coaches, and we were bringing to our program outstanding young men and women. In football, these athletes were winning enough games for us to maintain consistency in selling season tickets. Our contributors were very loyal with their support, although some people would complain when we failed to win enough, especially in those up and down years in the seventies.

As I have already mentioned, it was an advantage for us that we were the state university. When Ray Goff finished high school football in 1973, he was recognized for his passing efficiency. There were a lot of people in his hometown of Moultrie who encouraged him to enroll at Florida State, which featured the drop-back passing system.

But Ray chose Georgia and says today that since it was his state university and he planned to live in the state, it just made sense to come to Georgia. He felt that if he worked hard and gave the right effort, everything would work out okay.

It did, and I'm pleased with the way his career developed . . . even though I have endured a lot of ribbing through the years about taking the greatest passer in the state and making an option quarterback out of him. While you must always work hard in recruiting, a school like Georgia will always attract many Ray Goffs. It is winners like that with whom you build a successful program.

When I think of all the players I have coached, I am reminded of Tommy Lawhorne, who was valedictorian of his class and became a distinguished surgeon. Many other of our athletes have become doctors (more than twenty-five), including Happy Dicks, George Pilcher, Billy Darby, Mixon Robinson, Chuck Heard and Rosy Gilliam. Many have become lawyers (also more than twenty-five) including Trav Paine, John Griffin, Wayne Bird, Ed Allen and Billy Payne, who is heading up Atlanta's Olympic effort. Ronnie

Rogers became a sheriff, and Jim Wilson and Dan Spivey became professional wrestlers. Kent Lawrence became a judge. Many have played professional football, and a variety of others have attained outstanding success in business. Many also had have successful careers in the teaching and coaching professions. One is always proud of what his former players accomplish. Of all the professions represented by our former players, it is interesting to note that several former Bulldogs who toiled between the hedges have entered the ministry. I am especially proud of that.

But some have not succeeded. Some have experienced difficulty and have fallen on hard times. Others have made a mess of their lives. Some have let drugs ruin their dreams. It would be unfair to bring their names up here, but I have compassion for them. All I can do is support them and their families and offer a prayer that they will find a way to redirect their lives and utilize the values of sport to overcome the problems and complications that face them.

One of the accomplishments particularly appreciated in football is a player who walks on and becomes a noticeable success.

Robert Miles, who is a member of our counseling staff, walked on and played for our 1980 national championship team. Bob Chandler, a walk-on reserve punter, is now head of Patcraft Mills in Dalton, Georgia.

HILTON YOUNG — *"I was never a star. In fact I never thought I'd have an opportunity to play between the hedges, growing up in the projects in Athens. I was a Coke boy at the stadium which was about as close as I ever thought I'd be to the Bulldogs. But then Coach Dooley asked me to walk on and I later got a scholarship. That scholarship, that opportunity, gave me the desire to be productive and successful and do something in the community."*

Richard Tardits, determined and talented

Punter Spike Jones was a walk-on who made it all the way to the National Football League. Spike is now a successful salesman. Dale Williams was good enough to earn a starting position as a defensive back on our national champions, and so was Nate Taylor at linebacker. Tommy Nix, the center in 1980, is now a banker. Two walk-ons from 1988 will be heard from later, center Mark Lewis and linebacker Mike Guthrie. Rusty Russell, Erk's son who has remained in coaching, walked on and earned a position with our 1985 Cotton Bowl team.

Since 1964, we have enjoyed seeing players not rated high enough for a scholarship join our football program and achieve success.

The most remarkable athlete ever to walk on at Georgia was Richard Tardits, the Frenchman who was one of the Silver Seniors of 1988.

Richard's story, to me, is the most incredible in NCAA football history. In his native Biarritz, France, he played rugby very well. His father was a rugby player of note and still is with the Biarritz Archiballs, who travel the world participating in exhibition matches.

A friend of the family, Eduoard Servy, who became a doctor and settled in Augusta, Georgia, invited Richard over one summer. While in Augusta, he began watching old NCAA and NFL films on the cable channels. He inquired about this American game and learned from Servy, an active sportsman, that it was possible to try out for the team and earn a scholarship.

The odds against a player from the States achieving that goal are pretty steep, and these are usually kids who have been active in football all their lives. What would be the odds of an athlete who has never played the game earning a scholarship? If someone had asked me that before Richard joined our team, I would have suggested that it would have been next to impossible.

But, like everybody else, I didn't know the determination and commitment of this young Frenchman, whose capacity for life and competition exceeds that of most American athletes.

Dr. Servy called Dr. Mixon Robinson of our medical staff, and through Mixon, who had played for us, arrangements were made for Richard to give college football a try. To prepare himself for the game, he checked out books from the library on American football and read them, learning the basics of blocking and tackling. When he first joined us in the spring of 1985, we put him in a blocking drill, but he tackled the player he was sup-

159

posed to block. That is how little he knew about the game.

Right away, we realized that in teaching him to play football we had to keep it as basic as possible, since he had no background. You could take any number of college athletes across the country who did not make impressive college board scores and put them at defensive end, and instinctively they would recognize what was taking place on an option. They had seen it, in many cases, since the fourth or fifth grade and would know how to react. Richard had none of that experience. He had not developed any basic football reactions. Terminology alone was enough to keep him busy, but Richard learned quickly, motivated by a fierce desire and love of competition. His lack of football experience meant defense and special teams were his only hope, although his rugby background involved what would correspond to offensive positions. When I asked him if he would like to play on the kickoff team, he asked with his charming accent, "Is it fute-bahl?"

Because of his well-conditioned body, his speed and quickness and an alert mind, Richard gradually learned the rudiments of football. There was no mistake about his commitment. He was determined to learn the game and succeed, even though it was a challenge for him. He went all out every practice, and in his second spring practice he had reached the point of having learned enough defense to make some progress. He had learned to "get amongst them," which is a term defensive coaches like to use for sticking your head into the fight. He particularly showed a knack for rushing the passer.

Richard was having a great day rushing the passer in one of our Saturday scrimmages, and after the fifth quarterback sack, I stopped practice and awarded him a battlefield promotion right on the spot. From that point, Richard moved up from our special teams to a pass rush specialist. In his last season, he set the school sack record of twenty-nine and season sack record of twelve.

It was a great thrill to watch him enthusiastically develop into a full-time starter and All-SEC player his senior year. He would have achieved further all-star honors if he had not been hurt mid-season (severely sprained ankle) and missed a couple of our late season games.

Here was a young man who identified with the work ethic of football, one who was thrilled to have the opportunity to play the game in the purest sense. The thought of anything under the table would have never occurred to him, and to become the beneficiary of a college education by playing a mere game was for him and his family too good to be true.

It is interesting just how naive he and his father were about his scholarship challenge. His dad, a practical man, told Richard he would pay his way to Georgia for a year, and if he couldn't earn a scholarship in that period of time, he would have to return to France. If I had been aware of their plan, I am afraid I would have had to suggest that they consider an alternative. The odds against him were just too great.

By his senior year of football, he had completed his undergraduate degree requirements and was earning a master's while playing his last season with the Bulldogs. He also received an NCAA post-graduate scholarship and plans to study law at Arizona State while playing for the NFL Cardinals, who picked him in the fifth round.

Of all the athletes that I have ever coached, perhaps none is more appreciative of his scholarship and what football meant to him than Richard Tardits.

CHAPTER 13
Answers To Questions Few People Ever Thought To Ask

During the past twenty-five years, Vince Dooley was interviewed by the press innumerable times. Even so, many interesting questions were never asked. Following are questions that I always wanted to ask Coach Dooley.
— *L.S.*

1. If there is to be a national college football playoff, and all indications are that one will come about someday, why is a one-game playoff, which you support, so important? What will we gain? Will we not wind up with the rich getting richer since lesser schools really can't compete? If we are to have a playoff, why not take the money and give it to some charity or worthwhile cause rather than to the competing schools, which would make it tougher on the have-nots to stay in business?

I am very much against playoffs, but I am very much in favor of a national championship football game to be played after the bowl games.

Obviously, if you could design a playoff system, that would be what all fans and the media would like to see. It would be a great thing for college football. But I do not think it's practical for a couple of reasons: (1) It would do away with the bowl games which have been so good to college football. These bowl games are extremely important to the communities in which they take place, and I would be very much against hurting bowl games. (2) When you get into a complicated playoff system such as the pros have, I believe that it would have a very bad effect academically. We do have some constant problems in our drive to make the student athlete truly a student athlete. I think this would really distract from the basic concept and would hurt academically and take too many days away

from classes. I think one of the great things about the sport of football is that a player misses fewer classes than those in any other sport, and we want to keep it that way.

What I see down the road is a one-game college super bowl, which I think would grow to an event that would be comparable to the pro Super Bowl. It would be comparable to the final four in college basketball, would be comparable to the championship NBA basketball or the World Series. In any event, this sporting event would be a great promotion of the game and would bring a tremendous amount of money into the NCAA that could be divided among all of the schools. Both the participating teams would receive approximately what a team gets for going to a major bowl game. Outside of that, the money could be divided among all the other schools in Division 1A.

2. What is your position on a Super Conference?

A committee has been appointed by the Southeastern Conference to look into the possibilities of a "super conference," which could come about as a result of expansion of the Southeastern Conference. Basically that talk stems from the idea of the addition of perhaps Texas and Texas A&M from the Southwest Conference, Florida State, Miami and perhaps South Carolina.

There is talk that the reason for such an expansion is that the courts and the Federal Trade Commission could possibly rule against some of the existing television consortiums, such as the CFA and possibly Division 1A football. If such a consortium were ever formed, then the conferences might be the only legal entities that could enter into a television contract. Obviously, being a strong super conference would increase the potential of having the best television contract.

In any event, the Southeastern Conference will study it. My base position at this time is a conservative approach. I believe in the Southeastern Conference, the way it is, the way it has been and the great rivalries that we have in the conference. I certainly would be open-minded to hear what our committee has to say in the future, but at the present, I would be against any expansion to a super conference.

3. Should fans have to pay $18 to $20 and up for a ticket when it is going to support so many things other than football?

Nobody likes to pay an increased amount for football tickets, but that traditionally has been the new source of revenue as institutions continue to find ways to balance their budgets. Every athletic director has to make economic decisions, and they are based on the old supply and demand theory. Again, what will the market bear? We have always adopted a philosophy of not taking a leadership role in raising ticket prices. We have always been secondary in that respect and have been a year or two behind most of the institutions in our conference in raising prices.

I believe that our fans have appreciated that philosophy. But on the other hand, I think that most of them understand that we do it only when it becomes necessary. Obviously, a portion of the ticket price goes to support all of the other sports programs, men's and women's. If we had to fund football alone and not have all the other men's and women's sports, the price of a ticket would be around $10.

With the higher priced tickets, we are able to fund other sports, and I think our fans have been understanding and agreeable. However, I am very concerned about a saturation point in raising ticket prices. We must find other sources of new revenue. But more impor-

tantly, we must find ways to contain costs nationally, which is now the No. 1 issue of study in intercollegiate athletics.

4. Enlarging Sanford Stadium is always listed as a long-range project, but the ensuing debt will be a real challenge, especially if for whatever reasons there is a decline in current season ticket sales. How do you feel about adding on to Sanford Stadium?

Since I have been at Georgia, we have had two additions to Sanford Stadium. The first addition came after the 1966 championship team when it became apparent that the interest in Georgia football had picked up considerably as a result of our success the first three years. We had no problems selling the seats. The cost of the addition was around $3 million, which was quite a contrast to the cost of the original stadium, which was approximately $300,000. The second addition was much more questionable. It added some eighteen thousand seats at a cost of $12 million with the seats in the end zone. There was quite a bit of discussion and debate on this issue, but I felt strongly that we should move forward with the project, which was aided by restructuring our ticket priorities in order to help finance the stadium costs.

This proved to be a wise decision. It would be difficult to imagine how we could have survived financially as well as we did during the decade of the eighties without the additional seating.

Each addition to the stadium has blended extremely well with the base structure and has given us one of the most beautiful facilities in the country, with actually no bad seats. We ordered a feasibility study on closing in the west end zone, which is favorable. It would bring the capacity to 100,000, but as the architect told us, this would be the last addition ever to Sanford Stadium. We are basically talking about an additional eighteen to twenty thousand seats at a cost of approximately $20 million.

Our philosophy from the outset has been that we never want to put ourselves into a position of having too many seats, even though we know that we are graduating a tremendous number of students each year and that the population continues to expand in the Atlanta-Greenville corridor. These are all potentially new season ticket buyers. Still, our posture has been to move forward with caution.

At this time, I am personally against enlarging the stadium. Television has played an important part in college football in recent years and has the potential to play an even greater role in the future. But our attitude has again been conservative regarding television, and we must make sure television is not a negative influence on ticket sales.

We have even considered the possibility of adding ten thousand permanent seats without decking the end zone, which would round the bowl off at the height of the bridge, enabling people to maintain the spectacular view that we're all so proud of. According to the architect, this can be done immediately without creating problems with decking the end zone at a later date.

Despite all of these considerations, my philosophy at this time is not to enlarge but to keep studying the possibility to see what the future holds, again with the idea of never having empty seats and always having seats in demand.

5. Athletic dorms are still controversial on many college campuses. Why do you support the idea of a dorm?

There are indeed strong arguments for and against athletic dorms. Overall, I am in favor of athletic dorms, but I would also be in favor of a modification of the rules.

First of all, it is essential that athletic dorms be thoroughly supervised. There is the potential, with so many athletes in one place, for serious discipline problems, even though the traditional concept of the dorm was for better control and discipline. Dorms must be supervised. The athletes must be part of the supervision by assuming positions of leadership and responsibility. Athletic dorms provide better means of controlling the athlete, which is necessary in a structured environment such as football. They also provide easy accessibility to the coaches and, perhaps most important of all, the opportunity to better organize the academic support unit through a centralized academic achievement center.

I would like to see athletes after their sophomore year be given the option to live in the dorm or move out. This would be a healthy modification to the rules. But it is extremely important the first two years for the student athlete to live in the dorm under the proper supervision to get him off to a good start, both athletically and academically.

6. Athletic funds are very big in our college system today and money comes easy when there is success. Should the Athletic Association funds be shared to any extent with the other departments on campus?

Approximately two-thirds of college athletic programs in the country are in serious financial difficulty. Only one-third are well-off, and we happen to be one of the prosperous ones. For a long period of time, we have had a very sound business operation that has allowed us to generate enough revenue to support all of our sports programs, both men's and women's. Also we have set aside revenues for continuing capital improvement for all facilities.

We are proud of the fact that we have generated our own revenue — that we have not taken any state funds, all of which should be directed toward academics. We have pledged $1 million to the university to be used for non-athletic related scholarships at the discretion of the president. The pledge of a million dollars is for ten years at $100,000 a year, and we are approximately halfway finished with that pledge at this point.

As we look to the future, we grow increasingly concerned over rising expenses and limited new sources of revenue. This is of particular concern as we move forward to meeting our debt obligation. There is a widespread sense of affluence in Georgia athletics but very little attention given to the approximately $12 million in debt service. Obviously, being in that position does not allow us to arbitrarily share our funds with other departments on the campus other than the pledge that we are proud to have made to the university for scholarship purposes.

7. Students complain that since they all don't go to athletic contests that athletic fees are unfair. What do you think about student fees?

The student athletic fee program is a fair and equitable way to provide athletic services to the greatest majority of students. As a matter of fact, every institution in the University System of Georgia that provides athletic programs levies a student athletic fee. Our fee is the lowest in the system.

The University of Georgia Intercollegiate Athletic Program is open to all students, and like other services within the university, such as health and transportation, all students are assessed to support the program whether they are directly involved or not. By sharing the cost within the student body, the assessed fees are considerably reduced.

The revenue from the fees goes into our general operating budget and is returned indirectly to the students in services. It allows us to continue to offer substantially reduced

ticket prices in football and basketball and to offer free admission to all other athletic events. It also helps to offset the maintenance costs on the track, the Coliseum, Stegeman pool and tennis courts, which are used by the students. When the university builds the Spacenter, we will make a contribution of $5.5 million to this multi-purpose building, which our students greatly need.

8. Some feel that shoe contracts are a conflict of interest. There is the perception that the coach gets the big contract and then the school's athletes wear the manufacturer's product. If that is the case, shouldn't the money go to the school?

Shoe contracts can be a conflict of interest, and those contracts should be reviewed by the athletic director and the president to ensure that there is no conflict. A conflict can develop if a coach requires his athletes to use the brand that he is endorsing. Of course, some would argue that if professors can require their students to use their textbooks in class, why shouldn't coaches require their athletes to use their products?

A case in point is that at one time I was under contract to endorse Spalding footballs, but our quarterbacks actually used the Wilson ball because of a personal preference. It is also true while I have for a long time endorsed Nike footwear, we have had several athletes who used other equipment, which certainly was fine with me.

It has been my experience that the endorsement opportunities like shoe contracts have resulted from the success of individual coaches at a particular school. If those kinds of endorsements are passed on to other coaches strictly because of the school name involved, then there might be some consideration given to the income being divided between the coach and the school. But basically I believe that this is a justifiable benefit to the coach.

And most shoe contracts do provide for a substantial savings in shoe costs for athletic departments.

9. On the subject of commercials, should there be any ground rules, any restraint (legislation or anything self-imposed) on coaches participating in commercials? After all, it does involve an institution although athletic associations are private.

Endorsements in commercials are part of the coach's outside income. I believe that it is incumbent upon the coach to show good judgment in the use of commercials. Obviously, it is important that the coach believes the product worthwhile, that it will not reflect badly on him or the university. It certainly should be one that is done in good taste. I think it is also important that the coach be sensitive to an overexposure of commercialism that can result from doing too many commercials.

The coach has many responsibilities and constantly is going to find himself in the position of searching for the safe, middle ground of being able to earn income for himself and his family, but yet at the same time not coming across to the public as being too commercial.

This is part of the normal criticism that any coach will have to endure. For every decision that he makes, there is going to be a certain amount of criticism. As someone once told me, the best way never to be criticized is to never say anything or never do anything. Obviously, no one is going to be a successful coach in a major institution like the University of Georgia without saying or doing things. But the bottom line is being able to make sound judgments about decisions, to minimize criticism, to show a concern for what is in the best interest of the university and its alumni and supporters, and also being able to reflect favorably overall on the institution.

10. Are coaches' salaries getting out of hand?
   a) Rick Pitino at Kentucky is supposedly getting $800,000 to a million. Doesn't the faculty have a right to be offended by that?
   b) Assistant coaches' salaries are getting higher than professors with doctorates. Is that out of line?
   c) Should the football and basketball coaches make double, triple and more than the president of the university?

The enormous salaries of some coaches raise the eyebrows of the general public and certainly have caused great criticism. The base salary of coaches should be generally in line with the top executives of the university. Certainly the president's base salary should be higher than anyone else's, and no coach should ever have a salary higher than the president. The difference, of course, comes in the outside income. There are many top faculty members who are drawing huge consulting incomes but are never the subject of public controversy. There is, of course, tremendous public interest in the outside income of coaches, and in many cases the income is exaggerated.

Nevertheless, the amount of income is determined the old-fashioned, American way — that is, what can the market bear? The professional life expectancy of coaches is often very short, and while their income might be outstanding for a period of time, coaches can find themselves unemployed on relatively short notice. Most faculty members have tenure, while there are very few coaches who enjoy such a privilege.

Salaries of assistant coaches are now to a point of being substantial. Assistant coaches have more responsibility and are expected to produce, which means winning. I'm not in favor of this increased pressure but feel assistant coaches' salaries are commensurate with the demands of the job.

165

11. You fought to keep your personal income from being made public. Yet the president's is public. Why do you feel that a coach's income should not be disclosed?

I am not against my personal income being made public. As a matter of fact, my budgeted salary is disclosed to the public.

My income from outside sources is a different matter. There are no faculty members that I know of whose outside income is subject to public review. I don't believe that my outside income should be made available to the public mainly as a matter of principle. You may recall that once we went to court to prevent the review of our outside income from the newspapers. Then once litigation began, I opened my outside income to review by the public. I don't believe that the newspapers have a right under the guise of the Open Records Law to obtain my outside income just to help them sell newspapers or to let the public become the premature judge of any conflict of interest issues. The president is empowered with that prerogative, since each year the coach through the AD has a responsibility of disclosing to the president all outside income.

12. Why play Georgia Southern?

When I came to Georgia twenty-five years ago, we had to play so-called "money games" by scheduling a one-game series at their place without their returning the game in Athens. As an example, we played Michigan in 1965 and Michigan never came to Athens. One of our goals was to increase our home schedule to six games. In order to do that we had to bring teams in for one game with the possibility of a good payoff for them. We developed our six-game home schedule the last twenty years by bringing teams in for one game, such as Baylor, UCLA, several teams in the Pac-10, and teams from the ACC. But now that is becoming increasingly difficult

because many of those teams are in a position to demand home contracts. It has required many major schools to schedule teams in a lower division for the one-game arrangement in order to maintain a six-game home schedule. In the past, we have played such teams as Richmond, VMI, William & Mary, and will play similar teams in the future.

Georgia Southern, under Erk Russell, has built a fine program. Playing Georgia Southern will create a tremendous amount of interest around the state. I believe our team will be more ready to play Georgia Southern than they would Richmond or some of the other schools because our players are likely to be familiar with the Georgia Southern players and will have greater respect for them as a result of this familiarity. At the same time, I think it is a way of helping a state school that I don't believe in any way is recruiting competition for Georgia. Obviously, if it were we would not have scheduled Georgia Southern.

13. Why did you choose to run (or consider running) for political office as a Democrat?

Basically, I have always been a Democrat and grew up identifying with the Democratic Party. My family had come through the Depression, and consequently I saw what President Roosevelt was able to do for the country during a very difficult period. I have also been for the "little man," or the underdog. The Democratic Party traditionally has been the party of the have-nots. However, during my lifetime, I have seen the enactment of much legislation that has been helpful to the little man, and consequently I have grown progressively conservative over the years. The old saying, "Yesterday's liberals are today's conservatives," would be appropriate in my case.

Thus I can be classified today as a Southern Democrat — one who is indeed conservative, one who has concern for the have-nots. But I

166

also believe in a "hands up" philosophy as opposed to a "hand out" philosophy; I believe strongly in fiscal responsibility and a balanced budget. The conservative wing of the Democratic Party is where I would put myself as contrasted to the party on a national level. I have a growing concern about the party on a national level and wonder where a Southern Democrat will fit into the party in the future.

14. Does it bother you that there is a $10 million Butts-Mehre building on campus and no art museum?

We are very proud of the Butts-Mehre Heritage Building. Our ability to raise the money as part of the capital funding project is a testimony to the importance of athletics to the supporters of the University of Georgia. I personally contributed $100,000 to this fundraising effort to demonstrate my support for it. The building is a state-of-the-art athletic complex that, in addition to being a first-class football facility, provides splendid athletic offices that were much needed. It also houses a marvelous hall of fame museum that has been extremely well-received by the public. We have been amazed at the tremendous number of visitors who have come to view the facilities. I believe it is a great point of pride to many Georgia fans and supporters.

The complex is referred to as the standard by which all other athletic complexes are judged. Many institutions now in the country are in the process of planning such a facility on their own campus.

Some, of course, would argue that it is excessive to spend that much money on an athletic complex when there are other areas of the campus that are hurting. I would be the last one to take money that should go to academics, but I do not believe that it's the same money involved. There are certain people who will donate to an athletic complex but would not necessarily contribute money to

any other part of the university. I believe that all of the money we have been able to raise for athletics in the Butts-Mehre Building is money that would not have been available for any purpose other than athletics.

15. Do you support barring coaches from the profession if they are caught cheating, especially if there is a major offense?

I am definitely in favor of suspending coaches from the profession for a period of time, depending upon the seriousness of the offense. If a coach has been directly involved in a recurrent pattern of cheating, then that particular coach should be suspended for the same number of years as the institution is placed on probation. After that period of time, any coach should be given the opportunity for reinstatement.

16. How much should a coach be held accountable for the actions of his assistants, staff and alumni supporters? You can't police the actions and conscience of every person close to your program, but how much should a coach be held accountable?

Obviously that is a very difficult position for a coach to be in — to be responsible for the actions of all who could get the program in trouble. However, there is no question in my mind that a coach is one hundred percent responsible for all of his assistants and his staff. They are directly employed by him, and he has direct contact and influence over their actions. The coach also has a responsibility for his alumni and supporters. Obviously he cannot control them all, but he has the responsibility of setting the tone of his program with his alumni and supporters. By setting the tone, he can influence the greatest portion. However, it is still very, very difficult to know what all alumni are doing. One of the great things that has happened within the last couple of years is the NCAA's getting all of the alumni and boosters out of recruiting, which, incidentally, came out of the college football association meeting as a recommendation by the football coaches. It certainly makes it a lot easier on the football coach as far as his responsibilities are concerned.

Regardless of the challenge, it still is the coach's responsibility, and he should be held accountable for his assistants and staff, and also for his alumni and supporters.

17. Some in the media feel that you were a little misleading in the case of Herschel playing against Clemson in the season opener in 1982. What are your thoughts and recollections?

That is a good question. To be quite honest with you, I had no idea that Herschel would be able to play in the game against Clemson. That was actually the case right up to game time. From the very minute that he was hurt, I got the impression from the doctors that there would be no way he would be able to play against Clemson. But as time went on, the doctors realized that those types of things depend on the individual, and in the final analysis, Herschel displayed an incredible ability to heal faster than most and to mentally block out pain, as in the case of the Sugar Bowl with his shoulder.

It was not until I arrived in the dressing room that I first learned from Dr. Butch Mulherin that Herschel Walker would be able to play, if needed. Dr. Mulherin had in mind playing Herschel in a limited capacity, and that was Herschel's understanding. Quite frankly, perhaps the three of us should have sat down and discussed the situation in more detail. Herschel's impression was that he would be used a limited amount, and that was probably the impression of Dr. Mulherin. My interpretation from pre-game discussions

with the doctor was that Herschel could be used in a limited capacity at the proper time.

There is no question, as I look back on it now, that we probably used him a little bit too much in the second half. He enabled us to maintain offensive consistency late in the game when we needed to control the football by making the first downs. But at that time, I did not think that I was violating the boundaries under which Dr. Mulherin agreed that Herschel could play.

Quite frankly, again, I never intended to deceive the public or the media. I was absolutely convinced that he was not going to play any up until game time when Dr. Mulherin told me that he could be used in a limited capacity.

18. Many senior athletes, after eligibility is established, quit going to class, then there are those who go to class but flunk out as a result of little or no effort, yet under NCAA rules they are allowed to play in bowl games. You have allowed some Georgia athletes to participate in bowl games when they would not be admitted the next quarter of school. How do you justify that?

The NCAA rules state that once an athlete has rendered himself academically eligible for a sports quarter or semester, he is eligible for athletic competition during that entire period, which includes both bowl play and post-season play, despite the fact that the athlete might be in academic trouble at the end of the quarter or semester while the entire playing season is not over.

We do not totally agree with that philosophy, but we understand the NCAA position. For instance, if an athlete decides not to attend class during the period in which he is eligible, then it is the school's responsibility to declare him ineligible immediately for competition. In order to have the right to participate at Georgia, he must be attending class and making a good faith effort toward school and graduation. If this is not the case, not only will he will ineligible for the bowl game but he will be ineligible for any football games during any period when he quits classes completely.

When the season is over and the athlete finds himself in academic difficulty, then a value judgment is made on each athlete since the circumstances can be different. For example, if an athlete has not made a good effort in class during the quarter or if the athlete has exhausted his right of appeal, then he might be ruled ineligible for the bowl game. This was the case with Nate Lewis, one of our receivers, for the 1987 Liberty Bowl. On the other hand, we have had other examples such as Gary Moss, Tim Worley and Keith Henderson who made good faith efforts to attend classes on a regular basis but nonetheless came up short. Those are value judgment cases in which the final decision rests with the president, based on a recommendation by the athletic director and the coach.

19. Are one-year scholarships really fair?

The one-year scholarship is a fair way to eliminate the potential abuse that might come with the granting of a four-year scholarship without any obligation on the student athlete's part.

Several years ago when the four-year scholarship was in effect, there were several players who decided to give up football and to keep their scholarships with two or three years remaining. The rulings in those cases were in favor of the athlete.

In order to make the scholarship contract more equitable, the scholarships were reduced to one-year renewable scholarships. A requirement on the athlete's part would be to participate and be academically eligible for participation by the NCAA and SEC rules.

If an athlete decides to give up his sport, he would normally be allowed to keep his scholarship for the remainder of the school year, which in most cases would be proper.

20. Are athletes being exploited by the colleges today?

I don't think so. We must always be sensitive to student athletes and be supportive of opportunities for them. For example, a freshman athletic cannot attend summer school on scholarship before his freshman year. I am in favor of athletes attending summer school on scholarship because it would give them an opportunity to adjust to college and get their feet on the ground. However, I understand the objection and concerns. The fear is that some schools would take advantage of summer enrollment with illegal participation in pre-season practice.

There remain many inequities. The NCAA, for example, allows summer employment for the student athlete if he is is enrolled in school, but he can't be employed during the regular school year. I think that's wrong. A football player outside of the fall quarter, for example, should be allowed to earn some income during the winter and spring quarters where he could find a reasonable part-time job that would have the approval of the head coach. There are not too many that fall into that category since most of them are affluent enough to get help from home or they can qualify for a PELL grant, designed to help disadvantaged student-athletes. A job opportunity could take care of the middle group, which is too well off to qualify for a PELL but not affluent enough to receive help from home.

On the other hand, I think that the college athlete has a splendid scholarship. Scholarshipped athletes are entitled to room, board and tuition for a period of five years which includes all summer school. After that they are eligible for a minimum wage work-type program, which enables them to get their tuition and books paid for. Most student athletes earn a degree in five years, or should be able to, and their situation is enhanced by having participated in athletics, which in many cases opens a lot of doors. But if the prevailing philosophy is that they deserve more, then you are faced with the old giveaway concept that has adversely affected many of our young people today.

21. Do we let TV dictate too much, as in kickoff times, etc.?

Television, for better or worse, is here to stay. It has had a tremendous impact on the college game, and I think it is important that we do our best to maintain a sense of balance from the extremes that television can bring upon a particular program.

Case in point: We are, by our location and tradition, not a night-playing football program at the University of Georgia. We have too many people who come from too far in South Georgia and return home on the same day for night football to make sense. Therefore, in our dealings with television, we are bound by certain viewpoints and customs. For instance, being part of the CFA package, we have a responsibility to that organization but we also have our own institutional objectives.

Consequently we have a rule that we will play only one night football game a year, and that game must be played prior to November. This is best for our fans. LSU, on the other hand, has the opposite problem. They are by nature a night playing football team and that is best for their fans, so they must deal with it differently. I think it is important that every school minimize the inconvenience that it causes for its supporters.

We try to keep the fans' interest in mind. For instance, we start our games at 1:00 P.M. That timing helps us with our conference package with TBS, which requires a 12:40 P.M. start — only a twenty minute difference. This is a very easy adjustment compared to those who operate on Central Standard Time. They must start their games with TBS at 11:40 A.M., a great inconvenience.

Despite the inconveniences, there is no question that television is a tremendous opportunity to support the university and its athletic programs. It also is a tremendous recruiting advantage. As we send out questionnaires, we get a lot of interest from all over the country. Much of this interest in the university and our program has been boosted by kids who have grown up watching Georgia on television. When we are critical of television, we must never forget the benefits it has brought to the University of Georgia in the way of promotion, as well as the economic benefits.

CHAPTER 14
New Challenges And The Warm Glow Of Memory

In 1966 when I received write-in votes for governor, I was quite surprised and gratified. A football coach who has some measure of success at the state university is the beneficiary of a happy and enthusiastic response from some of the state's loyalists.

Running for governor was the furthermost thing on my mind in those days, even though I had begun to pay attention to what was going on politically in my adopted state. That natural interest and curiosity in politics has always been there.

HEARTACHES — During the Vanderbilt game in 1987, we were behind, 21-7, and the place was rocking. It looked as if their wishbone/passing attack would fool us forever. When Vandy scored its third touchdown, I experienced a tight pain in my chest. At that moment, I had a very peculiar thought that struck me as being funny: "Won't this be a heck of a way to go out, getting beat in Nashville by Vandy." Sometimes in a crisis you have to laugh to keep from crying.

We got ahead and the pain went away, but it came back the next day, making me believe it was severe indigestion. But when it continued, I went to see Dr. Ham Magill, an Athens cardiologist who told me I had to undergo the angioplasty treatment. It was the week of the Kentucky game, and I began telling Ham when I would be able to schedule the treatment.

He laughed and informed me that I would be heading to Emory Hospital in Atlanta that very minute. I wasn't even able to take care of any pressing matters, other than telling George Haffner, our assistant head coach, that he was to take over until further notice.

On Monday, October 12, Dr. John Douglas performed the first of three angioplasty procedures. In about twenty-five percent of the cases — the so-called balloon treatments — the arteries will become narrow again. I happened to be in the twenty-five percent category, so I underwent the treatment twice, which led to a lot of speculation that I was physically not well.

Even though my parents suffered from heart disease, I have never worried about my health, mainly because I have kept reasonably good health habits over the years and because there is such remarkable technology in treating heart disease.

Since the treatments, however, I have been more careful about my eating habits, and I continue on an active exercise routine as I have done since college. For a while, I smoked a pipe when I first arrived at Georgia, and through the years I would smoke a cigar on special occasions. But I have not smoked any the last three or four years.

After the first treatment at Emory, I returned mid-week for the Kentucky game, which was a tough day for us on the field. We had to come from behind late in the game to win it, 17-14. Early in the action, I was very irritated at an obviously missed call by the officials and immediately expressed my displeasure to the official on my side of the field. I never gave any thought to the fact that it might not be good for my heart. I have to admit, however, that after the excitement of the game subsided, my imagination led me to believe that I was having another attack. I checked with Dr. Magill, who assured me that I was okay. I was just doing what came naturally.

Apparently the publicity from my treatment stimulated many heart patients to realize that the procedure is not that difficult, and some were encouraged by what took place in my case. The doctors at Emory say that patients for some time have come in and said, "I want one of those Dooley jobs," meaning, "Let's get this thing done overnight and let me get on home and get about my business."

After the developments involving the senate race in 1986, however, I began considering the possibility of running for governor of Georgia. When I dropped out of the senate race, naturally there was that media question of whether I would consider office in the future. At the time, I was devoting all of my energy and attention to Georgia athletics, but I had privately concluded that down the road I might reevaluate a political opportunity.

With that in mind, I said at the press conference that I would never say "never" to any future political possibilities.

People associated with politics have long memories, especially the columnists and political editors. Until I provided any hard evidence to the contrary, I would be considered a potential candidate. On top of that, most people who really knew me and my attitude could easily have speculated that my coaching days were numbered.

On December 23, 1979, I was quoted in *The Atlanta Journal* as saying that I anticipated getting out in about four years, maybe a little longer. A coach thinks in terms of a recommitment for four years, and I had made that statement, but the story was played up far bigger than I had anticipated. As it turned out, my exit took five years longer than that projection. Although there are several big-name coaches near or past their sixtieth birthdays who are still actively coaching — Joe Paterno, Jerry Claiborne, Bo Schembechler, Bobby Bowden, Hayden Fry and Lavelle Edwards, for example — I don't think that will be as common in the future. The pressures associated with being a head coach today are not likely to produce long careers. You can't have it much better than Royal and Broyles had it at Texas and Arkansas, and they retired at fifty. I thought they got out too soon, but I didn't want to stay on until I could do nothing else.

My personality and attitude, the earlier senate interest, the timing — all those things kept the speculation active about my getting out. Some of that speculation was fanned enthusiastically by opposing recruiters, although I approached each recruiting class with the assurance that I had no specific plans to do anything but coach. I wanted to level with any player or parent who asked the question.

In fact, up until the fall of 1988 I could look every player in the eye and say that I had no immediate plans to get out of coaching. But as we approached the 1988 season, which would be my twenty-fifth with the two hundredth victory opportunity on the horizon, I began seriously to think about calling it quits. I kept thinking about running for governor, but I put it all aside until the season was over. It was that old matter of self-discipline. Even if I were going to quit coaching, I still had to decide whether I wanted to remain as athletic director or run for office. Naturally I did not want to give up the AD job if I weren't going to run, but in order to make serious political plans, the Georgia relationship had to be addressed.

For the last couple of years, I had thought about quitting but had not made a decision, then it became clear to me in the spring and summer of 1988 that I was more serious about getting out. The next recruiting class would have to be told, but in order to avoid hurting Georgia's recruiting efforts, I had to keep it quiet until the appropriate time. Besides, I wasn't absolutely sure that it was time to quit.

What happened with the governor's race was that I discovered that my political interest was not what I thought it was. In fact, those who said I did not have the fire in the belly were right. As I traveled the state, I realized that in order for this thing to make sense, it had to be the most important thing in my life. I didn't feel that way.

In order to come to a conclusion on the political thing, I had to move out of coaching and jump into the political rat race, which is exactly how I came to view the situation.

Over a period of time I talked with a number of people, including my attorney, Nick Chilivis (his wife Patti was a cheerleader for our 1964 team that played in the Sun Bowl), DeLoss Walker in Memphis and former Carter White House aide Hamilton Jordan.

It was their consensus that I should resign as athletic director if I were going to run for governor. As we got closer to the end of the season and the two hundredth victory milestone, I had to make some serious decisions. After the Tech game, the rumors were really building. Our assistant coaches were being asked by prospects if I would continue coaching. On my talk show the question kept coming up. It was a hot item all over the state. The newspapers speculated almost daily. And since I hedged, there appeared to be some substance to the rumors.

It is funny how the speculation seems to land on target. Nobody knew anything, absolutely nothing, except Barbara and me, and we really hadn't made a firm decision yet. But early in fall practice a South Carolina newspaperman came to our campus to check out the rumor that I was going to resign after the season and that Dick Sheridan of N. C. State would succeed me.

When you reach the point in your career that I had reached, the speculation flies. It is a guessing game with rumors, fanned by opposing recruiters, media and your own fans. When the question of retirement kept coming up, I told everybody it was a compliment. They retired Coach Bryant every year for the last ten years of his career, usually during recruiting season.

It was not until the first week in December, while I was in New York for the annual induction ceremonies of the National Football Foundation and Hall of Fame, that I finally made a decision. I would resign as football coach and athletic director and run for governor.

Barbara and Vince at retirement announcement

173

As I went about ending my coaching career, preparing the team for the Gator Bowl, I had to devote some time and thought to the political campaign. It could not interfere with the coaching responsibility, but there had to be some planning and organizing. I may not have been in a rush, but everyone else was. Everywhere I turned people were asking questions and offering advice. They still wanted to know how the team was doing and if we would be up for Michigan State, but they wanted to talk politics, too.

Some offered good advice. Some were optimistic, some less than encouraging. I am not naive enough to believe that all of my good Georgia friends and supporters would not have other political commitments, but by and large it was mostly positive encouragement. There seemed to be a feeling that a political outsider would appeal to a large segment of the voters. In fairness to the university and the football team, I did not become involved with any political activity except for reacting to the inevitable calls and questions.

I did talk to my advisors, but there were no appearances or speeches. As a matter of fact, I was an unannounced candidate and wanted to emphasize that position until the Gator Bowl was over.

After the game, the first order of business

DAN MAGILL — *"'Vince Who?' was the big question being bandied about twenty-five years ago.*

"Barbara Dooley, in her inimitable way, tells the priceless story of trying to locate Vince at a meeting shortly after he arrived in Athens. But since he was a newcomer and unknown, she was asked to describe him.

"'Well, he's a little bit short, a little bit fat, a little bit bald, and he has a big nose,' replied Barbara. And with that graphic description, according to Mrs. Dooley, Vince was immediately located.

"Now a quarter of a century later, Vincent Joseph Dooley is not 'a little bit short.' He is a giant of a man, towering over his peers in the coaching profession: seven times SEC coach-of-the-year, six times district coach-of-the-year, twice national coach-of-the-year; and president of the Football Coaches' Association. He stands tall.

"He is not 'a little bit fat,' but is lean as a bean; and despite a little trouble with his 'ticker,' he appears in better condition than ever. He has also cut the lard from the Athletic Department. During his tenure the GSEF has made grants to the Art Department, Debate Team, Redcoat Band and Alumni Society. A $1 million endowment fund has been made for nonathletic activities at the University. He recently donated $100,000 to the university library.

"Not only has Coach Dooley accomplished such feats as whipping Notre Dame for the national championship, but he has also accomplished the even more remarkable feat (especially from my vantage point) of appearing to have more hair on his head today than he did twenty-five years ago. Does Coach Dooley walk on water? It would surely seem so.

"Unlike Pinocchio, whose nose grew longer as he told untruths, Vince's nose has seemed to grow shorter — or at least more Grecian — as his strengths and accomplishments have become evident to all.

"For years he worked tirelessly for crippled children in Georgia through the Easter Seals program; by tightening scholastic requirements for student athletes, he has emphasized the value of a college education; by introducing drug testing for student athletes, he has helped deter the spread of drug use on campus.

"What this really boils down to and what I'm trying to say is that after twenty-five years, we really love this guy — warts and all."

for the university was to announce that it had hired Ray Goff as my successor and to begin the search for an athletic director to succeed me, probably in March.

There was plenty for me to concern myself with in regard to athletics since I was still the AD, but now I was free to devote time and effort to the race for governor. But I had no idea what awaited me.

It was unbelievable how many requests I got for appearances and speeches. My calendar was immediately booked solid. For a political novice, I was getting the biggest rush of any of the potential candidates. It wasn't long before I felt like a ship floating about without a rudder.

A professional politician has his machine already in place when he enters a race. He can follow an orderly process, to some degree, that enables him to begin slowly and build to a peak at the right time in the later stages of the campaign. That was not a luxury I would enjoy. I was overwhelmed. What I wanted to do was organize a staff, set up a fund-raising campaign (I was already way behind in that category) and develop an orderly game plan for the campaign.

That never happened. With no organization in place, I was pulled in every direction for an appearance or a speaking engagement. My whole life had been based on organization, but suddenly I was out of control.

Frustration set in. I was not enjoying myself, and most importantly of all I didn't feel good. In the mornings I normally wake up early and look forward to the day. I am excited about what will take place, even if it is routine. There has always been something to do in my professional life, and if there weren't, I would find something to keep me occupied, even if it meant going fishing or getting to a book which had been resting on the corner of my desk for some time.

That eagerness was no longer there. I just couldn't get a handle on things. I began to realize that my mind was telling me to run for governor, but my heart kept saying no.

That prompted me to call my doctor, Ham Magill, and consult with him. He felt that the tension and stress of the potential political campaign were probably worrying me, but he assured me that physically I was fine, that I wasn't doing anything to injure my health.

After an engagement in Columbus on a Friday in late January, I stayed with Don and Betsy Leebern and planned to fly with Don to Atlanta the next day for another speaking engagement.

I had told my son-in-law, Lindsey Cook, who was to be my campaign manager, that I wasn't feeling good about things, and he called DeLoss Walker, outlining to him my hectic schedule. DeLoss concluded that he had misjudged my situation, that my name recognition and being in such demand called for a different type of campaign. This overwhelming response was an indication that I had a lot of support out there and it needed to be addressed. I couldn't afford to go through the motions. Most candidates were seeking appearances, and I was, out of necessity, trying to avoid them.

For example, I spoke to the Rome Rotary Club at the request of an old friend, Frank Barron, and there were several writers there and numerous TV cameras. Besides the Rotarians, the guest list totaled about 170. The situation was practically the same at every speaking engagement.

Nobody would allow me to quietly figure out what I wanted to do and start out with a casual approach and build to a climax. There is no way we could have developed a campaign with a build-up at the finish that would have exceeded what was already happening.

On that flight to Atlanta, I told Don Leebern that I just didn't feel good about things and that I had to meet with DeLoss. Don, who had been a true and loyal friend since my first year at Georgia, quickly said, "Take the plane and go on up there today."

Later that same day, DeLoss and I met at a restaurant near the Memphis airport and talked about the campaign and my feelings. First he outlined the opportunities and offered to restructure the campaign to take advantage of what was taking place. With every point he made, I countered with, "I

although I was bothered at my family's having to suffer with such unfounded rumors.

The GBI incident developed in January of 1983 when I checked into the Atlanta Hilton Hotel and received a message from our line coach, Alex Gibbs, to meet him in the lounge. This was during recruiting time for us. A couple of women came over, said they were big Georgia fans, and asked for autographs. That is the kind of thing you come to expect from fans when you are a head coach, and I thought nothing about it. They did invite themselves to sit down, and in the course of

DELOSS WALKER — *"The thing that impressed me most about Vince as a potential political candidate was that he had a tremendous ability to communicate his thoughts and position in a believable way. Some articulate people don't have the believability.*

"Another reason I thought he would be successful is that a man who knows his history has a better chance of success. He is familiar with what is happening, he has a sense of understanding what is taking place and what to do and what not to do."

can't explain it, but I just don't feel right. My heart is really not in it the way I know it should be." Finally, he said, "If you truly feel that way, if you are not totally committed, then you shouldn't do it. You shouldn't run."

Immediately I began to feel better, and I returned home with plans to devote full-time effort to being athletic director. For the third time in the eighties, I had considered an option that would take me away from Athens, and each time it boiled down to the percentage decision that I should not leave.

Some people speculated that I decided not to run because of an incident involving the Georgia Bureau of Investigation. I would have been the subject of intense scrutiny from every direction they suggested, and the publicity from that episode was what turned me off a political campaign. That is not true,

the conversation they identified themselves as being with the GBI. After ten or fifteen minutes, I felt uncomfortable with the situation, so I excused myself and returned to my room.

Later I was in my room, talking on the phone to my brother Billy, when I heard a knock on my door. When I opened it, there was a woman standing there. I told her she would have to wait until I finished my phone conversation. When I moved to continue my phone call, she stepped into the room. When I asked her what she wanted, she was guarded and acted strange. Then she began making a sniffing-like gesture to her nose. Immediately I got her outside, assuming that somebody on drugs or involved in a drug deal had knocked on the wrong door. The next morning I told Alex Gibbs about it, and even while telling him I still considered it a very strange incident.

I didn't think anything else about it until Don Leebern called me several months later and asked me, "What is this I hear about a GBI report involving you and drugs?" I was stunned and had no idea what he was talking about. Don didn't have a lot of details, but he had learned that something had been filed with the agency, enough to make me retrace my activities for the previous months.

Finally, after putting two and two together, I concluded there must have been some connection with the incident at the Hilton. I immediately called my attorney.

Nick laughed at the rumor. He couldn't believe anything so ridiculous would ever be written up and placed in the GBI files. Later on he realized, while involved with another case, that a report may have been created. Under the open records act, Nick asked for a copy of the file on me, and sure enough, there was a written report, albeit almost totally baseless. Nick said the report on file, about drugs being offered in exchange for sex, defied logic and common sense. The reporting officer had been reprimanded for her actions, which I attributed to her being overzealous, but that information was not made public until much later.

GBI policy was that it destroyed such records after two years, but Nick's feeling was that an accurate copy of the records should be kept in case someone made an issue out of it down the road.

He asked the Attorney General's office to agree to preserve all copies of the report under seal. When he didn't get complete cooperation, he filed a lawsuit, and the judge, apparently realizing that the report was facially ludicrous, agreed that the reports should indeed be preserved under seal. Under the Superior Court Rules, the judge's order had to be transmitted to the Supreme Court of Georgia for review.

Some in the newspaper community had heard rumors but didn't know too many details. After making the decision to run for governor, I knew that the situation would lead to one of those whisper campaigns that had to be addressed. I chose to address it head on. Up front. I wanted it out and done with. I had nothing to hide and my conscience was clear. Even so, there was the apprehension on how it would be played. This is why we agreed that we should reveal what was under seal once I chose to run for governor.

I thought it turned out okay, considering the grilling I took by a couple of investigative reporters. That is a hard fact of political life. If you are not guilty of anything spicy or sensational, somebody will make something up. As my friend Earl Leonard of the Coca-Cola Company told me when he was asking why I would want to run for governor, "That is part of the game, to hint something off base and let everybody speculate. They will even look you in the face and accuse you of something bizarre. There are no holds barred in politics." But none of that bothered me. I felt that I had some experience in dealing with tough decisions and challenges. My decision not to run was based on being out of control and having no organized schedule or pattern to follow. If I could have enjoyed the luxury of a "normal" campaign, it might have been different. Who knows? All I know is that I didn't feel good about the race.

All during the last two years I coached, I asked myself this question: "If I quit coaching, what will I do?" My age and my energy level are such that I would not be happy retiring to inactivity. There had to be something for me to do.

In 1986, a couple of insiders had suggested that one of the things that appealed to me about the senate race was that when I quit coaching, just being athletic director would not be enough to keep me busy or happy. Being a U.S. Senator certainly would have been enough.

At the time I would have agreed with them. But now that I have made the decision to remain in athletics, I am redoubling my efforts to stay involved. I am taking on more charity work. I am traveling, speaking and representing Bulldog athletics in new and various ways. Some of it had to do with my prior plans to run for governor, but the first six months of 1989 were without a doubt the busiest time of my life. I was more involved with more projects and traveled more than at any point in the past. I expect to be an active, involved athletic director. There will be little time to spare, and, thanks to the support of our President, Charles Knapp, in the fall I will be working football games for ESPN as a color analyst. Dr. Knapp and I both agree that my national exposure in that job will benefit the university. I think I will enjoy being athletic director, and after what I went through in early 1989, I don't think I'll have any doubts again about whether I'll be busy enough as athletic director.

Now the speculation is that I won't remain as athletic director very long, but I don't look that far down the road. I am enjoying my responsibilities as athletic director, my work with ESPN, and not worrying every day about the football team. By that I mean that I am not consumed every day, everywhere I go with what I am going to do about my next football team or the next game. It is difficult for a person who has never had the responsibility of coaching a major college team like Georgia to understand this. When you are a head coach, the affairs of the team are always paramount in your thinking, even in the off season. You are always thinking how you will organize something, or how you will deal with a personnel problem. Early in the year you begin thinking how you will approach the opening game. Your mind is always on football. You don't relax at a cocktail party, you don't enjoy sitting around with people and doing nothing. Now I can do that. How Ray Goff's team fares will be important to me, naturally. I am there to help him in the role that an athletic director has with a head coach, but the day to day worries and responsibilities of the team are on his young shoulders. Ray is strong, and in my opinion he will do well.

The first thing I learned about Ray was that he had a winner's attitude. Winning was important to him. He showed his leadership ability early on, becoming the center of our leadership group. He was voted captain by a substantial margin. In fact, I think the two players over the years who got the most votes for captain were Ray and Willie McClendon.

We never had a more effective option runner than Ray. We used to kid him about being deceptively slow. He appeared slow because of his size, but he was really pretty fast. He was a swivel-hipped runner with the great leg strength. But he was also a sitting duck for people to take a shot at. He got pounded a lot, but he kept coming back for more. I don't believe we ever had a player with more bruises and "hurts" on his body who still played.

When we played Auburn for the championship in his senior year, Ray's arm was so sore he could not bring it parallel to the ground. We did not throw a single pass that day and won the game and the title. He couldn't raise his arm to throw, but if we had asked him he would have given it a try. Whatever it took to win, he was willing to do.

Ray was a team player all the way. He shared the credit with his teammates.

He had strong convictions and a good ability to say the right thing. He was proud of his religion and said what he felt, and I always respected him for that. I knew that he was sincere. I believe that Ray's outstanding attitude can be traced to his strong family ties; his mother and father did a good job.

Football coaching today is being able to survive a series of crises, both on and off the field. You can count on it. It used to be that a coach's job would not be seriously challenged by off the field crises, but today there is more off the field responsibility than ever before.

If you are going to succeed as a coach, you have to survive those crises, and I look forward to sharing with Ray Goff my experiences when he thinks they might be helpful. It's his football team, and I will never interfere, but when he feels I can help in any way, my door will be open, just like it always was when he was an assistant and I was the head coach.

One thing I am really looking forward to is having some time to enjoy and relive some of the memories of the past twenty-five years, which went by so quickly.

I want to visit with our old players and the great fans and friends of the university. I expect to take the time to get more involved with the people over the state. I'll be busy as athletic director, but I look forward to the opportunity to relax more with the people who have helped make our program successful.

Our greatest strength is the Georgia people. They have been generous, loyal and supportive and are an integral part of the team that has achieved the success of the past twenty-five years.

While I am excited about doing some television color commentary. I also will enjoy sitting in the stands and shouting, "How 'bout them Dawgs!" I'm ready to enjoy some football weekends without the pressure.

I might even take up golf, but on second thought, I'll probably be too busy. But not too busy to have some fun with Patrick Dooley Lindsey Cook, and his sister, Catherine Barbara, and their cousins as they come along.

Some may find it hard to believe that I have become sentimental, but every day now I appreciate more and more what my friend the late Bill Munday wanted inscribed as his epitaph: "I was Bulldog born and Bulldog bred. When I die, I want to be Bulldog dead."

PHOTO CREDITS

Rich Addicks, page 145

Jimmy Cribb, page 59

Wingate Downs, dust cover photo, pages 66, 173

Travis Ellison, pages 91, 107

Steve Ellwood, pages 58, 59

Florida Publishing Company, page 126

George L. King, Jr., pages 98, 122, 124, 136, 142, 143, 144, 147

Randy Miller, page 135

Loran Smith, pages 1, 12

Danny White, page 3

Thom White, page 141

Special thanks to the University of Georgia Sports Information office for use of photos from its files, and to Terry Atkinson for her assistance in collecting them.

INDEX

INDEX

The Dooley Years

1964 (7-3-1)
Coach: Vince Dooley, Auburn
Capt.: Barry Wilson, DE

9/19	3	Alabama 31	Tuscaloosa, AL*
9/26	7	Vanderbilt...... 0	Nashville, TN*
10/3	7	S. Carolina ... 7	Columbia, SC
10/10	19	Clemson........ 7	Athens
10/17	14	Florida State....17	Athens
10/24	21	Kentucky....... 7	Athens
10/31	24	N. Carolina..... 8	Athens
11/7	14	Florida.......... 7	Jacksonville, FL
11/14	7	Auburn 14	Auburn, AL
11/28	7	Georgia Tech ... 0	Athens
SUN BOWL			
12/26	7	Texas Tech 0	El Paso, TX

1965 (6-4-0)
Coach: Vince Dooley, Auburn
Capt.: Doug McFalls, DB

9/18	18	Alabama 17	Athens
9/25	24	Vanderbilt....10	Athens
10/2	15	Michigan 7	Ann Arbor, MI
10/9	23	Clemson 9	Athens
10/16	3	Florida State.10	Tallahassee, FL*
10/23	10	Kentucky....28	Lexington, KY*
10/30	47	N. Carolina .35	Chapel Hill, NC
11/6	10	Florida......14	Jacksonville, FL
11/13	19	Auburn 21	Athens
11/27	17	Georgia Tech 7	Atlanta

1966 (10-1-0)
SEC CHAMPIONS
Coach: Vince Dooley, Auburn
Capt.: George Patton, T

9/17	20	Miss. State ..17	Jackson, MS*
9/24	43	VMI........ 7	Roanoke, VA*
10/1	7	S. Carolina ...0	Columbia, SC*
10/8	9	Ole Miss 3	Athens
10/14	6	Miami 7	Miami, FL*
10/22	27	Kentucky....15	Athens
10/29	28	N. Carolina . 3	Athens
11/5	27	Florida......10	Jacksonville, FL
11/12	21	Auburn 13	Auburn, AL
11/26	23	Georgia Tech 14	Athens
COTTON BOWL			
12/31	24	SMU........ 9	Dallas, TX

1967 (7-4-0)
Coach: Vince Dooley, Auburn
Capt.: Kirby Moore, QB

9/23	30	Miss. State...... 0	Athens
9/30	24	Clemson........17	Clemson, SC
10/7	21	S. Carolina 0	Athens
10/14	20	Ole Miss 29	Jackson, MS*
10/21	56	VMI........ 6	Athens
10/28	31	Kentucky....... 7	Lexington, KY*
11/4	14	Houston........15	Houston, TX*
11/11	16	Florida........17	Jacksonville, FL
11/18	17	Auburn 0	Athens
11/25	21	Georgia Tech ...14	Atlanta
LIBERTY BOWL			
12/16	7	N.C. State......14	Memphis, TN

1968 (8-1-2)
SEC CHAMPIONS
Coach: Vince Dooley, Auburn
Capt.: Bill Stanfill, T

9/14	17	Tennessee 17	Knoxville, TN
9/28	31	Clemson........13	Athens
10/5	21	S. Carolina 20	Columbia, SC*
10/12	21	Ole Miss 7	Athens
10/19	32	Vanderbilt...... 6	Athens
10/26	35	Kentucky.......14	Lexington, KY*
11/2	10	Houston........10	Athens
11/9	51	Florida......... 0	Jacksonville, FL
11/16	17	Auburn 3	Auburn, AL
11/30	47	Georgia Tech ... 8	Athens
SUGAR BOWL			
1/1/69	2	Arkansas 16	New Orleans, LA*

1969 (5-5-1)
Coach: Vince Dooley, Auburn
Capt.: Steve Greer, DG

9/20	35	Tulane 0	Athens
9/27	30	Clemson........ 0	Clemson, SC
10/4	41	S. Carolina 16	Athens
10/11	17	Ole Miss 25	Jackson, MS
10/18	40	Vanderbilt...... 8	Nashville, TN*
10/25	30	Kentucky....... 0	Athens
11/1	3	Tennessee 17	Athens
11/8	13	Florida.........13	Jacksonville, FL
11/15	3	Auburn 16	Athens
11/29	0	Georgia Tech ... 6	Atlanta
SUN BOWL			
12/20	6	Nebraska 45	El Paso, TX

1970 (5-5-0)
Coach: Vince Dooley, Auburn
Capt.: Tommy Lyons, C

9/19	14	Tulane 17	New Orleans, LA*
9/26	38	Clemson........ 0	Athens
10/3	6	Miss. State..... 7	Jackson, MS
10/10	21	Ole Miss 31	Athens
10/17	37	Vanderbilt..... 3	Athens
10/24	19	Kentucky....... 3	Lexington, KY*
10/31	52	S. Carolina 34	Athens
11/7	17	Florida.........24	Jacksonville, FL
11/14	31	Auburn 17	Auburn, AL
11/28	7	Georgia Tech ...17	Athens

1971 (11-1-0)
Coach: Vince Dooley, Auburn
Capt.: Royce Smith, OG

9/11	56	Oregon State....25	Athens
9/18	17	Tulane 7	Athens
9/25	28	Clemson........ 0	Clemson, SC
10/2	35	Miss. State..... 7	Athens
10/9	38	Ole Miss 7	Jackson, MS
10/16	24	Vanderbilt...... 0	Nashville, TN*
10/23	34	Kentucky....... 0	Athens
10/30	24	S. Carolina 0	Columbia, SC*
11/6	49	Florida......... 7	Jacksonville, FL
11/13	20	Auburn 35	Athens
11/25	28	Georgia Tech ...24	Atlanta*
GATOR BOWL			
12/31	7	N. Carolina 3	Jacksonville, FL

1972 (7-4-0)
Coach: Vince Dooley, Auburn
Capt.: Robert Honeycutt, FB

9/16	24	Baylor 14	Athens
9/23	13	Tulane 24	New Orleans, LA
9/30	28	N.C. State......22	Athens
10/7	7	Alabama 25	Athens
10/14	14	Ole Miss 13	Jackson, MS
10/21	28	Vanderbilt..... 3	Athens
10/28	13	Kentucky....... 7	Lexington, KY
11/4	0	Tennessee 14	Athens
11/11	10	Florida......... 7	Jacksonville, FL
11/18	10	Auburn 27	Auburn, AL
12/2	27	Georgia Tech ... 7	Athens

1973 (7-4-1)
Coach: Vince Dooley, Auburn
Capt.: Bob Burns, FB

9/15	7	Pittsburgh 7	Athens
9/22	31	Clemson........14	Athens
9/29	31	N.C. State......12	Athens
10/6	14	Alabama 28	Tuscaloosa, AL
10/13	20	Ole Miss 0	Athens
10/20	14	Vanderbilt......18	Nashville, TN
10/27	7	Kentucky.......12	Athens
11/3	35	Tennessee 31	Knoxville, TN
11/10	10	Florida.........11	Jacksonville, FL
11/17	28	Auburn 14	Athens
12/1	10	Georgia Tech ... 3	Atlanta
PEACH BOWL			
12/28	17	Maryland.......16	Atlanta*

1974 (6-6-0)
Coach: Vince Dooley, Auburn
Capt.: Keith Harris, LB

9/14	48	Oregon State....35	Athens
9/21	14	Miss. State......38	Jackson, MS*
9/28	52	S. Carolina 14	Athens
10/5	24	Clemson........28	Clemson, SC
10/12	49	Ole Miss 0	Athens
10/19	38	Vanderbilt......31	Athens
10/26	24	Kentucky.......20	Lexington, KY
11/2	24	Houston........31	Athens
11/9	17	Florida.........16	Jacksonville, FL
11/16	13	Auburn 17	Auburn, AL
11/30	14	Georgia Tech ...34	Athens
TANGERINE BOWL			
12/20	10	Miami (Ohio) ...21	Orlando, FL

1975 (9-3-0)
Coach: Vince Dooley, Auburn
Capt.: Glynn Harrison, RB

9/6	9	Pittsburgh 19	Athens
9/20	28	Miss. State...... 6	Athens
9/27	28	S. Carolina 20	Columbia, SC*
10/4	35	Clemson........ 7	Athens
10/11	13	Ole Miss 28	Oxford, MS
10/18	47	Vanderbilt.......3	Nashville, TN
10/25	21	Kentucky.......13	Athens
11/1	28	Richmond 24	Athens
11/8	10	Florida......... 7	Jacksonville, FL
11/15	28	Auburn 13	Athens
11/27	42	Georgia Tech ...26	Atlanta*
COTTON BOWL			
1/1/76	10	Arkansas 31	Dallas, TX

1976 (10-2-0)
SEC CHAMPIONS
Coach: Vince Dooley, Auburn
Capt.: Ray Goff, QB

9/11	36	California 24	Athens
9/18	41	Clemson........ 0	Clemson, SC
9/25	20	S. Carolina 12	Athens
10/2	21	Alabama 0	Athens
10/9	17	Ole Miss 21	Oxford, MS
10/16	45	Vanderbilt...... 0	Athens
10/23	31	Kentucky....... 7	Lexington, KY
10/30	31	Cincinnati 17	Athens
11/6	41	Florida.........27	Jacksonville, FL
11/13	28	Auburn 0	Auburn, AL
11/27	13	Georgia Tech ...10	Athens
SUGAR BOWL			
1/1/77	3	Pittsburgh 27	New Orleans, LA

The Dooley Years

1977 (5-6-0)
Coach: Vince Dooley, Auburn
Capt.: Ben Zambiasi, LB

Date		Opponent		Location
9/10	27	Oregon	16	Athens
9/17	6	Clemson	7	Athens
9/24	15	S. Carolina	13	Columbia, SC*
10/1	10	Alabama	18	Tuscaloosa, AL
10/8	14	Ole Miss	13	Athens
10/15	24	Vanderbilt	13	Nashville, TN
10/22	0	Kentucky	33	Athens
10/29	23	Richmond	7	Athens
11/5	7	Florida	22	Jacksonville, FL
11/12	14	Auburn	33	Athens
11/26	7	Georgia Tech	16	Atlanta

1978 (9-2-1)
Coach: Vince Dooley, Auburn
Capt.: Willie McClendon, TB

Date		Opponent		Location
9/16	16	Baylor	14	Athens
9/23	12	Clemson	0	Athens
9/30	10	S. Carolina	27	Columbia, SC*
10/7	42	Ole Miss	3	Athens
10/14	24	LSU	17	Baton Rouge, LA*
10/21	31	Vanderbilt	10	Athens
10/28	17	Kentucky	16	Lexington, KY*
11/4	41	VMI	3	Athens
11/11	24	Florida	22	Jacksonville, FL
11/18	22	Auburn, AL	22	Auburn
12/2	29	Georgia Tech	28	Athens

BLUEBONNET BOWL
Date		Opponent		Location
12/31	22	Stanford	25	Houston, TX*

1979 (6-5-0)
Coach: Vince Dooley, Auburn
Capt.: Gordon Terry, DE

Date		Opponent		Location
9/15	21	Wake Forest	22	Athens
9/22	7	Clemson	12	Clemson, SC
9/29	20	S. Carolina	27	Athens
10/6	24	Ole Miss	21	Oxford, MS
10/13	21	LSU	14	Athens
10/20	31	Vanderbilt	10	Nashville, TN
10/27	20	Kentucky	6	Athens
11/3	0	Virginia	31	Athens
11/10	33	Florida	10	Jacksonville, FL
11/17	13	Auburn	33	Athens
11/24	16	Georgia Tech	3	Atlanta

1980 (12-0-0)
NATIONAL CHAMPIONS
SEC CHAMPIONS
Coach: Vince Dooley, Auburn
Capt.: Frank Ros, LB

Date		Opponent		Location
9/6	16	Tennessee	15	Knoxville, TN*
9/13	42	Texas A&M	0	Athens
9/20	20	Clemson	16	Athens
9/27	34	TCU	3	Athens
10/11	28	Ole Miss	21	Athens
10/18	41	Vanderbilt	0	Athens
10/25	27	Kentucky	0	Lexington, KY*
11/1	13	S. Carolina	10	Athens
11/8	26	Florida	21	Jacksonville, FL
11/15	31	Auburn	21	Auburn, AL
11/29	38	Georgia Tech	20	Athens

SUGAR BOWL
Date		Opponent		Location
1/1/81	17	Notre Dame	10	New Orleans, LA*

1981 (10-2-0)
SEC CHAMPIONS
Coach: Vince Dooley, Auburn
Capt.: Buck Belue, QB

Date		Opponent		Location
9/5	44	Tennessee	0	Athens
9/12	27	California	13	Athens
9/19	3	Clemson	13	Clemson, SC
9/26	24	S. Carolina	0	Athens
10/10	37	Ole Miss	7	Oxford, MS
10/17	53	Vanderbilt	21	Nashville, TN
10/24	21	Kentucky	0	Athens
10/31	49	Temple	3	Athens
11/7	26	Florida	21	Jacksonville, FL
11/14	24	Auburn	13	Athens
12/5	44	Georgia Tech	7	Atlanta

SUGAR BOWL
Date		Opponent		Location
1/1/82	20	Pittsburgh	24*	New Orleans, LA*

1982 (11-1-0)
SEC CHAMPIONS
Coach: Vince Dooley, Auburn
Capt.: Wayne Radloff, C

Date		Opponent		Location
9/6	13	Clemson	7	Athens*
9/11	17	Brigham Young	14	Athens
9/25	34	S. Carolina	18	Columbia, SC*
10/2	29	Miss. State	22	Starkville, MS
10/9	33	Ole Miss	10	Athens
10/16	27	Vanderbilt	13	Athens
10/23	27	Kentucky	14	Lexington, KY*
10/30	34	Memphis State	3	Athens
11/6	44	Florida	0	Jacksonville, FL
11/13	19	Auburn	14	Auburn, AL
11/27	38	Georgia Tech	18	Athens

SUGAR BOWL
Date		Opponent		Location
1/1/83	23	Penn State*	27	New Orleans, LA

1983 (10-1-1)
Coach: Vince Dooley, Auburn
Capt.: Freddie Gilbert, DE

Date		Opponent		Location
9/3	19	UCLA	8	Athens*
9/17	16	Clemson	16	Clemson, SC
9/24	31	S. Carolina	13	Athens
10/1	20	Miss. State	7	Athens
10/8	36	Ole Miss	11	Oxford, MS
10/15	20	Vanderbilt	13	Nashville, TN*
10/22	47	Kentucky	21	Athens
10/29	31	Temple	14	Athens
11/5	10	Florida	9	Jacksonville, FL
11/12	7	Auburn	13	Athens
11/26	27	Georgia Tech	24	Atlanta

COTTON BOWL
Date		Opponent		Location
1/2/84	10	Texas	9	Dallas, TX

1984 (7-4-1)
Coach: Vince Dooley, Auburn
Capt.: Knox Culpepper, LB

Date		Opponent		Location
9/8	26	Southern Miss.	19	Athens
9/22	26	Clemson	23	Athens
9/29	10	S. Carolina	17	Columbia, SC*
10/6	24	Alabama	14	Birmingham, AL
10/13	18	Ole Miss	12	Athens
10/20	62	Vanderbilt	35	Athens
10/27	37	Kentucky	7	Lexington, KY
11/3	13	Memphis State	3	Athens
11/10	0	Florida	27	Jacksonville, FL
11/17	12	Auburn	21	Auburn, AL*
12/1	18	Georgia Tech	35	Athens

CITRUS BOWL
Date		Opponent		Location
12/22	17	Florida State	17	Orlando, FL

1985 (7-3-2)
Coach: Vince Dooley, Auburn
Capt.: Peter Anderson, C

Date		Opponent		Location
9/2	16	Alabama	20	Athens*
9/14	17	Baylor	14	Athens
9/21	20	Clemson	13	Clemson, SC
9/28	35	S. Carolina	21	Athens
10/12	49	Ole Miss	21	Jackson, Miss.*
10/19	13	Vanderbilt	13	Nashville, Tenn.
10/26	26	Kentucky	6	Athens
11/2	58	Tulane	3	Athens (HC)
11/9	24	Florida	3	Jacksonville, FL
11/16	10	Auburn	24	Athens
11/30	16	Georgia Tech	20	Atlanta*

SUN BOWL
Date		Opponent		Location
12/28	13	Arizona	13	El Paso, TX

1986 (8-4)
Coach: Vince Dooley, Auburn
Capt.: John Little, SAF

Date		Opponent		Location
9/13	31	Duke	7	Athens
9/20	28	Clemson	31	Athens
9/27	31	S. Carolina	26	Columbia, SC*
10/4	14	Ole Miss	10	Athens
10/11	14	LSU	23	Baton Rouge,LA*
10/18	38	Vanderbilt	16	Athens
10/25	31	Kentucky	9	Lexington, KY*
11/1	28	Richmond	13	Athens (HC)
11/8	19	Florida	31	Jacksonville, FL
11/15	20	Auburn	16	Auburn, AL*
11/29	31	Georgia Tech	24	Athens

HALL OF FAME BOWL
Date		Opponent		Location
12/23	24	Boston College	27	Tampa, FL*

1987 (9-3)
Coach: Vince Dooley, Auburn
Capt.: Kim Stephens, OG

Date		Opponent		Location
9/5	30	Virginia	22	Athens
9/12	41	Oregon State	7	Athens
9/19	20	Clemson	21	Clemson, SC
9/26	13	South Carolina	6	Athens
10/3	31	Ole Miss	14	Oxford, Miss.
10/10	23	L.S.U.	26	Athens
10/17	52	Vanderbilt	24	Nashville, TN*
10/24	17	Kentucky (HC)	14	Athens
11/7	23	Florida	10	Jacksonville, FL
11/14	11	Auburn	27	Athens
11/28	30	Georgia Tech	16	Atlanta*

LIBERTY BOWL
Date		Opponent		Location
12/29	20	Arkansas	17	Memphis, Tenn.*

1988 (9-3)
Coach: Vince Dooley, Auburn
Capt.: Todd Wheeler, C.

Date		Opponent		Location
9/3	28	Tennessee	17	Athens
9/10	38	T.C.U.	10	Athens
9/17	42	Miss. State	35	Starkville, MS*
9/24	10	S. Carolina	23	Columbia, SC
10/1	36	Ole Miss	12	Athens
10/8	41	Vanderbilt	22	Athens
10/22	10	Kentucky	16	Lexington, KY
10/29	59	Wm. & Mary	24	Athens
11/5	26	Florida	3	Jacksonville, FL
11/12	10	Auburn	20	Auburn, AL
11/26	24	Georgia Tech	3	Athens

MAZDA GATOR BOWL
Date		Opponent		Location
1/1/89	34	Michigan St.	27	Jacksonville, FL*

*Denotes Night Game